WHAT'S RIGHT WITH
ISLAM

A New Vision
for Muslims
and the West

IMAM FEISAL ABDUL RAUF

HarperSanFrancisco
A Division of HarperCollins*Publishers*

HarperCollins books may be purchased for educational, business, or sales promotional use. For information please write: Special Markets Department, HarperCollins Publishers, Inc., 10 East 53rd Street, New York, NY 10022.

HarperCollins Web site: http://www.harpercollins.com
HarperCollins®, ☝®, and HarperSanFrancisco™ are
trademarks of HarperCollins Publishers, Inc.

FIRST HARPERCOLLINS PAPERBACK EDITION PUBLISHED IN 2005

Library of Congress Cataloging-in-Publication Data is available.

ISBN 0–06–075062–6 (pbk.)

05 06 07 08 09 RRD(H) 10 9 8 7 6 5 4 3 2 1

To my beloved children, family, and students,
that they may become light-beacons of wisdom.

O Lord, grant that we perceive truth as true, and the good fortune to follow it; and that we perceive falsehood as false, and the good fortune to avoid it.

—Islamic benedictory prayer

Contents

Foreword

Karen Armstrong

At the beginning of the twentieth century, almost every single Muslim intellectual was in love with the West. They wanted their countries to look like Britain and France, at that time the leaders of secular, democratic modernity. Some even went so far as to say that the Europeans were better Muslims than the Muslims themselves, because their modernized societies approached the egalitarian ideals of the Quran more closely than anything that prevailed in traditional, Islamic countries. Muhammad 'Abduh (1849–1905), Grand Mufti of Egypt, was profoundly disturbed by the British occupation of his country but was well versed in European culture and felt entirely at home with Western people. After a trip to Paris he is reported to have said, "In France I saw Muslims but no Islam; in Egypt I see Islam but no Muslims." In Iran, mullahs fought alongside secularist intellectuals for democratic, representative government. When the new parliament was established in 1906, Shaykh Muhammad Husain Naini (1850–1936) argued that it was the next best thing to the coming of the Shiite Messiah, who was expected to establish a rule of justice in the last days, because it would curb the tyranny of the Shah.

It is important to remember this early enthusiasm. When Muslims first encountered the modern, democratic West, they did not recoil in visceral disgust but recognized that it resonated with their own religious traditions. Today many Muslims and Westerners regard one another with deep distrust. After the atrocities of September 11, many in the West have come to believe that, as Samuel P. Huntington had predicted, there is indeed a clash of civilizations because their religion renders Muslims unfit for modernity. Many are convinced that "Islam" somehow compels Muslims to commit acts of terror and violence, that it applauds suicide bombers, and that it is inherently incompatible with liberal, Western democracy. This is understandable, since most Americans and Europeans have very little understanding of either Islam or the political conditions that have contributed to our present perilous predicament.

If we are indeed fighting a "war against terror," we need accurate information. We cannot afford to remain in ignorance because the stakes are now too high. It is vital to know who our enemies are, but it is equally important to know who they are *not*. Only a tiny proportion of Muslims take part in acts of terror and violence. If our media and politicians continue to denigrate Islam, accepting without question the stereotypical view that has prevailed in the West since the time of the Crusades, we will eventually alienate Muslims who have no quarrel with the West, who are either enjoying or longing for greater democracy, and who are horrified by the atrocities committed in the name of their faith. We urgently need to build bridges with the Islamic world. I can think of few projects that are more crucial at the present time.

That is why this book is so important. Instead of concentrating on *"What went Wrong?"* like Bernard Lewis, Imam Feisal Abdul Rauf shows what Islam has going for it and what it has to offer the West. He himself is a bridge figure because he has deep roots in both worlds. He was educated in Egypt, England, Malaysia, and the United States, and his mosque in New York City is only a few blocks away from the site of the World Trade Center. After September 11, people often asked me, "Where are the moderate Muslims? Why are they not speaking out?" In Imam Rauf, we have a Muslim who can speak to Western people in a way they can understand.

One of the most important assets of the United States in their struggle against terrorism is the Muslim community of America. Many American Muslims have long been aware that they can practice their religion far more creatively in the United States than they could in their countries of origin. Years before September 11, they were trying to build a vibrant and strong "American Islam," bringing up their children to be good Muslims and patriotic Americans. When I visited such a community in 1999, I suggested that they should—at least in some respects—look at the example of American Catholics. At the time of the War of Independence against Britain, only 1 percent of the colonists were Catholic. Catholics were a hated and despised minority: they were thought to be in league with Antichrist, ruled by a tyrannical pope, and indelibly opposed to freedom and democracy. Nobody would have dreamed that a Catholic would one day become the president of the United States. Those were bad times for American Catholics, but in the nineteen sixties, it was the bishops of the United States who were largely instrumental in pushing forward the reforms of the Second Vatican Council. Their faith had been invigorated by the American ideals of freedom, equality, and transparency in leadership, and, like Pope John XXIII, they wanted the bracing air of modernity to sweep through the musty corridors of the Vatican. Had this spirit prevailed, the Catholic Church might have avoided some of its present problems.

American Muslims could exert a similar influence on the Islamic world and prove that it is indeed possible to live according to the ideals of the Quran in the United States. But they cannot do that if they are shunned as potential terrorists and feel constantly on the defensive. It is vital that Western people realize that Islam is not an alien creed but that this tradition is deeply in tune with their own ideals. In these pages, they will see that for centuries Muslims created societies that were far more tolerant and pluralistic than European Christendom; that there are important principles of Muslim law that are highly congenial to democracy; and that the Quran stresses the importance of justice and equity, which are so central to the Western ideal. They will learn that Muslims helped Europeans rebuild their culture after the long trauma of the Dark Ages by reacquainting them with the philosophical, scientific, and mathematical heritage of ancient Greece.

But herein lies the rub. During the twelfth and thirteenth centuries, while European scholars were sitting at the feet of Muslim scholars in Spain, the European Crusaders were slaughtering Muslims in Palestine and Syria. There was, at this formative period of Western civilization, an unhealthy imbalance. In their efforts to build a new identity, Western Christians saw Jews and Muslims, the two victims of the Crusades, as a foil, a symbol of everything that they believed they were not (or feared that they were). They tended to project buried anxieties about their own behavior onto these two "enemies of civilization." Thus it was during the Crusades that scholar-monks of Europe stigmatized Islam as the religion of the sword, even though Christians themselves had instigated brutal holy wars against Muslims in the Middle East. During the Crusades, hatred of Jews became a chronic disease in Europe, and this shameful tradition led to some of the worst crimes of Western history. But our Islamophobia is equally ingrained, and the cruel atrocities of September 11 have confirmed many in the old crusading prejudice.

We now need to cultivate a more just and balanced view of Islam. The old medieval hatred was fueled by denial. It is always difficult to forgive people we have harmed. Crusading Christians found it impossible to appreciate the strengths of Muslim civilization because at a subconscious level they knew that they themselves had sinned. Jesus, after all, had told his followers to love their enemies, not exterminate them. Today Western people must become aware that during the last century their foreign policy has contributed to the present crisis. As Imam Rauf shows in these pages, by supporting undemocratic regimes in the Middle East, for example, Britain and America not only have failed to live up to their own ideals, they also have unwittingly fostered the growth of extremism. Nothing can excuse the massacre of September 11 or the suicide bombings in Israel and Palestine. Imam Rauf explains the causes of the malaise and abuse of religion in some parts of the Muslim world. Western people rightly demand that Muslims become more openly self-critical, but they cannot therefore turn a blind eye to their own shortcomings.

Imam Rauf's book has a positive message. It helps Muslims and Western peoples see a way out of the present impasse, in which atrocity leads to retaliation, attack to counterattack, to preemptive strike and a new spate of terror. If we are to break out of this vicious cycle, we must learn not simply to tolerate but to appreciate one another. The West has lost much of the admiration that it enjoyed in the days of Muhammad 'Abduh, partly because of its own misguided policies.

In the middle of the twentieth century, the Canadian scholar Wilfred Cantwell Smith issued a solemn warning. A healthy, functioning Islam is crucial for world peace because for centuries it helped Muslims cultivate values and ideals that we in the West also share, because they spring from a common tradition. Muslims must learn to accommodate the West and not fall prey to the lure of extremist rejection of Western power. But the peoples of the West must also realize "that they share the planet not with inferiors but with equals." If they fail, Smith concluded, both "will have failed to come to terms with the actualities of the twentieth century."[1] The blazing towers of the World Trade Center symbolize, perhaps, our collective failure to pass this test. This book shows that the only possible way forward is by the assiduous cultivation of mutual respect. It should be read, but then—even more important—it should be acted upon.

Preface

Most readers cannot afford to spend a lot of time mastering nuances of another religion that are important only to scholars. Most seek the insights into Islam that really matter—those that can help explain and illuminate the world of Islam vis-à-vis the issues of the day. And most readers want simple direct answers to heartfelt basic questions.

WHY READ THIS BOOK?

You may be an American congressional representative, concerned about U.S. national security, needing to know why anti-American rage is widespread in the Muslim world, why Muslim political movements are often couched in the vocabulary of Islam, and what spawns these movements. You also want to know what the American government might do differently to make our citizens safer, both domestically and abroad.

You may be a devout American Christian, offended that Iranians have called your beloved country the Great Satan and wondering if Islam is intrinsically anti-Christian.

You might be a religious conservative like George W. Bush, genuinely believing that Islam is a religion of peace yet puzzled as to why Muslims don't quite agree on Iran's membership in an "axis of evil."

You may be an American Jew, deeply attached to Israel, worried about the rise of anti-Semitism in the Muslim world, and anxious that 1.2 billion Muslims are out to destroy the land of your historical religious longing.

You may be a spiritual seeker, wondering why Islam is the fastest growing religion in the world.

You may be an American feminist intrigued by Barbara Walters's documentary on Saudi women and impressed by how strong-minded they were under their billowing black robes.

You may be a young American Muslim woman or man, confused between the picture of Islam that you see projected in the American media by Osama bin Laden and that practiced by your sweet grandmother who sits forever on her prayer rug praying that you will marry a devout Muslim boy or girl.

All the questions in this book were among those asked during my post–September 11 lectures, and I'm grateful to all the questioners who especially delighted in asking the tough ones.

WHY I SEEK A NEW VISION

Since September 11, Islam, a religion I love and that comprises my essential identity as a human being, has become broadly perceived in the United States as a national security threat, while America, a land whose values I cherish, has aroused broad antagonism and anguish in much of the Muslim world. Today American Muslims bear the pain of witnessing this growing divide, and my fellow Americans have challenged me to offer some urgently needed fresh ideas on how to bridge this yawning chasm.

The U.S. military victory over Saddam Hussein's regime in Iraq means that America is now responsible for shaping a new Iraq, a land deeply associated in the Muslim mind with some of Islam's greatest historical heritage. Iraq's capital, Baghdad, was the seat of the Abbasid Islamic caliphate for five centuries, from 750 CE to 1258 CE, a period of great development in all the Islamic sciences, from jurisprudence and philosophy to the physical sciences and fine arts.

Returning from a battle, the Prophet Muhammad once remarked to his companions that they were returning from the *lesser* jihad to the *greater* one, meaning from the battle fought with swords to the battle we wage within our hearts and minds to live the godly and good life. America has now won the lesser jihad, that of toppling the Saddam regime. Its larger challenge lies ahead: winning the hearts and minds of the Iraqis and, through them, the rest of the Muslim world. This waging of peace is now America's greater jihad.

For their part, American Muslims, those who have harmonized and integrated their American and Muslim identities, are uniquely positioned to help meet the challenge of waging peace. They have learned to speak to America about Islam, to the Muslim world about America, and to each about both the concord and the friction between Islamic values and American values. They are urgently needed if we are to bridge the chasm between the Muslim world and the West.

The burning question is how the horror of September 11 occurred in the name of Islam, and Americans legitimately fear that Islamic values seem to be inherently hostile to Western and democratic values.

In attempting to fathom the underlying issues, my non-Muslim American friends have probed: Is Islam's theology to blame? Does the problem arise from Islam's concept of jihad or a belief that suicide bombers enjoy the embraces of seventy-two virgins in Paradise? Or is the problem linked to the suppression of women in some Muslim societies, to the widely held Muslim belief in the nonseparation of church and state, to the erosion of moderate Islam at the hands of puritan Wahhabis, or to the lack of a Reformation like that in Christianity?

After a two-hour session of such questions and answers, the gauntlet is inevitably thrown before me: Well, how *do* we heal the relationship between the Muslim world and the West? This is the critical question of our time, and as an American Muslim fulfilling the obligations of an imam, I am compelled to attempt an answer.

For the last thirty-five years, in lectures at schools and universities, churches and synagogues—and yes, mosques too, every Friday and sometimes Sundays—I've been explaining the faith of Islam to Muslims and non-Muslims alike. Both groups need to clear their many misconceptions about Islam and Islamic thought, which has been grievously caricatured by non-Muslims and by Muslims insufficiently educated in their faith. It's a surprise to many—though not much of a secret, as many of my interfaith friends readily lament—that too many people in our respective Abrahamic faith traditions suffer from *misunderstanding* their own religion or not understanding it well enough. And while this is true *in spite of* attending churches, synagogues, and mosques, some argue that that is partly *because of* it. Many are dissatisfied, turned off, angered, frightened, or confused by their experiences at their places of worship. This happens at mosques too.

But ignorance of our own and others' faiths is not the only problem. Americans have become a religiously illiterate people, by-products of an era in which a gross misunderstanding of the separation of church and state led to such a cleavage between them that it became unfashionable or embarrassing to practice our religious heritage and passé to study it. While religious illiteracy poses no threat in those who are not religious practitioners, it does become dangerous in those who decide to take religion seriously: they don't know that they don't know—a category of believer that our wise teachers have advised us to flee from![1] And when these become our teachers of religion, is it any surprise that an important book must be written whose title is *When Religion Becomes Evil?*[2]

There is little doubt today that the rise of religious fundamentalisms represented the reaction of religion against the antireligious secular modernism that peaked in the mid-twentieth century.

I am both a Muslim and an American citizen, as proud of the important and fundamental principles that America stands for as I am proud of the important and fundamental principles for which Islam stands. Both America and the Muslim world have nourished me in important ways, yet I'm pained by what they have done to each other.

September 11, a day that will live in infamy for having provoked the United States into a war, confused and frightened many non-Muslim Americans about Islam. Being told that Islam is a religion of peace doesn't jive with images of Muslim spokesmen railing against America or publicly attacking Christians and Jews or with television images of Iranians screaming "Death to America!" No longer did the news reports cover suicide bombers attacking military targets thousands of miles distant. Now the attack had taken place at home, and Americans could no longer afford to be complacent.

The attack on the World Trade Center changed the equation in critical ways: CNN's "America at War" headline became a household fixture; and for the first time since the War of 1812, America had been attacked in the contiguous forty-eight states. American civilians were at risk of foreign attack from a faceless enemy directly associated with *my religion*—Islam. And to drive home the point, this attack targeted the most important symbols of U.S. power:

- The World Trade Center, symbol of Wall Street and U.S. economic power

- The Pentagon, headquarters of the U.S. military complex, the most powerful military in the world, whose annual budget is equal to the military budgets of the next twenty countries combined

- The U.S. Capitol building, symbol of our democracy

This was much too close for comfort, and no nation could suffer such an assault without responding in a very robust way.

All the while, continuing news of suicide bombers in Israel and in Muslim countries such as Pakistan, Indonesia, and Iraq, and more recently in Saudi Arabia and Morocco, have further reinforced American stereotypes about and fear of Muslims.

Fear breeds a number of things: hatred of anything associated with "the enemy"—from ethnic appearance to clothing to religion—and a circling-of-the-wagons mentality. This country veered uncritically to the right, going overnight from a nation where burning the flag, offensive as it might be, was a constitutionally protected right to one where you were politically incorrect if you did not sport a flag on your lapel; from partisan politics to (briefly) the most nonpartisan political scene in our lifetimes. Was Samuel Huntington right? Were we witnessing a "clash of civilizations" between the West and the rest—in this case between Western civilization and Islam? It seemed too simple: How could America hate some five to seven million of its own?

The attacks on the World Trade Center and the Pentagon also changed me personally. Before September 11 I was an Islamic teacher focusing on the theological, spiritual, and jurisprudential side of my faith and active in interfaith work in New York City. I went from refusing to get dragged into politics because I saw it as a no-win situation to being forced to explain myself and defend my faith. The events of that day in 2001 pulled me out of the warm mahogany pulpit at my mosque twelve blocks north of ground zero in New York City. Inundated by requests to "explain the Islamic viewpoint," I hurried from one television and radio interview to the next, trying to explain in a few sound bites the depths of the issues.

My commitment to improving relations among the religious communities and to ministering to the hurts in life to which we humans are subject propelled me onto a speaking circuit of synagogues, churches, seminaries, and interfaith groups, seeking ways to help others understand and recognize the higher ground that unites our faith traditions.

This book is dedicated to that effort. Here we will analyze the divide between the Muslim world and the United States and identify what is precious in the heritage of each. We will address some of the burning questions raised since September 11 on issues of religion, politics, economics, sociology, and psychology. Through increasing our understanding of how the relationship between the Muslim world and the West went wrong, we can begin to discover ways to rebuild it.

Imam Feisal Abdul Rauf
New York, 2004

Overture: A Cordoba Lost

After two wars, the first to end the authoritarian Taliban regime in Afghanistan, the second to end the authoritarian secular Baathist regime in Iraq, the United States finds itself more estranged than ever from the Muslim world.

Under a June 2003 headline, "Muslims Reveal Fear and Loathing of America," the *Financial Times* reported a new survey by the Pew Global Attitudes Project, "Views of a Changing World 2003: War with Iraq Further Divides Global Publics." The report concluded, "The bottom has fallen out of support for America in most of the Muslim world."[1] It cited as an example that only 1 percent of the citizens of Jordan hold a "favorable impression" of the United States. Meanwhile, the twentieth-century "arc of crisis," stretching across the Muslim world from South Asia to the Mediterranean, continues to seethe, and the polarization between the United States and the Muslim world now is as bad as it has ever been. Even though we don't know if he's still alive, Osama bin Laden still receives significant backing from Muslims for being the leader most capable of "doing the right thing regarding world affairs," according to the Pew study. Clearly, something is deeply wrong in America's relationship with the Muslim world.

Yet, how can this be? Core Islamic values overlap with core American values. The three Abrahamic religions—Judaism, Christianity, and Islam—share the two greatest commandments:

1. To love God with all our heart, mind, soul, and strength

2. To love our neighbors—that is, our fellow human beings—regardless of race, religion, or cultural background as we love ourselves

Whenever each religious tradition has honored these command-ments, it has contributed to humanity's growth and progress. Where one has failed, it has contributed to conflict and disease both within its own society and between its society and that of others.

What Muslims have done right, and still do well, is to fulfill the first commandment through acts of worship: the five "pillars" of daily sacramental prayer, public charity, fasting, and pilgrimage. All these actions express and are devoted to the primary pillar of faith: adoration and remembrance of the one God.   *to one more shudada*

At a social level the Muslim world, by and large, fulfills the second commandment through a strong sense of valuing community over in-dividualism and teaching a deep-seated responsibility to help others through charity and other acts. In the past Muslims successfully insti-tutionalized the second commandment by establishing pluralistic so-cieties that respected religious, racial, and ethnic differences while including them all within the greater community. Islamic history offers models of pluralism that could be quite instructive for modern Amer-ican society, such as a court system that decided cases according to different religions' laws. Throughout most of Islamic history, laws dif-fered not only from region to region but also within a given region. Laws were applied based upon the litigants' beliefs, especially in mat-ters of marriage and divorce, custody, and inheritance. Such individu-alized judicial systems presided over Muslim, Jewish, and Christian communities in the Middle East and over Muslim, Hindu, and other religious communities in South Asia. A Jewish couple engaging in a custody case, for example, could opt to have their case heard under Jewish law.

For many centuries, Islam inspired a civilization that was particu-larly tolerant and pluralistic. From 800 to 1200 CE, for example, the Cordoba Caliphate ruled much of today's Spain amid a rich flowering of art, culture, philosophy, and science. Many Jewish and Christian artists and intellectuals emigrated to Cordoba during this period to es-cape the more oppressive regimes that reigned over Europe's Dark and Middle Ages. Great Jewish philosophers such as Maimonides were free to create their historic works within the pluralistic culture of Islam.

This flowering of Islamic culture, however, reached a plateau after the thirteenth century while European civilization entered its age of enlightenment and experienced a period of dramatic advancement. The repercussions of this turnaround in the fortunes of the two civilizations are still felt today in the Middle East, and they form the background for much of today's dysfunctional relationship between the Muslim world and the West. One of this book's goals will be to illuminate this historical reversal and the role that it continues to play today.

Meanwhile, by the seventeenth century, two extremely powerful ideas arose in Europe, ideas that paradoxically formed the core of its institutional support for the second commandment:

- The notion that reasonable interest on a monetary loan does not amount to usury—an idea that made possible a certain system of banking

- The invention of the corporation, especially the notion that the corporation is a separate "person," with owners (shareholders) protected from responsibility for any liability, such as unpaid debt or crime, incurred by the company

It is ironic that enormous good has come from the inventions of banking and the corporation—two practices that were once major sins in all the Abrahamic faith traditions: charging interest for moneylending and eliminating the obligation to fully repay one's debt. But these two institutions combined with the emergence of modern liberal democracy to radically improve the fortunes of the Western world. The beginnings of modern capitalism—made possible by the limited liability company and its ability to borrow money and invest it in highly profitable but risky ventures without completely wiping out its owners' assets—led to the creation of enormous wealth and fueled the rise of the West to economic dominance, which continues to this day. Not being able to accept these ideas is one of the primary reasons the Muslim world lagged behind the West and the Asian Pacific nations, which did not have to contend with the religious compunctions that held the Muslim world back. The problem was that Muslim jurists equated any amount of interest, no matter how small, with usury, which the Quran absolutely forbids. This strict prohibition on charging interest still prevails in the Muslim world and has largely prevented it from robustly developing the financial market's institutions of banking, capital markets, and stock exchanges—the foundations of capitalism. Neither could Muslim nations effectively control their own monetary policies, since raising and lowering interest rates is the chief way a nation's central bank controls inflation and the amount of money in circulation.

The rise of European capitalism went hand in hand with the spread of European colonialism. And with colonialism comes the issue of race, another factor that would affect the relationship between the Muslim world and the West.

European assumptions of supremacy over non-European peoples included components of culture and religion as well as race. Although Samuel Huntington calls it a "West versus the rest" fault line of conflict, deeming it civilizational, I believe the conflict more accurately emanated from assumptions about race. More broadly, however, the fault line lay between Europe and the rest of the world, which it deemed an "other" that could be freely dominated, exploited, and subjugated—a gross violation of the second commandment shared by the Abrahamic religions.

European assumptions of superiority over non-Europeans were projected onto religion and created subsidiary fault lines of conflict: the divide between Western European Christianity and Eastern (Orthodox) Christianity; the fault line between European Ashkanazi Judaism and non-European Sephardic Judaism.

The effort of European colonial powers to Europeanize Muslim and other societies sowed seeds of conflict by deeply confusing the subject people's identity in two ways. First was the conflict—what Huntington calls the "tear"—in these societies caused by creating a new elite of natives in a European image. For example, the British tried to create a race of "brown Englishmen" ruling over India, thereby tearing a segment of Indian society from itself culturally, linguistically, and religiously. The French did this in their colonies of Algeria and other places in West Africa, the Spanish in the New World of Central and South America. Where external colonialism did not succeed, as in Turkey and Iran, Westernized locals such as Kemal Atatürk (in the 1920s) and the Shah of Iran (in the 1930s) militantly Europeanized their societies. The process created a cultural tear between a society and its rulers, who belonged racially to the indigenous civilization but aspired mentally and culturally to the West, thereby belonging fully to neither.

The second fault line created by European colonialism resulted from splitting traditional identities by creating new nation-state identities based upon *geography*. Many non-European peoples identified themselves traditionally by tribe, language, and religion; geography was a secondary definition. Yet colonial powers divided peoples like the Kurds and the Uzbeks among two or more nation-states. The Kurds were denied their own state and forced to belong to Turkey, Iraq, or Iran. The Uzbeks were divided between Uzbekistan and Afghanistan, and the Tajiks (who are an Iranian people) between Tajikistan and Afghanistan. Splitting a people who feel part of one nation into two or three is a recipe for conflict. The reverse trend, combining different peoples into a new identity that is based on nothing but geography, completed the picture of conflict seeded by colonialism. A good example of this is Nigeria, where two hundred and fifty different religious, tribal, and language groupings were pooled by the British to create the nation-state of Nigeria.

The founders of America inherited European prejudices against other races, but they also shared with the world's colonies the experience of oppression under a colonial power.

Having created two historic documents reflecting the ideals of liberty and religious pluralism, the Declaration of Independence and the Bill of Rights, Americans continued to operate from a Eurocentric worldview that excluded Native Americans, African Americans, Asians, and other races from the family of human rights and protections until the twentieth century. Nonmainstream Protestants, Catholics, Jews, or people of other faith traditions were not fully admitted to the American family until that time.

Capitalism in Europe diffused the landed aristocracy's monopoly on power by creating new owners of wealth who could provide sizable loans to the aristocracy—even to the royal families and the state. Capitalism, by spreading wealth to nonnoble landless classes of society, sparked agitation against the monarchical systems of rule, eventually feeding the human desire to experiment with new forms of governance: democracy and socialism or communism.

The experiences of the twentieth century proved that democracy worked better than authoritarian totalitarian rule, and capitalism better than socialism. *Democratic capitalism*, a term describing the potent combination of democracy with a free-market economy, has demonstrated its success over a command economy, which typically requires authoritarian rule.

The West's dramatic material advancements over the last four centuries, fueled by the simultaneous development of democracy and capitalism, are perceived as companions to the rise of reason and the beginnings of secular humanism. This philosophical trend of secularism promoted the West's concept of religious freedom, which was enshrined in the First Amendment of the American Constitution as the separation of church and state. America's founding fathers believed strongly that religion cannot and must not be entrusted to the halls of power. The rise of science and secularism peaked in the twentieth century, when a strong antireligious secularism became viewed as the impulse of modernity.

Yet the American notion of the separation of church and state was not intended to develop an atheistic or agnostic society. Rather, the objective was to allow any and all religions to thrive while preventing the state from using its powers to establish one religion or religious doctrine over any other.

But in the twentieth century, a more militant secularism gained currency in America, and the separation of church and state was reinterpreted in ways that were increasingly antireligious. In a sense, antireligionism crept in as a new state religion, in my opinion, violating the intent of the First Amendment authors.[2]

The rise of an aggressive antireligion sentiment in the West and within the ruling elite of much of the remaining world, dismissing as it did the religious voice from participating in society's political and economic boardrooms, created an equal and opposite reaction in the twentieth century: the rise of religious fundamentalisms worldwide, as Christians, Muslims, Jews, Hindus, Sikhs, and Buddhists all experienced fundamentalism and its attending expressions of militancy. All fundamentalisms shared one common enemy: "secular modernity"— not because of secularism or modernity per se, but because secular modernity was viewed as actively antireligious.

The Muslim world still perceives that the West distrusts religious voices and will not brook their presence in the discourse on building the good society. Muslims believe that America needs to reestablish its original understanding of the First Amendment, which balances the separation of church and state with freedom of religion by allowing all religions equal standing and by honoring the role of religion in building the good society. This balance is enormously important to Muslims.

Muslims have yet to fully incorporate the institutional expressions of democratic capitalism, defined as the combination of democracy and capitalism, into their various essential institutions: the rule of law (an independent judiciary), human rights, a stable currency, equal opportunity, free markets, social safety nets, and so forth. These principles, in my view, are among the most important *institutional* expressions of the second commandment that humanity has invented. They are one of the most important contributions Western Judeo-Christianity has made to the good society in the United States.[3]

By helping its masses enjoy greater economic well-being and a better quality of life and by allowing them to participate in the decisions governing their lives, democratic capitalism has contributed to the betterment of the "neighbor"—humanity at large.

America has continued improving and perfecting democratic capitalism, but too often it has confined its idealism to the West, while its efforts to encourage democratic capitalism in Muslim societies have been less than robust: In addition, the West's perceived alliance with authoritarian regimes ruling over Muslim populations, which have discouraged and suppressed the rise of democratic institutions, along with America's seeming refusal to support the rise of Islamic forms of democracy, have deepened the historical divide between the Muslim world and the West.

We have now identified several of the key historical threads that begin to explain the rise of Islamic religious fundamentalism. These include:

• The rapid accumulation of Western wealth, fueled by democratic capitalism, and the perception that this wealth is used to aggravate the plight of the poor

- A psychological sense that the Islamic world had "fallen behind" and that its civic institutions were not living up to the second commandment in terms of providing for its people, even in Islamic terms

- The social tears and fault lines of conflict etched in the unnatural landscape left behind by European colonialism

- The rise of a "militant" modern secularism, which threatened traditional Islamic culture and religion

- The perception throughout most of the twentieth century that Western nations restricted their political and military support to undemocratic regimes

These currents, taken together, fertilized the soil of frustration in which twentieth-century Islamic religious fundamentalism grew and flourished.

HOW DO WE HEAL THE RELATIONSHIP?

So how do we set about healing the relationship between the Muslim world and America?

What America has done *right* institutionally in perfecting democratic capitalism reflects the extent to which its democratic capitalism enables the fulfillment of the second commandment. And while the United States in the past often denied many of its rights and benefits to non-Europeans (Native Americans and African Americans), and while it retains vestiges of this attitude toward the non-European world, what the Muslim world wants now is be included as a full, welcome member in the family of humankind, meriting equal treatment from the United States and the European community. (For example, the Muslim world perceives that Turkey is denied admission to the European Union solely because it is a predominantly Muslim country.)

America has had a profound impact on global religion. American Protestantism created a healthy separation between church and state and bequeathed its ideas of pluralism to European Protestantism. American Catholicism influenced global Catholicism, helping bring about Vatican II and its very American ideas about pluralism and church-state separation. American Judaism by and large reconfigured world Jewry. It is time for an American Islam that will translate into the Islamic vernacular, for the Muslim and non-Muslim worlds, the best of the American dream, namely, its pursuit of the second commandment through the benefits of democratic capitalism.

In return, the heritage of Islamic civilization has much to offer the West. It could contribute substantially to an expanded cross-cultural dialogue, an enhanced pluralism, and the exploration of new ideas. Islam could make its own invaluable contributions to American understandings of the ideal role for religion and culture in a multiethnic good society. And a healthy Western Islam could be critically important in mediating differences and improving the relationship between Muslim countries and America.

By anchoring ourselves deeply within the true fundamentals of our faith traditions, without excluding the ethics of a secular humanism (which I strongly believe are the ethical injunctions of the second commandment stated separately from the first), we can chart a fresh course for resolving the conflict between the West and the Muslim world. The American Muslim perspective is indispensable if we are to successfully bridge the chasm between America, today's sole military and economic superpower, and the 1.2 billion Muslims around the globe.

We strive for a "New Cordoba," a time when Jews, Christians, Muslims, and all other faith traditions will live together in peace, enjoying a renewed vision of what the good society can look like. In this good society all religious voices are welcome and given maximum freedom, and no one religion (or even atheism) is allowed to inhibit any other. Toward this dream we aspire.

CHAPTER 1

Common Roots

Many of the earliest civilizations believed in a plurality of gods. From the ruins and temples of ancient Mesopotamia and Egypt in the Middle East and Greece and Rome in Europe to India and China in the Far East, the majority of early civilizations worshiped a pantheon of gods, with each god ruling over a sector of the universe and all of them ruled by a greater God. Representing their gods in the forms of statues, early people practiced idolatry, worshiping the gods' physical representations.

HE WHO CARVES THE BUDDHA NEVER WORSHIPS HIM

In such societies, the pharaoh, emperor, caesar, or king was generally regarded as divine, a son of God, and the priestly class (like the Brahmins in India) a privileged one that supported his function as semi-divine. Worldly society reflected the structure of the divine court, the pharaoh or king with his consort ruling over society just as the Great God had a consort and children who were gods, ruling over the many lesser gods. As the son of God, the king was God's representative on earth.

Together with such beliefs about the God-human relationship came a belief in the structure of human society. People were born into classes or castes reflecting the structure of the divine court, showing life "on earth, as it is in heaven." In society were found the royal and noble classes, the priestly class, the warrior class, the merchant and farming classes, and all those who did the most menial and undesirable work. Social mobility was not typically the norm; one was born, worked, married, and died within the boundaries of one's class. One's status in life, profession, and choice of spouse were predetermined by the family and class one was born into—by the social structure—and one's destiny was deemed in some societies as karmic.

In many of these societies, rejecting the state religion was not a simple matter of exercising freedom of human conscience (something we in America take for granted today). It was typically regarded as treason against the state, an act punishable by death, not to mention a violation of the institutional social structure on which society was built. Literally, one had no place in society, for such a person would be like an ant rejecting the structure of its colony, unprotected by its institutions. The possible freedom one had to exercise such inner convictions and to be true to oneself was to opt out of society and live as a hermit in a cave. Pre-Islamic Arabs called such people, driven by their conscience and desiring to live by its standards, *hanif*.

Such powerful social constraints may sound strange to the contemporary American reader, but a mere fifty years ago in America, "unless one was either a Protestant, or a Catholic, or a Jew, one was a 'nothing'; to be a 'something,' to have a name, one [had to] identify oneself to oneself, and be identified by others, as belonging to one or another of the three great religious communities in which the American people were divided."[1]

To be independent and step out of sociological norms and deeply embedded thought patterns is very hard for people to do. And if it was hard for us in America, a country where we prize individual freedom, you can imagine how hard it must have been a few thousand years ago in the earliest known ancient Middle Eastern civilizations that straddled the area between Egypt and Persia.

In that region, and in such a society characterized by a polytheistic religious, political, and sociological climate, a *hanif* man called Abraham was born in a town in Mesopotamia, the area now called Iraq. He found the idea of polytheism unacceptable. Biblical and Islamic narratives inform us that Abraham's father was a sculptor of such idols. We can well imagine the young boy Abraham seeing his father fabricating such statues from the raw material of wood or stone and perhaps occasionally cursing when the material cracked. The reality of the Chinese proverb "He who carves the Buddha never worships him" must have been apparent to Abraham, who probably observed, in the way children see through their parents' absurdities, the creature creating the Creator.

The Quran quotes Abraham as debating with his contemporaries: "Do you worship that which you yourselves sculpt—while God has created you and your actions?" (37:95–96). After going on a spiritual search, and after rejecting the sun, the moon, and the stars as objects of worship (objects his community worshiped), Abraham realized that there could be only one creator of the universe—one God (Quran 6:75–91 describes Abraham's search for God). Today Muslims, Christians, and Jews regard Abraham as their patriarch, the founder of a sustained monotheistic society subscribing to the belief that there is only one God, the Creator and Sustainer of the Universe.

The monotheism that Abraham taught was not only *theologically* radical, in that it decried the plurality of gods as false, it was also *socially* radical. The idea that God is one implied two significant things about humankind.

First, it implied that *all humans are equal,* simply because we are born of one man and one woman. "O humankind," God asserts in the Quran, "surely we have created you from one male [Adam] and one female [Eve] and made you into tribes and clans [just] so that you may get to know each other. The noblest of you with God are the most devout of you" (Quran 49:13). This meant that all of humankind is a family—brothers and sisters, equal before God, differentiated only by the nobility of our actions, not by our birth. Showing preference for one human over another on the basis of accidents of birth, like skin color, class structure, tribal or family belonging, or gender, is unjust and therefore has no place in a proper *human* worldview. Although it grossly violates reason and ethics, showing preference on the basis of these categories is the very way people traditionally judged others and structured their societies.

Second, because we are equal and have been given free will by our Creator, we have certain inalienable liberties. The most significant liberty we have been given is to accept or reject God, our Creator. Every other choice is a distant second to this, from the liberty to choose between a host of right and wrong actions to the liberty to choose our spouse or profession instead of being born into them. Because we are free to think for ourselves, thought control is anathema to this ethic of free will. Even today, in many parts of the world people are still socially coerced into a certain religious belief, job, spouse, or way of thinking. Our delight in movies that depict the love story of a prince who wants to marry a poor farmer's daughter demonstrates how much this commitment to free will is embedded in us—how we sympathize with those prohibited from marrying "outside their class" by such social rules of propriety.

"There shall be no coercion in religion; the right way is clearly distinct from error," asserts the Quran (2:256). In verses such as "The Truth is from your Lord; *so let whomever wills, believe, and let whomever wills, disbelieve*" (Quran 18:29, italics mine), the Quran asserts that God created us free to choose to believe in or reject God. "Had God willed He would have made you into one community (*ummah*); but [it was His will] to test you in what He gave you. So compete with each other in doing good works. To God you are all returning, and He will inform you about how you differed" (Quran 5:48).

Human free will, the liberty to make our own individual choices—and our own mistakes—is essential to human dignity. Only if we have free will can we be held individually accountable for our choices and actions. Only then can we grow and mature, *learning* to be responsible agents. Without the freedom to choose, how could we be held responsible?[2]

But because individual humans can and do freely exercise their will in ways that sow inequality and limit the liberties of others, an ethic of free will judges such violations as wrong, unjust, and tyrannical. Jews, Christians, and Muslims therefore have a particularly strong sense of social justice; they are keen to seek retributive justice.

We shall call this cluster of monotheism's core ideas and its concomitants of human liberty, equality, fraternity, and social justice the *Abrahamic ethic*. These ideas constitute the essential core of Abrahamic religion and the later iterations and reformations of the Abrahamic religion known today as the faith traditions of Judaism, Christianity, and Islam.[3] The Abrahamic ethic required that society allow its individual members the freedoms appropriate to human dignity, the freedom to stand before the Creator and exercise individual choices without society's coercion. This ethic speaks not only to *theology*, that is, that our ideas about God should be built upon the idea of God's oneness, transcendence, and ineffability, but also to issues of sociology and politics, about how society should be structured, namely, that society should be structured on the basis of human equality, human liberty, and social justice.

Readers may wonder why monotheists call Abraham the "father of us all" rather than exclusively of the monotheistic faith traditions. While it's true that India, China, and Japan are not generally monotheistic societies, increasingly they are implementing democratic systems of governance—systems anchored in the concept of human equality and thus emanating from the Abrahamic ethic. This is an ethic that is embedded in our human nature.

In the polytheistic society of Abraham's time, it was politically and sociologically incorrect to claim that liberty, equality, fraternity, and social justice were essential to the human condition; such talk was not only revolutionary, it would have required a paradigm shift in social thought. While a prophet conveying this message might be popular with the poor and disenfranchised in society, the message itself threatened to deprive the higher classes of their special status in society. In most cases entrenched power elites vigorously fought any prophet who conveyed such a message. Abraham tried unsuccessfully to convince his people to believe in only one God, a God who is beyond human capacity to fully comprehend, who bears no resemblance to humanly sculpted likenesses. The Quran says that those who rejected Abraham's message urged their people to move against Abraham for his perfidy against their gods: "Burn him and defend your gods—if you're going to do something!" Abraham was saved by God, who commanded the flame to "be lukewarm and a safe haven for Abraham!" (Quran 21:68–69).

The Quran laments the human tendency to reject God's prophets sent to guide humanity: "We indeed gave Moses the Book, and sent a string of messengers succeeding him, and We gave Jesus son of Mary clear arguments, aiding him with the Holy Spirit. Why is it then that whenever a messenger came to you with what didn't match your desires, some you rejected, and others you slew?" (Quran 2:87). Prophets were not welcomed; rather they were attacked, punished, and chased out of town for trying to convince their contemporaries of the truths of monotheism. Abraham suffered the same fate, leaving town with his followers.

THE ABRAHAMIC ETHIC: JUST HUMAN NATURE

The Quran states[4] that monotheism and its social concomitants, as true or right religiousness, were embedded by God in human nature as part of human conscience and that God commanded humanity to honor it: "Be religious in accordance with your truest inclinations [literally, *hanif*-ly], the immutable nature (*fitrah*) of God upon which He created people—there is no altering God's creation—that is right religiousness, but most people do not know" (Quran 30:30).[5] The idea of this verse is that any person who listens to his or her heart and conscience would recognize that God is One, that humanity is one family, that humans should be free and should treat each other fairly and with justice.[6]

Muslims therefore call their faith *din al-fitrah*, "natural religiousness," meaning the goodness that flows out of human nature, action that we regard as self-evidently right and ethical, a gift of God to all humans, a piety that we are born into before our parents shaped us into their socially accepted beliefs. Those who practice what their hearts tell them are therefore practicing the right religion for them at that moment.

God calls this natural religiosity "His own religion" (*din Allah*, Quran 3:83, 110:2), something God has bestowed to the human critical faculties of reason and understanding. Its content is universally imperative; all humans ought to fulfill it since they have been equipped at birth with all that is required to know it. Its primary component is the recognition that God is One, is indeed God, and that no one else is God. The rest of it revolves around our creatureliness vis-à-vis the Creator, a relationship that can be nothing but loving worship and service: "I have not created jinnkind[7] and humankind except to worship Me. I desire no aid from them, nor do I desire that they feed Me" (Quran 51:56–57). This relationship involves the observance of His patterns, which are knowable by reason, with which He equipped all humans. Recognition of God is everybody's business, everybody's prerogative, everybody's possibility, and everybody's supreme duty.

The Quran emphasizes the universality of the Abrahamic ethic by asking, "And who desires other than the Abrahamic ethic (*millati ibrahim*) except the one who depreciates himself?" (Quran 2:130). Implicit here is that the Abrahamic ethic honors human dignity and demands that a human being respect his or her dignity as human, and it holds no countenance for religious or social practices that discriminate between humans at birth, deeming some capable and others incapable by nature of knowing God. Such doctrines absolve those whom they declare incapable of the supreme duty of acknowledging and worshiping the one God and thus rob them of their essential humanity.

This natural religiousness or natural piety is absolutely normative for all humans. By definition, it admits of no exception. While it may not coerce anyone into observing its tenets, it is categorically opposed to, and condemning of, those who violate them or permit their violation; otherwise, it would not be consistent with itself. God describes Himself in the Quran as "Nature's God" by using a variety of descriptive expressions of Nature, such as Lord of the worlds (Quran 1:2), Lord of the heavens and the earth and what is between them (Quran 78:37), Lord of the east and the west (Quran 73:9), and so forth. The Abrahamic ethic, as the defining feature of Jewish, Christian, and Islamic praxis, presents its case as a demand of nature, a necessary requisite of reason, and a critical truth.

It was therefore no accident that the cry of the French Revolution was for human "liberty, equality and fraternity," essential components of the Abrahamic ethic. Neither was it an accident that the authors of the American Declaration of Independence expressed the Abrahamic ethic as "self-evident Truths: that all men are created equal, endowed by their Creator with certain unalienable rights," a Creator whose laws of creation are by definition the laws of nature. And since nature is a manifestation of God's creation, nature's laws are therefore God's laws: natural law is divine law. So, the argument goes, what you feel in your heart as good and right is the very foundation of divine law.

KNOWING GOOD FROM EVIL

Throughout human history, all religious thought, whether mono-, poly-, or pantheistic, was based on people's inner conviction that everything in the universe is the outcome of a creative, conscious all-embracing power or, simply stated, God. This power creates by an act of will, which we call the divine will, and therefore all that exists is by definition in accord with that will.

Human existence is a product of that will and power and is there-fore subjugated to it. We are again by definition "submitted" to that will and power. Our physical being, for example, is created and shaped by it, as are the appetites of our physical being. We are created to feel hunger and thirst, and we submit to hunger by feeding ourselves, sub-mit to our thirst by quenching it. When satiated, we submit to that feel-ing by stopping eating or drinking. Although we have a will of our own, there are limits to that will. We can choose to drink or not to drink, we can overeat or overdrink, but at a certain point we can eat no more even if we want to. In addition to our physical being, we also have a passionate or emotive aspect to our being, an intellectual think-ing capacity, a mind; and we have a spiritual side to our being, our soul. We directly know that overeating is not right, even without exer-cising our thinking capacity; we observe that it is not in our interest; it is harmful, thus wrong.

What is good for a creature is that which benefits it, what is bad is what harms it. Our idea of what is good is therefore what benefits me, and what is bad is what harms me. This dynamic of self-interest sows disagreement and conflict when what benefits me harms you. Har-mony between two or more individuals is when a means is figured out whereby each side feels benefited. The public good, or what is right, is what maximizes the good for each member of the group and for the in-terest of the group as a whole.

But our own will exists because of the divine will, empowered and embraced by it. The question that arises is, does the divine will have an interest in or a preference for a given outcome when humans exercise their will? The short answer is yes. And the divine preference is for the human to submit his or her will to—freely choosing—that which God has recommended. The recommendation is most succinctly stated in two requests that God has made of humanity:

1. To love the one and only God with all our heart, mind, soul, and strength

2. To love our neighbors, that is, our fellow human beings, re-gardless of race, religion, or cultural background, as we love ourselves

Doing this means that we align ourselves with the Creator's definition of good. Rejecting these principles means we have aligned with the Creator's definition of bad or evil. And since the Creator is by definition the Absolute, the Creator's definition of the good is the closest that we relative and contingent beings can get to the absolute good. All morality, all public good, all ethics, are anchored on the fulfillment of these two principles in practice.

When we love someone, it is natural that we love that which she or he loves; we express our love by aligning our love with the beloved's loves and preferences. To love God, the Absolute Being, must therefore mean that we ought to love God's preferences.

Many deeply religious people focus on the first commandment to love and worship God but have no regard for their fellow human beings. Jesus Christ was once asked what the greatest commandment was, and after mentioning the first, he emphasized the equal importance of the second commandment when he prefaced it by saying, "And the second is like unto it," adding, "On these two commandments hang all the law and the prophets" (Matthew 23:36–40).

When a pagan once challenged Hillel to summarize the whole of the Torah while he stood on one foot, Hillel answered, "What is hateful to you do not do unto your fellow human being, this is the whole of the Torah; the rest is commentary, go and learn" (Shabbat 31A). Rabbi Akiba affirmed that the central principle of the Torah is, "You shall love your neighbor as yourself " (Bereshit Rabbah 24).[8]

Loving God is not complete unless we love what God loves. Loving God is necessarily incomplete if we do not love God's prophets and messengers and, in the words of the Quran, "not separate, or differentiate, among them" (Quran 2:285). This means not saying that "my prophet is better than yours." God certainly loves His prophets, all of them, and we are therefore to love all the prophets, and not differentiate between them. This also suggests that we are not to claim that the prophets came with different messages but to assert that they came with the same message.

My father once told me that when he was a young boy, his father (my grandfather) told him, "Muhammad, my son, can you imagine that someone would love someone else more than he loves himself?" Puzzled by the question and not knowing how to respond, my father was overwhelmed when my grandfather added, "I love you more than I love myself." This is the love of parenthood, which sacrifices its own self for the benefit of the child.

The relationship between parent and child echoes God's love toward humanity.[9] The first commandment is God's request that humanity reciprocate the divine love extended to it, and the second commandment is that human beings act toward each other with reciprocal love. God is Absolute Being; we are contingent beings. We therefore must love God as "absolutely" as we can, therefore "with all our heart, mind, soul, and strength." And because we are all equal, born equal, of one man and one woman, we must strive to love each other equally as we love ourselves.

The prophets are exemplars to us, windows through which we see the divine presence and will expressed in the purest and most highly refined form of human behavior and ethics. The prophets therefore represent the best of humanity and are a select group from what God calls in the Quran his "friends," (*awliya'*, plural of *wali*), those we call "saints" in English. Of all humanity, we should love and honor the saints more than we love and honor any other class of humanity, and because they are imbued with God's presence, they deserve to be loved more than those of humanity who are not imbued with that presence. The Prophet once said, "If you love me, then love those whom I love," which flows from the principle that if we love God, then our love is incomplete if we don't love those whom—and that which—God loves.

When Jews, Christians, Muslims, and all people of any faith discover a way to help each other truly adhere to these shared teachings, treating each other as they want themselves treated, religious conflict between them will cease.

ABRAHAM'S IDEA OF THE GOOD SOCIETY

The above-quoted Quranic verse, which points out that whoever desires something other than the religion of Abraham has disgraced himself (Quran 2:130), goes on to say that God commanded Abraham to "Submit!" (*aslim*), whereupon he responded, "I submit myself (*aslamtu*) to the Lord of the worlds." The Quran calls Abraham a *muslim* (Quran 2:130–36, also 22:78) and defines *Islam* as the human act of submitting oneself to God in accord with the principles we have described above as comprising the Abrahamic ethic.[10] The Quran continues, "And Abraham enjoined his sons, and so did Jacob: "O my sons, surely God has chosen religion for you, so don't die except that you are submitted" (*muslimun*, that is, muslims). "Or were you witnesses when Jacob was on the verge of death, when he said to his sons, 'What will you worship after me?' They answered, 'We shall worship your God and the God of your fathers Abraham, and Ishmael and Isaac; one God only, and to Him we are submitters'" (*muslimun*, Quran 2:130–33).

Abraham enjoined his sons Ishmael (born from Hagar) and Isaac (born from Sarah) to worship only this one God, and they in turn enjoined the same upon their children. Isaac's son Jacob, later renamed Israel, had twelve sons, each who fathered the tribes collectively known as the Children of Israel. The Arabs are regarded as the descendants of Ishmael and the Jews the descendants, or children, of Israel.

The monotheistic principle is enshrined in the Hebrew Shema, which the Prophet Moses taught his followers: *Shma yisrael adonai elohenu adonai echad:* "Hear, O Israel, the Lord our God, the Lord is One." Although Moses addressed the Children of Israel, it is a call that is in fact addressed to all humanity—that the Lord our God, the Lord is One. The human response to this call is cogently expressed in the Arabic declaration of faith (*shahadah*) that the Prophet Muhammad taught his followers: *Ash hadu an la ilaha illallah:* "I declare that there is no god but God."

The Quran regards all the prophets named in the Bible who came to announce this teaching, including Aaron, Moses, John the Baptist, and Jesus Christ, as beings completely submitted to God, thus *muslim*. They all were sent by God to reiterate the same message of submission to only the one God, to judge by God's standards and laws (Quran 5:44), all of which are anchored on practicing the two greatest commandments that Moses and Jesus preached and that bears repetition: to maximally love God, and to equally maximally love our fellow human beings.

After fleeing his hometown, Abraham traveled in the lands that today are called Iraq, Jordan, Palestine, Arabia, and Egypt, seeking to establish a monotheistic community "under God" that lived and institutionalized these principles. It was just not possible to do that in the existing social milieus of the time. He had to start with a clean slate, in a frontier place where there were no preexisting social norms.

The story of Abraham's descendants, depicted in the biblical narratives as well as in the Quran and the Hadith (the sayings of the Prophet), demonstrates the difficulties of establishing a monotheistic tradition in a world where the dominant tradition was a robust polytheism with its sociologically stratified societies.

After domestic tensions developed between Sarah and Hagar, the Egyptian mother of Abraham's firstborn son, Ishmael, Abraham resolved the dispute by separating them. As we shall see later in our discussion of separation of powers, there is always an ideal distance between any two parties, which if reduced causes pain. Abraham took Hagar and their infant, Ishmael, and left them alone in a desolate valley. Muslim narratives locate this valley as present-day Mecca, in the western part of the Arabian peninsula, about forty miles inland from the eastern coast of the Red Sea. Hagar asked Abraham if it was God's will to leave them there, and when he affirmed it, she surrendered to the divine will. When her water ran out she ran to and fro between two small hillocks in search of water and miraculously discovered the well now known as Zamzam.[11] Nomadic passersby noticed birds flying above the well and paused to check. On finding Hagar, they asked her permission to obtain water from her well, for a water well in the desert at that time was more valuable than an oil well is today, and they wouldn't presume to take Hagar's water without her consent. She gave her permission, and some of them remained with her, becoming the first inhabitants of Mecca. This is the story of how Abraham, Hagar, and Ishmael founded the city of Mecca.

From time to time, Abraham would visit Hagar and Ishmael to check on their welfare. Years later, after Ishmael had grown to adulthood, Abraham returned and together with Ishmael was commanded to build there the very first temple, a simple cubical structure, the Ka'bah, devoted to the worship of the one God: "We enjoined Abraham and Ishmael, saying: Purify My House for those who visit it, those who abide there for devotion, those who bow down and those who prostrate themselves . . . and when Abraham and Ishmael raised the foundations of the House: Our Lord, accept from us; surely You are the Hearing, the Knowing. Our Lord, make us both submitted to You, and raise from our offspring a nation submitted to You; show us our rites, and turn to us in mercy. Surely You are oft-turning in mercy, the All-Merciful. Our Lord, raise up from them a Messenger from among them who shall recite to them Your messages and teach them the Book and Wisdom, and purify them. Surely You are Almighty, All-Wise" (Quran 2:125–29).

The Quran quotes Abraham as praying to God to "make this [the fledgling town of Mecca] a secure town, and grant its people fruits, such of them as believe in God and [human accountability on] the Last Day" (Quran 2:126).

IDEALS VERSUS REALITIES:
KEEPING THE FAITH IS HARD TO DO

As much as the Abrahamic ethic is embedded in human nature, human nature has a strong inclination to violate it. I have quoted above the Quranic criticism of contemporaries of the Prophets, ostensibly his followers, who violated its message.

The challenge of maintaining the pure monotheism and ethical principles of the Abrahamic faith required a succession of prophets to remind and restate the primordial message of Abraham. Why the reminder? Because, as the Quran says, humans are forgetful. If there is anything in the Islamic view that approximates the Christian idea of original sin, in the sense of something that can be described as the universal human flaw, it is that humans *forget*. It does not mean a lapse in memory as much as a lapse in applying what we know. We know better, but we do what we know to be wrong anyway—and perhaps even delight in doing it.

Generally, although we recognize the commandments we are given as ethically correct, we have a strong tendency not to follow them. And loving someone "like a brother" is not very helpful if you love your brother the way Cain loved Abel, by killing him. That's why I advise my congregation to probe the one who tells you, "I love you like a brother." The prophets understood this very well, which is why the golden rule is to love others *as we love ourselves.* Anything less just won't do. Knowing that loving your fellow human being as a brother or sister wasn't quite enough, and perhaps because we sometimes treat our neighbors more generously than our own siblings, the Prophet

Muhammad phrased the second commandment by saying to his companions, "None of you is a believer (*mu'min*) until he loves for his brother what he loves for himself."[12] Ironically, the closer we are to someone, the stronger the tension and the conflict. This certainly raises the bar. How many of us feel happiness and not envy when others succeed or when others receive something not given to us?

One factor contributing to the challenge of fulfilling the Abrahamic ethic is the difficulty humans have in understanding something unless they can relate it to themselves, individually and/or collectively. For example, the word *Jesus* evokes different images for different people. European Christians often depict him as blue eyed and blond haired; Mexican Christians depict him as black eyed and black haired. Obviously, Jesus could not have been both, but the point is that humans tend to create in their minds their own image of what something is; often this image is inaccurate, imposed upon the object of their understanding. If European and Mexican Christians, however, decided that this was important to the truth about Jesus and something worth fighting for, then this example would not be so harmless.

More significant issues arise in how Christians regard Jesus spiritually. Catholics regard Jesus as the "unbegotten son of God." Those who denied the divine sonship of Jesus disputed this, and until the 1600s they were burned as heretics for this difference in opinion.

When it comes to religion, each of us holds in our mind an image of what our religion and our God is. We're not that different from little Johnny, who was drawing something on the school chalkboard. His teacher asked, "What are you drawing, Johnny?" "God," he answered." "But," his teacher retorted, "nobody knows what God looks like." And Johnny proudly puffed up his chest and exclaimed, "They will after I'm done!" Because God created us in His image, we can't seem to help returning the favor, creating God in ours, and in spite of knowing that our idea does no justice to divine reality, we can't resist the urge. If someone debates us on our understanding of God, we get quite upset about it, but when prophets come to correct our understanding, we tend to treat them worse—like Abraham or Jesus, seeking to burn or crucify them as heretics.

The Quran points out this human tendency, asking, "Do you propose to teach God what your religion is? While God—Knower of all things—fathoms what is in the heavens and the earth?" (Quran 49:16). An example of this tendency to fabricate God in our own image is found in the story of the Children of Israel. Invited by Joseph to escape the famine in Palestine, they emigrated to Egypt and prospered there for several centuries, until the reign of the tyrannical pharaoh Rameses, who enslaved them. God sent them the prophet Moses, an Israelite brought up in the palace as a prince, to free them. After some very dramatic miracles of changing the Nile to blood, having locusts ravage the land, and so forth, finally Pharaoh grudgingly allowed Moses to free the Israelites from his yoke. He was angry at Moses, for he thought that he, Pharaoh, was God's son; how could this putatively illegitimate person with a speech impediment (Moses spoke with a lisp), brought up as his stepbrother, be the one to wield the kind of power that Pharaoh was supposed to have? Discovering that Moses's God was more powerful than his was enough to make Pharaoh livid. But at last Moses crossed over into the Sinai with his people and along the way left them under the watch of his brother and fellow prophet, Aaron, when he climbed Mount Sinai to thank God and converse with Him.

The modern reader finds it peculiar that the Israelites, after all the miracles, the freedom from slavery, and the exodus from Egypt, agitated very hard with Aaron to fabricate and worship a golden calf (Quran 7:148ff. and 20:83ff., also Exodus 32). They wanted to appreciate God in the manner they were accustomed to after centuries of Egyptian living had shaped their cultural outlook and culinary tastes; why, they even got tired of the manna that God sent them from heaven and complained about it!

KEEPING THE FAITH ACROSS CULTURES AND GENERATIONS

While roaming in the Sinai desert, Moses's followers faced the challenge of being satisfied with the manna sent to them from heaven. Numbers 11 of the Bible paints a dramatic picture: "And the Children of Israel wept again, and said, Who shall give us meat to eat? We remember the fish we freely ate in Egypt; the cucumbers, melons, leeks, onions and garlic. But now our soul is dried away: there is nothing at all, beside this manna before our eyes." The Quranic version of the Israelites' plaint is: "O Moses, we cannot endure one kind of food [the manna from heaven], so pray to your Lord on our behalf to bring forth for us the kind of food that sprouts out from the earth; of its herbs, its cucumbers and garlic, its lentils and onions . . ." (Quran 2:61). Presumably, they wanted earth food, not heaven food.

Before we rush to criticize the Israelites for this, let's look at our first-generation, religiously observant immigrant Americans. I know a friend whose father, a *Norwegian* Lutheran, refused to go to church for a long time after his minister died and was replaced with a *German* Lutheran minister. He wanted to worship God in the way he was accustomed to. Many Indo-Pakistani Muslims in my mosque insist on rolling up their trouser cuffs, having been taught back home that their prayer is invalid if their pants fall below their ankles (which is not true)! And I have observed that the most pious American Muslim immigrants from Egypt, Turkey, Pakistan, Senegal, and Indonesia are not satisfied indefinitely with steak and potatoes and pumpkin pie. In the language of the Bible, their "souls will dry up" and probably their prayers and Ramadan fasts as well, if not fortified with their beloved fava beans, *doner* kebabs, lamb curries and chicken *biryani, sopo de kanja,* and prawn *sambals,* not to mention the splendid baklava "done just the way we do it back home" and the heavenly *ras malais* and *gulab jamons.*

An American professional colleague with whom I once worked frequently traveled to Paris on business. After a week of French food, he would suffer from a Big Mac attack, seeking the nearest McDonald's for a hamburger with french fries and a large Coke. The ecstasy in his eyes was the stuff of legend—and could not be matched by anything from Fauchon's. I also know a Muslim fellow who attends the weekly Friday prayers at a particular mosque in the Queens section of New York City for what he claims is the most sublime chicken *biryani* he's ever tasted, which he obtains after the prayers for three dollars. The route to our souls is often through our hearts, and the route to our hearts through our stomachs and taste buds.

Lest the reader think I am not speaking seriously, let me remind you that this is scriptural truth, mentioned in the Bible and Quran. Feeding the poor is a fundamental good deed in all religions and is a duty that any wise and caring government will fulfill, for hungry people foment hostile rebellions against rulers who allow their people to starve. Not only do we hunger for food, we hunger for specific kinds of food..

The time that the Israelites wandered through the desert of Sinai—forty years—was required perhaps less to filter out their attachment to polytheism and idolatry than to allow a whole new generation of the Children of Israel to be born into a pure monotheism under Moses's watchful eye. To paraphrase an American proverb, Moses could take the Israelites out of Egypt, but he couldn't take Egypt out of the Israelites. Old habits die hard, or perhaps never, which is why it often takes the dying out of a generation and coming into age of a new one to shift a society's norms or prejudices on deeply felt issues.

From stories like this, we see that the development of a religious community is very hard work. The American Muslim community today, at the dawn of the twenty-first century, is not unlike the Israelites roaming for forty years in search of their promised land. A cross-section of some seven million people from all parts of the Muslim world, struggling to find its American legs, the American Muslim community is now birthing a second generation anchored in American culture. Shaping such an American Islamic identity from the diversity of its immigrant and African American backgrounds requires a prophet-like wisdom to navigate the struggles, diversity of opinions, moments of deep despair, and enormous challenges along the road.

During the course of our individual lives, our images and understandings of God and religion usually evolve. The same happens at a societal level. Each society also develops, as a community, its own ideas of religion and God. At best, we worship, not God as He knows Himself, but rather the image of God we have in our mind's eye, which is why an essential description of God is that He is fundamentally unknowable to us.

When a prophet is sent to teach us things we need to know, the message is received in the cultural, linguistic, and intellectual environment of the local people; in this process of translation, errors creep in. From one generation to the next, the problem is repeated, and the new generation, with its slightly different viewpoint, begins to see the message a bit differently. After several generations, the original understanding can be quite skewed.

Every religious tradition faces the perennial challenge of translating its faith into the terms relevant to its time. The problem in its most general form is: "What are the eternal principles of our faith, and how do we restate them in the changed here and now?" Every era brings its own challenges to the way we do things or have historically thought about and understood things.

Muslim society faced its first critical challenge after the death of the Prophet. How would the faith be maintained? Who would be society's leader? Within a few years after the Prophet's death, many companions who had memorized the Quran died, and the crisis was how to keep the Quran, which resided in the collective memory of the community, from being lost. How could they ensure the Quran would be recited correctly by the increasing numbers of non-Arabic-speaking peoples (Egyptians, Syrians, and Iranians), whose accents could alter the purity of the divine scripture and its meanings? This led to the formal collecting and writing of the Quran in an authorized manuscript form, and eventually it was sent to each country with an authorized reciter to teach correct Quranic pronunciation (*tajwid*). Originally, some thought this a heretical innovation (*bid'ah*), for the Prophet had neither done nor authorized such a thing. And how to teach the increasing numbers of Muslims the essentials of their faith, and to recognize good and permissible (*halal*) from unethical and forbidden (*haram*) behavior? This led to the rise of the field of Quranic exegesis (*tafsir*) and jurisprudence (*fiqh*) within the first three centuries after the Prophet's death. Again, some then regarded Quranic exegesis to be most presumptuous and bordering on blasphemy; how could any mere human dare to comment on God's words?

This perennial challenge is a significant theme in the history of all faith traditions. Every time God sent a prophet to reiterate and reform the Abrahamic message, the followers of the prophet wound up with differences of opinion that were substantial enough to result in splitting themselves into sectarian groups. The most well known split between the inheritors of the Abrahamic heritage was the split of Christianity from Judaism, an unintended outcome of Jesus's mission. And whereas the Prophet Muhammad was sent to revive the Abrahamic ethic in the cultural mind-set and language of the Ishmaelite branch of the children of Abraham, most people have come to regard the Prophet Muhammad's mission as conveying a different message from that of Jesus and Moses, seeing it as a distinct and separate religion.

Observe in our day how orthodox Jews regard Reform Jews as outside the fold of Judaism, how Catholic Christians in Ireland regard Protestant Christians as belonging to the enemy camp, and how Pakistani Sunni Muslims have made the Sunni and Shiite divide so acrimonious that we read about Pakistani Shiites being shot and killed in the mosques while attending Friday prayers!

Meanwhile the Quran, which both Sunnis and Shiites believe is God's word, asserts that God "ordained[13] for you of religion that which He enjoined upon Noah, and which We have revealed to you, and which We enjoined on Abraham and Moses and Jesus—to establish religion (*din*) and not to be divided therein. Hard upon the polytheists is what you invite them to" (Quran 42:13). According to this verse, divisive attitudes and practices are signs of a non- or antimonotheistic, anti-Abrahamic ethic, for an authentic religious practice would not lapse into religious triumphalism and self-aggrandizement but instead adhere to the teachings of the Quranic verse "Surely those who believe, and the Jews, the Christians, the Sabians, whoever believes in God and the Last Day and does good, shall [all] have their reward with 'their Lord; there is no fear for them, nor shall they grieve" (Quran 2:62, 5:69).

The Abrahamic ethic of monotheism had a difficult time surviving in the polytheism and idolatry of the powerful civilizations of its early time. As I have pointed out, *theological* polytheism represented only half of the battle in establishing the good society. The other half was made up of *sociological* leftovers from polytheistic societies: the stratification of society by tribe, race, class, gender, and slavery, which ran against the principles of human liberty and human fraternity. No less pernicious were the attempts to manipulate and control people's thought.

Across eras and cultures, the battle for God in the best sense has been the struggle to establish a human society that is the good society, namely, one that authentically reflects the Abrahamic ethic, especially its second commandment. Humans, being what they are, found this difficult. They kept lapsing into their pre-Abrahamic paradigms: theologically they reverted to polytheism and incorrect worship of God, while socially they disallowed others their freedoms of action and even of thought, treating human beings as unequal and denying them their rights.

We have already mentioned the story of Moses's people and how difficult it was for them not to lapse into Egyptian practice on such a central matter as the worship of God. The following are examples from Christian and Muslim history:

- As Christianity spread to Rome, many Romans couldn't help Romanizing Christianity, to the consternation of many of Jesus's other followers, especially those in the Christian capitals closer to Jerusalem, such as Antioch. Attributes of the emperor were projected onto him: Jesus was seen as King of Kings, although he himself demurred on that point, saying, "My kingdom is not of this world" (John 18:36). The notion of the emperor being appointed by God or in some way related to God was projected onto him, although he himself is not known to have made that claim either. In the fourth century Christianity became the state religion, and in later centuries any interpretation that differed from that of the official church was deemed heretical, an act against the state, thus treasonous and punishable by death. Jesus, by contrast, although deeply critical of hypocrisy and false ideas, invited people to correct their beliefs about God and never put anyone in danger for holding a different or wrong opinion, much less burned them at the stake as heretics.

- After the death of the Prophet Muhammad in 632 CE, certain aspects of the pre-Islamic mind-set (called *jahili* by Muslims) that were at odds with the Abrahamic ethic crept back into the Muslim community. Arab tribalism entered Muslim politics, and within thirty-five years the method of electing the Muslim ruler by a system of merit was discarded, much to the dismay of the Muslim community, in favor of a dynastic system (as we will see in greater detail in chapter 5). In 656 CE the Umayyads, of the tribe of Banu Umayyah, who from pre-Islamic times had been fierce competitors of the Hashemites (descendants of the Prophet's tribe Banu Hashem), established dynastic rule with a capital in Damascus.

Once dynastic rule was in place, other aspects of this polytheistic mind-set crept in: a privileged family, then a (privileged) noble class, which together implied a nonprivileged class, a gradual loss of freedoms for certain classes of human society, and a stratification of society that was at odds with the Abrahamic ethic. The first major intra-Muslim conflict erupted when the Muslim community split into the Sunni and Shiah, the Sunni believing that the Muslim leader need not be descended from the Prophet, the Shiites believing that he should be. Other pre-Islamic ideas continued to erode human liberty and freedoms. They include:

- Loss of the rule of law and an independent judiciary

- The ruling that apostasy, being equivalent to treason, was punishable by death

- The continuation of slavery, despite the many Quranic verses recommending the freeing of slaves

- The mistreatment and oppression of women

Societies and individuals face an ever-present challenge in bridging the gap between ideals and realities. We may think we value our ideals, but we often are unable or unwilling to make our reality match them. Even when we are willing, it takes hard work.

What is right about any religion or social structure is therefore the extent to which individuals and societies *fully* manifest the principles of the Abrahamic ethic. The corollary is no less true: an individual or society is unjust or undeveloped to the extent that the Abrahamic ethic is violated or not fully implemented. The Quran never tires of repeating that its task is to reestablish the Abrahamic ethic and that Muhammad and all the prior prophets came to do just that: "The nearest of people to Abraham are those who follow him, and this Prophet [that is, Muhammad] and those who believe" (Quran 3:68). Islam, as we shall see later, *defines* itself as the latest version, or reformation, of the Abrahamic religion. It is not so much the religion of Muhammad (which is why Muslims reject the name *Muhammadanism*, a name given to it by outsiders), but the religion of God, originally established by Abraham, cleansed by Muhammad of pagan and polytheistic encrustations that had accrued over the intervening centuries.

Not only is God's message to humanity one in its essence, the Quran describes the believers as those who "believe in God and His Angels and His Scriptures and His messengers," adding that these believers are to assert "we do not differentiate between any of His [God's] messengers; they say, 'We hear and we obey, we seek Your forgiveness, O Lord, and to You is our return'" (Quran 2:285). Not differentiating between God's messengers implies that we should also not seek to create violent differences between the messages that each of these messengers brought, for the differences lay more in details than in substance. God comments in the Quran regarding the history of the followers of Moses, Jesus, and Muhammad: "Surely this community of yours is one community, and I am your Lord, so be dutiful to Me. But they became divided into sects, each party rejoicing in what they had" (Quran 23:52; see verses 44–54 for the naming of the different messengers). The challenge still facing human society today is how to worship God without dividing ourselves and how to institutionalize such a unified understanding.

To recapitulate, the Abrahamic ethic embodies the fullest and most balanced individual and social institutional expression of these two commandments whose core ideas are:

- A radical monotheism, expressed in loving the one God with all of one's being

- Human liberty, equality, and fraternity, expressed in loving for others what we love for ourselves (that is, social justice) and in ensuring and protecting these principles

Whenever each religious tradition, Muslim or non-Muslim, has honored these commandments, it has contributed to humanity's growth and progress. When one has failed, it has contributed to conflict and disease both within its own society and between its society and that of others.

SOME OF YOUR BEST FRIENDS ARE MUSLIM?

A sincerely religious person who has as close friends devout members of other faiths learns to dispense with a number of common false-hoods. Primary among them are that all religions other than one's own may be ignored; that all religions are essentially the same; that all religions other than one's own are wrong; or that all adherents of other religions are bad and evil people.

A harmonious pluralistic society requires us to know ourselves and the others in our midst. No Christian can claim to be following the precedent of Christ unless she or he accepts the presence of other intelligent, compassionate, educated people who are deeply spiritual Muslims, Jews, Hindus, Buddhists, or atheists. The same applies to those of other religions as well as to atheists who regard themselves as decent, upright secular humanists. If a Muslim cannot find comfort in a world in which others are Christian, Jewish, Hindu, Buddhist, and agnostic, that person cannot claim to be following the teachings of the Quran and the Prophet Muhammad.

Today, interacting with Muslims politically, economically, and socially is almost inescapable, so we would do well to examine Islam and understand that Muslims too share in humanity's ultimate existential concerns.

MUSLIMS: NEW KIDS ON THE BLOCK

Muslims see their religion as the most recent iteration of the religion that God seeded on earth when He created humankind. Because Muslims believe their religion is intended to be a religion for all people, Muslims thereby relate to humanity on three levels: to all humanity as humans, to all religious communities as common heirs of a divinely revealed religious tradition, and to Jews and Christians as direct recipients of the Abrahamic ethic as such. These relationships are built into Islam's very nature. There is no Islam without it. Islam's natural impulse is a globalized religion based on a set of universal principles that all of humanity can agree on.

Muslims recognize all humanity as God's creatures, whom God blessed with reason and understanding so that they can know God;

that being so endowed, they must have recognized God as one who is transcendent and ultimate. Moreover, Muslims acknowledge that all humanity is capable of knowing God, true religion being embedded in the human heart, the natural religion, the *din al-fitrah*. No Muslim may deny this fact of nature without contradicting the Quran and hence abjuring Islam. Recognition of this truth is basic to a Muslim's faith.

The universalism of natural religion is buttressed by the Quran's understanding of history. It affirms that God did not leave humankind entirely to its own resources in the matter of acknowledging Him as God and Creator. In His mercy, God sent prophets to convey to them His divine message, that they owe religion to God alone. "We have raised in every nation a messenger, saying: worship God and avoid evil. . . . So travel all over the earth, and see what was the end of the rejecters" (Quran 16:36).

No matter how humans may have denied their humanity by refusing to perceive the truth of God, of His transcendence and unity, they were duly informed and warned by a messenger whom God sent to teach them that truth in their own language and idiom (Quran 14:4). The content was always essentially the same: "We sent no messenger before you except that We revealed to him that there is no god but Me, so worship Me" (Quran 21:25). Thus, all excuses for rejecting God fall down.

HINDUS AND BUDDHISTS: OLDER KIDS ON THE BLOCK

The monotheistic legacy of religion, Islam holds, continued after Adam with Noah. "God ordained for you the same religion He ordained for Noah," the Quran affirms (42:13). "God chose Adam, Noah, the people of Abraham and 'Imran over the other nations" (Quran 3:33); "We have revealed to you [Muhammad] as We revealed to Noah and the prophets after him, and We revealed to Abraham and Ishmael and Isaac and Jacob and the tribes, and Jesus and Job and Jonah and Aaron and Solomon, and We gave David scripture. *And [We sent] messengers We have mentioned to you before and messengers We have not mentioned to you.* And God addressed Moses, speaking [to him]" (Quran 4:163–64, italics mine).

Because the Quran informs its readers that there were many messengers not named, and that God "raised in every nation a messenger"

(Quran 16:36), Muslims therefore believe that God sent to all of humanity prophets "of the seed of Adam, and of those carried with Noah, and of the seed of Abraham and Israel, and of those whom we guided and chose" (Quran 19:58–60). The "seed of Adam" refers to prophets who came to all of humanity, and the narrower class the seed "of those carried with Noah" refers to all those prophets descended from Noah. The narrower still "seed of Abraham" includes prophets who were the progeny of Ishmael and Isaac, and "the seed of Israel" means of course those prophets descended from Isaac's son Jacob, later renamed Israel.

Therefore God must have sent prophets to India, China, and to every people in the rest of the world. While these prophets may not have been from the seed of Abraham, they would certainly have been from the seed of Adam, and probably among the seed of Noah. Based on such arguments from the Quran, Hindus and Buddhists are descendants from religious teachings originally brought forth from prophets descended from Adam and Noah.

This religion taught by all the prophets worldwide—globalized religion from an Islamic perspective—therefore consisted of five principles, which were repeatedly affirmed by all divine revelations:

1. God's *singularity* and *transcendence,* affirmed in His ontological separateness, otherness, or unknowableness from His creation. This means that our arms are just way too short to put around God, that as much as we try to speak about and understand God, God is at the end of the day The Greatest Unknown.

2. God as All-Being is *relevant* to His creation. God as Creator is our reason for being, gives purpose to our life, and forged the norms and ethics by which every creature is to live its life. This means that God is the most important thing in our lives, and the one through whom we learn to know right from wrong.

3. This divine relevance is *knowable* to us humans, which we get in any or all of three ways: by divination (that is, by reading or seeing it in the omens of nature, which include our inner selves and states of conscience); by science and the collected knowledge (history) of our ancestors, including discovering it in the inimitable patterns or laws of nature; and by prophecy, the

direct revelation of the will of God through words for the ready use of human understanding.

4. Humans are *capable* of fulfilling the divine imperatives. This is because we *know,* and because we *act* as the result of our free will informed by our conscious foreknowledge, and because God has made nature subservient to us. When we exercise our will in accord with divine preference, we have done good and avoided evil.

5. Humans are *responsible* and therefore shall be held responsible, which means we are subject to judgment—to reward in the case of compliance and punishment in the case of defiance or violation.

These five principles are the core and foundation of all religiosity. All those who belong to authentic religious tradition anywhere in the world have acknowledged these principles regardless of whether or not they observe them in their everyday lives and thereby establish their claim to the religion of God. These truths are integral to the faith of Islam, and they describe globalized religion.

JEWS AND CHRISTIANS:
SIBLINGS ON THE BLOCK

Jews and Christians are described by a special name in the Quran: "People of the Book," *ahl al-kitab,* or a "scriptured people." Muslims believe that God sent them God's Words—that is, scripture—through their prophets, containing the divine teachings of His message. If for some reason they had missed what is natural and hence necessary to them, they were given scripture freely as a gift from heaven, accompanied by prophecy. As such, Jews and Christians are people with the true religion, the *din al-fitrah,* strengthened and informed by scripture and prophets. No Muslim may deny this without contradicting the Quran. Therefore, religiously speaking, Muslims acknowledge that Jews and Christians are endowed with the religion of God twice, once by nature and hence necessarily and universally, and once by the grace of God through their scripture and prophets.

The foregoing acknowledgments are indubitable and indisputable to Muslims because they come as divine proclamations in the Quran, but they were further reinforced by a third kind of justification, the direct kind: "Those who have believed—and the Jews, the Christians, the Sabaeans, those who believe in God, the Last Day [of Judgment] and do good works—stand to be rewarded by God. No fear or grief shall befall them" (Quran 2:62). "Do not argue with the People of the Book except in the best way . . . and say [to them]: We believe in that which was revealed to us as well as that which was revealed to you. Our God and your God is One and the same. We all submit to Him" (Quran 29:46).

This text does not merely recognize the similarity of Jews and Christians to Muslims; it identifies Islam with them. This unity of the three religions makes the Muslims regard Jews and Christians as their brothers and sisters in faith, in submission to the one God of all. Disagreement between them certainly exists, but all disagreements are no more than family disputes.

Just as it distinguishes between the righteous and the unrighteous of the Prophet Muhammad's followers—and in order to dispel any such confusion of the superiority of the outer definition of Muslim over non-Muslim—the Quran explicitly distinguishes the righteous from the unrighteous of Jews and Christians (and by implication of all religious groups): "Of the People of the Book there is an upright party who recite God's messages in the night-time and they adore Him. They believe in God and the Last Day, and they enjoin good and forbid evil and vie with one another in good deeds. Those are among the righteous; whatever good they do, they will not be denied it. And God knows those who keep their duty" (Quran 3:112–16).

Indeed, family disputes can be of the worst kind, but let us bear in mind that there is no criticism that the Quran has addressed to either Jews or Christians that Jews and Christians have not addressed to themselves or their tradition. Neither can any Muslim deny that many of these faults are universal ones, shortcomings that are present in any religious community and have also existed in the Muslim community.

For example, the Quran did criticize the Jews for failure to uphold the Torah (5:68–70), for excessive legalism and exaggerated authoritarianism by some of their rabbis (3:50, 5:66–68), and for nationalizing monotheism (2:111).

In distinguishing between the righteous and the unrighteous of the Prophet Muhammad's followers, the Quran asserts: "The [nomadic] Arabs are hardest in disbelief and hypocrisy, and least disposed to comprehend the bounds of what God has revealed to His messenger; God is Knowing, Wise. . . . And among those around you of the [nomadic] Arabs are hypocrites, and among the people of Medina—defiant in their hypocrisy. You don't recognize them—We do. We will castigate them twice, then repeat upon them a painful punishment" (Quran 9:97, 101). And if there existed hypocrites in Medina at the Prophet's own time, why should we believe that that reality changed? But the Quran distinguished between them and the righteous, for next to this verse we have, "And of the Arabs are those who believe in God and the Last Day, who regard their expenditures and the Messenger's prayers as drawing them near to God; truly these [efforts] bring them near [to God]; God will admit them into His mercy; God is truly forgiving, merciful" (Quran 9:99).

As to the Christians, the Quran criticizes the deification of Jesus (Quran 9:30) as well as the doctrine of trinitarianism and exaggeration in matters of religion (Quran 4:171). The Quran reproaches Christians for not bringing out the full worth of monotheism and of replacing or diluting it with another message. The Quran asserts that it is knowledge and awareness of, and submission to, the truth of the One God (monotheism) that saves; that is, humanity is saved by such a faith, and works depend upon the presence and then the sincerity of such a faith. One might say that Christians founded a faith based upon the saving miracle of God in the exclusive person of Jesus Christ, a faith in which one can approach God only through Jesus.

Christianity and Islam differ from Judaism in its emphasis on ethnicity and accomplishment of prescribed acts as the Divine Imperative. Christianity and Islam both shattered the borders of ethnic Israel. Christianity replaced it with a spiritual Israel and gave precedence to the love of God ("to adore God in spirit and in truth") over prescribed acts. But Christianity asserted that humanity is corrupted by sin and that Christ alone can deliver us from this state. Islam is founded upon the axiom that humanity is created in the divine image (agreed to by Jews and Christians); therefore, something exists in us that, participating as it does in the Absolute—but for which humans would not be human—makes salvation possible provided we possess the necessary knowledge; and this knowledge is what scriptural revelation (the Quran) provides. Therefore, although we need a specific human "revealer," the purpose of the revealer is to convey the more important *revelation* as such, comprising knowledge of the essential and unalterable content of humanity's relationship to God and made real in the transformative power of divine remembrance (*dhikr*), the mutual remembering by human and God of each other.

But the Quran has equally praised the Christians for their humility and altruism and for their fear of God and has declared them closest to the Muslims by their warm practice of neighborly love (Quran 5:82). True, the Quran rejects the Christian claim that the texts of scripture are integral records of the message Jesus conveyed. In this, however, the Quran is not alone. Biblical scholars and theologians have said the same thing. Even among the apostolic fathers, and certainly in the Nicene, anti- and post-Nicene Fathers, countless Christian scholars have maintained more or less exactly what the Quran did.

However, the Quran never totally condemned any people, since the critical verses stand side by side with those other verses that justify the righteous, both enjoying the same divine authority. To say it in colloquial terms, we—Muslims, Jews, and Christians—have all committed some mistakes in our understanding of God and in our practice, but basically we're all right as long as we believe in the one God, try to love God as best as we can, and make our best effort in treating humanity humanely. None will be rejected by God for what we call ourselves, but all of us will be judged by our character and the nature of our belief and actions.

Recapping, the Quran teaches its followers to treat all humanity well and especially Jews and Christians, with whom they share in a religious tradition that goes back through Abraham to Noah and ultimately Adam. This Abrahamic Semitic legacy of religion, the Quran maintains, gives life to the ethic that God "has ordained for you of religion that which He enjoined upon Noah, and that which We have revealed to you, and which We enjoined on Abraham and Moses and Jesus—*to establish religion and not be divided therein*" (Quran 42:13, italics mine). This is the mandate for all religious people, and especially for those working in the interfaith sector—to worship God well and not divisively break our communities into hostile factions on account of religion.

Given the above attitudes of Muslims toward Jews and Christians, attitudes demonstrated historically, American attitudes toward Muslims, who make up almost a quarter of the human race, cannot and must not depend on the opinion of a few Americans or of a news media whose knowledge of Islam is limited or not anchored in the ethics of the second commandment. An American media that continues to equate Muslims with anti-Americanism, terrorism, and a lifestyle that contradicts America's deepest values does America a great disservice. So does a Muslim world media that continues to equate America with values that are fundamentally opposed to Islam.

God's call in the Quran to Jews and Christians still stands as the Muslim call, as proper, relevant, and necessary today as it was when it was first revealed some fourteen centuries ago: "O People of the Book! Let us now come together under a fair principle common to all of us— that we worship none but God, that we associate nothing with Him, and that we take not one another as lords beside God" (Quran 3:64).

Nothing less than this position will do, namely the acknowledgment by Americans—especially American Jews and American Christians—of Muslims as a religiously legitimate global community worthy of sharing in the Abrahamic ethic, which is the foundation of our American Declaration of Independence, and making this principle the anchor of American policy toward the Muslim world.

CHAPTER 2

What's Right with Islam

There are valuable truths in the Muslim experience and worldview that it would behoove America to recognize and consider, and there are valuable truths about America that the Muslim world would do well to recognize, appreciate, and adopt. To highlight these truths, I have titled this and the next chapters, "What's Right with Islam" and "What's Right with America."

Muhammad, born in 570 CE, did not see himself as establishing a new religion. Rather, he was reinstating the primordial religion of God, the religion founded by Abraham, in a manner that would be accessible to all of humanity. The values that Prophet Muhammad taught were not intended to be new, but preexisting, eternal values expressing eternal truths.

The Arabs had a concept of proper humanness (*muruwwah*), which meant a complex of attributes such as generosity, courage, honesty, being true to one's word, the ability to right wrongs, protect the weak, and so forth—akin to the German *menschlichkeit* and the Yiddish *sei a mensch. Muruwwah* is what makes one a decent human being. In the Prophet Muhammad, Muslims find their definition of the perfect mensch, or the perfected human (*insan kamil*).

THE PERFECTED HUMAN

Muhammad's father, Abdullah, died before he was born, and his mother, Aminah, died when he was six. Uncommon in the Arab world, he was an only child, tenderly and lovingly cared for by his grandfather Abd al-Muttalib until he died—Muhammad by then barely eight years of age. Then he was cared for by his uncle Abu Talib, who loved him as dearly as his own.

When Muhammad was twenty-five, his employer, a wealthy forty-year-old widow named Khadijah, was deeply attracted to Muhammad's character and the honesty and efficiency with which he conducted her business affairs. She proposed marriage; Muhammad accepted her proposal and enjoyed almost twenty-five years of happy married life with her until she died in the same year as his uncle Abu Talib. Khadijah was the first woman he married, and she bore him six children, four girls and two boys. The boys died in infancy.

Muhammad's honesty, modesty, trustworthiness, good character, and gentlemanly conduct became proverbial so that he became known by the nickname *al-Amin* ("the trustworthy one"), so much so that travelers would deposit their money or other valuables with him for safe-keeping. His wisdom in arbitration is shown by a charming story that took place when he was thirty-five and the Ka'bah had to be rebuilt. When construction reached the point where the Black Stone (the surviving part of the original structure, which sits in the southwestern corner) had to be put back in place, a fierce argument broke out among the Meccan clans, each wanting the honor of placing the cornerstone. Muhammad was asked to arbitrate the matter. He called for a piece of cloth, took the stone and placed it at the center of the cloth, and requested each clan's representative to hold the cloth. Together they lifted and lodged it in place, thus dividing the honor among all the clans.

Disturbed by the paganism of his people, Muhammad (by this time around forty) would retreat from Meccan society to meditate, frequenting a cave on the outskirts of Mecca, spending as long as several weeks at a time. The archangel Gabriel appeared to Muhammad during one of these retreats and embraced him three times, each time commanding him, "Recite!" Frightened and bewildered, Muhammad responded each time, "I don't read." Gabriel then recited the first verses of the Quran: "Recite: By the Name of your Lord who created— created Man from a clot. Recite: And your Lord is the Noblest; who taught—via the Pen—taught Man what Man knew not" (Quran 96:1–5). This event evokes the archangel Gabriel's annunciation to Mary; Gabriel cast the Quran into Muhammad's heart, just as he cast the spirit of Jesus into Mary's womb; Mary was a virgin, and Muhammad was unlettered (*ummi*). In a later visit, Gabriel informed Muhammad that he was to be a prophet and messenger from God to his people.

Fearing for his sanity, Muhammad ran trembling home to Khadijah, crying, "Wrap me up! Wrap me up!" Convinced of her husband's sterling character and his sanity, she consoled him. To further reassure him, Khadijah took him to her aged cousin Waraqah Ibn Nawfal for a consultation. Ibn Nawfal was a Christian who was closely acquainted with both the Torah and the Gospel. Upon hearing Muhammad's story, he declared, "By the One who holds my soul in His hand, you are the Prophet of this people. The same Great Spirit has come to you that came to Moses. Your people will reject you, abuse you, and drive you out and fight you." Sighing, he wished he were young enough to stand by Muhammad's side.[1]

Khadijah was the first to believe in Muhammad's message of faith in the one God, and until the end of her life she remained a tower of strength for the Prophet, a comforter and a steadfast supporter through all difficulties. After Khadijah, his cousin Ali (then ten years old) and his closest friend, Abu Bakr, were the next to accept Islam.

Fearing the wrath of the pagan Meccans, the new Muslims practiced their faith discreetly for three years while Islam quietly spread among the Meccans. After this period the Prophet was commanded to openly proclaim God's religion to everyone: "Warn your clan, your nearest kin, and be compassionate to those of the believers who follow you" (Quran 26:214–15).

The Meccan unbelievers regarded this new religion as a threat to their way of life and their economy, which was based on the annual pilgrimage to Mecca. They tried to dissuade Muhammad, offering him anything he wanted—money, wives, even leadership over them—if he desisted from preaching. His response was, "Even if they placed the sun in my right hand and the moon in my left hand, I could not cease until I succeeded or died trying."

After thirteen years of persecuting the Prophet, the Meccans tried to assassinate him, and he escaped with his followers to Yathrib, a town some two hundred miles north of Mecca, later called "the Prophet's City" (*medinat un-nabi*, or Medina for short). Eight years of battle ensued with the Meccans until the Prophet finally returned victorious. On the day of his entry into Mecca, he addressed his previous enemies with the words "This day there is no vengeance against you, and you are all free," thus winning them over with his generosity.

The Prophet worked hard to eliminate class, gender, and economic distinctions, and Islam's message of equality, goodness, and freedom drew many of the poorest among the Meccans. He strongly encouraged the freeing of slaves—a companion of the Prophet and first person to call the daily prayers was Bilal, a freed Abyssinian slave—and he defined the measure of a man's piety on how he treated women: "The best of you are those who are best to their women," he said.

Because Muslims do not pictorially represent the Prophet Muhammad, they prefer to describe him by the classical description given by his cousin Ali ibn Abi Talib, often written up as a beautiful calligraphic piece called the *hilya:*

> He was neither too tall nor too short. He was medium sized. His hair was not short and curly, nor was it lank, but in between. His face was not narrow, nor was it fully round, but there was a roundness to it. His skin was fair. His eyes were black. He had long eyelashes. He was big-boned and had wide shoulders. He had no body hair except in the middle of his chest. He had thick hands and feet. When he walked, he walked inclined, as if descending a slope. When he looked at someone, he looked at them in full face.
>
> Between his shoulders was the seal of prophecy, the sign that he was the last of the prophets. He was the most generous-hearted of men, the most truthful of them in speech, the most mild-tempered of them, and the noblest of them in lineage. Whoever saw him unexpectedly was in awe of him. And whoever associated with him familiarly, loved him. Anyone who would describe him would say, I never saw, before him or after him, the like of him.
>
> Peace and blessings be upon you, O Messenger of God.[2]

Since he had enriched the lives of his people in so many ways, when the Prophet died the shock was so momentous that the Muslim community could not bear to hear it. On hearing the news, Abu Bakr, the first caliph, went to the mosque, hushed the crowd, and addressed them with these words: "Whoever worshiped Muhammad, be informed that Muhammad is dead. But whosoever worshiped God, be informed that God is alive and never dies." Then he read from the Quran: "Muhammad is but a messenger, preceded by other messengers." With these words, Abu Bakr quelled the possibility that Muslims might worship Muhammad. Muslims do, however, take his example, his *sunnah*, very seriously.

THE PROPHET AS EXAMPLE

Muslims see Muhammad as recapping the messages of all the previous prophets, just as the conclusion to a book recaps the themes of the whole book. He manifested the absolute submission and monotheism of Abraham, the dream-interpreting ability of Joseph, the spiritual warrior-kingship of David, the wisdom of Solomon, the law of Moses, and the spirituality of Jesus. He was tested by adversity and the need to be patient by a temporary loss of contact with God, like Job. He traversed the path from being not aware of God to enlightenment and God-discovery, a path most spiritual seekers tread. He was a prophet and spiritual guide; a head of state and leader of a community; a supreme judge and arbitrator of dispute; a reformer of society; a family man, loving husband, and father. In the way that Muhammad discharged these roles, Muslims see their exemplar, one who shows common men and women how to fulfill these roles in their own lives in a manner in keeping with divine intent. He was the perfected human (*insan kamil*), who journeyed to the utmost stage of human development and therefore is able to teach humanity how to journey through those stages as well.

Because Muslims are required to follow the Prophet's precedent (*sunnah*), Muslim spiritual masters described several qualities of self that a human soul embodies along its path toward perfection. These qualities of self are best thought of not as a linear progression in which at each new stage one loses the previous stage, but rather as layers added to one's personality. These qualities include:

1. The "self that incites toward evil" (*an-nafs al-ammarah*). This is the unregenerate, unrestrained, "lower" self, which urges us to commit evil.

2. The "self-blaming or conscientious self" (*an-nafs al-lawwamah*). This is the self that recognizes its wrongs, criticizes itself for the faults it commits, and seeks correction. We might call this our human conscience or "higher self," which helps us balance negative urges coming from our lower self.

3. The "inspired self" (*an-nafs al-mulhamah*). This is the self that recognizes inspirations coming from God, calling it toward Him, and responds. The individual begins to be a conscious channel for divine action in the world.

4. The "contented self" (*an-nafs al-mutma'innah*). This is the self that has found deep mutual satisfaction with God. It is both pleased with God (*radiyah*) and pleasing to God (*mardiyyah*). God calls upon this soul on Judgment Day, admitting it into His Paradise (Quran 89:27–30).

5. The "perfected self" (*an-nafs al-kamilah*). At this stage of spiritual development, the soul becomes completely transparent to God's will and completely submitted to it. It loves and is loved by God. One sign of this love, explains the Prophet in a hadith, is that "God becomes the sight by which it sees, the hearing by which it hears, the hand by which it acts, the foot by which it walks, and the heart by which it comprehends."[3]

How does one attain these various stages? How does one "walk the Prophet's walk" in order to become a completed or perfected human being (*insan kamil*)? The Prophet's contemporaries sought this by "befriending" him (in Arabic, becoming a *sahib*, "companion," of God's messenger), which meant imbibing from him a certain spiritual energy that made them light up with love for God. All of Islam is, in effect, the effort to follow the Prophet's normative example—to become a friend of the Prophet, so that we, like him, may radiate the presence of God into the world.

To follow his example, those of us who do not live in his time and place befriend him by heeding the message he delivered to all humanity. As the latest iteration of the Abrahamic message, Muhammad's message informs humanity about God from God's view of right religion.

MUHAMMAD'S MESSAGE: DRAW CLOSE TO GOD

Muhammad's message starts with a simple recipe. It speaks to what constitutes right action, right knowledge, and right virtue, namely *islam, iman,* and *ihsan. Islam,* or submission to God, refers to our *effort* in a set of right ritual actions. *Iman,* or faith, refers to right *beliefs* about God. *Ihsan,* or virtue, refers to living with a God-conscious attitude, what Buddhists call *mindfulness.* It encompasses both the states of loving God with all your heart and opening yourself to union or intimacy with God.

Muhammad's message therefore appeals to all distinct parts of the human being:

1. *Islam,* freely choosing to obey God (will)

2. *Iman,* seeking God's Truth with your mind (intellect)

3. *Ihsan,* loving God above all else (heart) and opening oneself to union with God (soul)

Islam is not about worshiping Moses, Jesus, or Muhammad, or the traditions that they came to teach. It is about *using* any one of these traditions, or any authentic tradition revealed by God to humans, to worship in submission to God so that we can get really intimate with God.

There is a famous *hadith,* or narrative about the Prophet, that says that the Prophet was seated with his companions one day when a stranger, later identified as the archangel Gabriel himself, walked into their presence. Gabriel proceeded to sit directly in front of the Prophet and asked him a series of questions. He first asked, "Tell me, what is submission (*islam*)?" The Prophet answered it by listing what became popularly known as the five pillars of Islam: testimony of faith, daily prayer, charity, fasting, and pilgrimage (which we will describe below). To the surprise of those watching, this unknown questioner said, "You are correct." Next he asked what faith is (*iman*), to which the Prophet answered by listing the five items of belief: in God, in the angels, in the Scriptures, in the Prophets, and in the Last Day, the Hereafter. Again the questioner responded, "You are right." Then he asked, "What is [mastery of] virtue (*ihsan*)?" To which the Prophet answered, "[Mastery of] virtue is to worship God as if you see Him; and if you don't see Him, then [worship Him with the conviction that] He sees you."[4]

Muslims read this hadith as outlining a path of religious evolution, from a mere external observation of religiosity to an inner expression of faith to a state of intimacy with God. Even among the religious, not all human souls are inclined to intimacy with God, any more than all souls are drawn to be expert in medicine. And among those who desire divine intimacy, few are capable of the self-discipline and hard work that is demanded of them to achieve it, just as few who want to become doctors are truly capable of expending the effort.

MUHAMMAD'S MESSAGE, PART 1: DO THE RIGHT THING

What Muslims have done best—and still do well—is fulfill the first commandment through their acts of worship known as the five pillars. Islamic law refers to this vertical dimension of faith (the God-human relationship) as the category of *'ibadat* (literally, "worship") comprising the set of required beliefs and ritual acts of worship that provide the seeking human soul with its personal discovery of God and teach it how to adore and magnify God.

Right Effort: The Five Pillars of Islam

Right action (*islam*) consists of what is commonly known as the five pillars of Islam—those things a dutiful God-believing human should do. Theologians call them "orthopraxis," those ritual practices one must do to be considered a practitioner of the faith.[5]

The Prophet taught these five pillars of Islam:

1. *Declaring that there is no god but God and that Muhammad is His messenger.* This is called the *shahadah,* or testimony of faith, and it sounds like this in Arabic: *ash-hadu al-la ilaha illallah, wa ash-hadu anna muhammadar rasul-ullah.* Saying this admits a person into the Muslim faith and community and is equivalent to the Pledge of Allegiance that a new citizen makes to the United States. The Prophet emphatically stated that any human being who says this must have his or her life and property protected and may not be harmed by the Muslim community.

The story that fleshes out this teaching took place during a time of hostilities between the Prophet, then in Medina, and the people of Mecca, who had rejected him and tried to assassinate him. A group of Muslim scouts crossed paths with a group of Meccan scouts; fighting ensued, and the Muslims dominated. One of the last survivors of the Meccans got down to his knees and uttered aloud the *shahadah*, whereupon the Muslim killed him. When they returned and the Prophet heard this news, he called the fellow in and asked him why he had killed the Meccan, whereupon the man responded that the Meccan had said that only to spare his skin and not out of a genuine belief. The Prophet asked him, "Did you open up his heart to determine if he spoke truly?" and kept repeating that question firmly until the fellow was overcome with the deepest regret.

I always recommend to my non-Muslim students to learn this phrasing: *la ilaha illallah, muhammad rasu-lullah;* it comes in handy when visiting the Muslim world, especially Arabic-speaking Muslims. You can use *la ilaha illallah* to conclude a bargain in the souk or bazaar in your favor, to stop an argument and bring about calm, or to express your condolences, and you can even utter it in a sigh to declare your sense of despair.

In the *shahadah* Muslims not only admit the oneness of God but also implicitly recognize the series of messengers, such as Abraham, Moses, and Jesus, as well as the many more unnamed and unknown to us. In this we hear the human response to the divine announcement in the Hebrew Shema addressed to all humanity: God asking humanity to heed the truth that God is One, and we responding by saying, "There is no god but You."

Chanting *la ilaha illallah* as a mantra has positive effects, especially when done in a group. It can bring people to ecstasy, soothe and calm, energize, and enable some to make more translucent the veil between them and God. It is therefore the central practice or chant of Sufi orders (the mystics of Islam), who do this collectively on a weekly basis a hundred or more times and individually daily up to tens of thousands of times. The word *ilah* is cognate to the Hebrew *el* or *eloh,* meaning "god," and *Allah* is a contraction of *al-ilah,* "*the* God." Jesus's words from the cross, "*Eloi, Eloi lema sabachtani?*" (Mark 15:33, Matthew 27:46, meaning, "My God, my God, why have you forsaken me?") would be pronounced in Arabic "*ilahi, ilahi lima sabaqtani?*"

2. *Adoring God in a sacramental ritual prayer five set times daily* (salah), *facing the Ka'bah in Mecca.* The five times of prayer are set to coincide with the cosmic clock: dawn, noon, midafternoon, sunset, and when the evening twilight has disappeared from the night sky. It consists of a choreographed set of movements: standing, bowing, returning to the standing position, and falling down on one's face in prostration, then sitting up, and prostrating again; this is one cycle of prayer (called *rak'ah*). After two cycles of prayer, there is a supplication done in the seated position. In the standing position, we initiate the prayer by saying, "God is Greatest" (*allahu akbar*) then recite the opening chapter of the Quran followed by a small chapter or any verse of the Quran.

The opening chapter translates as follows:

In the name of the Merciful, Compassionate God
Praise be to God, Lord of the Worlds
The Merciful, the Compassionate
King of Judgment Day
You alone we worship, and You alone we seek help from
Guide us along the right path: the path of those You have blessed, not
those upon whom is wrath, nor the lost.
Amen.

In the bowing position we say, "Glory be to God the Great," then rising up to the standing position we say, "God hears the one who praises Him," then we prostrate twice, in each saying, "Glory be to God the most exalted." A state of ritual purity is required, accomplished by an ablution (washing of face and of hands up to the elbows, wiping of hair and washing or wiping of the feet). When water is not available, we pat our hands on dry earth or sand and just wipe the face and the hands.

The prayer's choreography is based on the Prophet's night journey, when he was taken by the archangel Gabriel from Mecca to Jerusalem and from Jerusalem was raised to God's presence, where God "revealed to His servant that which He revealed" (Quran 53:10) and where the Prophet was shown "among the greatest signs of his Lord" (Quran 53:18). Along the way the Prophet witnessed countless angels in rows adoring God eternally in each of these positions. And because he found this sight so powerfully compelling (as it is even to non-Muslims when they witness the sight of thousands of Muslims moving in unison), the positions were combined and made into the choreography of prayer. The Prophet's ascension and the prayer given to him that night produced a popular saying in the Muslim world that the prayer is the ascension of the Muslim to his or her Lord (*as-salatu mi'raj ul-mu'min*).

The supplication recited at the end in the seated position includes blessings called down upon Muhammad and his family and descendants (*aali Muhammad*, which according to one interpretation means all the followers of Muhammad's message), upon Abraham and his family and descendants (*aali Ibrahim*, thereby, according to one interpretation, including supplications for all Jews and Christians), and upon all the righteous of humanity (thus the righteous of all religions) and is ended by expressing the greeting of peace (*as-salamu alaykum*) to the recording angels Muslims believe are seated on their right and left shoulders. The movements reflect a universal body language of respect. In ancient societies, and until very recently in Japan, people would prostrate before their lords and masters, and even still in Japan people bow to each other as a sign of respect, with the person lower on the social ladder bowing more deeply toward the one higher. The words are such that any Jew or Christian, or anyone who believes in one God, can perform without violating his or her faith.

Wherever one goes in the Muslim world, from Indonesia to Senegal, a Muslim can enter a mosque, stand shoulder to shoulder with another Muslim, and perform the prayer in the same language with the same movements. The person praying adjacent to you may have a different opinion on what an Islamic state means, may belong to a different school of Islamic law, may think that the war in Iraq was good or bad, may be a Republican or Democrat, Sunni or Shiite, but Muslims pray as one body. Like Christians who believe they are united in a body of Christ, Muslims are united in a body of ritual practice, and the five-times-daily prayer is a potent bonding activity.

3. *Paying the community treasury a minimum tax of 2.5 percent of one's wealth as a means of purifying that savings and transmuting one's work into worship* (zakah). The tax varies depending on the type of work one earns a living from. Income from mining (such as oil or diamonds) is

taxed at 20 percent. This is especially intended to help the poor, ensuring them a minimum standard of living, but it also may be used for other purposes benefiting the public welfare.

Islam makes this tax a *religious* duty, and to many this links Islam with governance (the state). Some scholars believe that the income and other taxes currently levied on Muslims satisfy the requirement of *zakah*. Not only are current taxes much higher than 2.5 percent, American Muslims pay well over 30 percent, so they say, "Give us a break." Other scholars say no and insist that the *zakah* be paid separately as a *religious* obligation, a position that is logical if one subscribes to the perception that the state is separate from religion.

4. *Fasting* (sawm) *for a month once a year, defined as abstaining from eating, drinking, smoking, and sexual activity from dawn to sunset daily for the month of Ramadan* (the ninth month of the Islamic lunar calendar). As Catholic Christians fast for forty days of Lent, so Muslims fast during the month of Ramadan. Ramadan is an enclosure in time, as a mosque, church, or temple is an enclosure in space. The respect we accord a house of worship is to be granted to Ramadan. It is a time for reflection, for self-purification, for retreating from the bustle of worldly life into a time of deeper contemplation. We wouldn't enter a house of worship and engage in gossip, commit sinful acts, or even read *People* magazine, although I'm sure there are those who do. Fasting without abstaining from evil actions such as gossip and foul conversation is therefore not fruitful, for the Prophet taught that a person who fasts and does not guard the tongue or avoid evil actions has accomplished little except perhaps to become hungry and thirsty. The Prophet once said that the silence of a fasting person is glorification of God; even his or her sleep is counted as worship.

The real objective of the Ramadan fast is to raise one's God-consciousness (*taqwa*). It is meant not as punishment but as an exercise that accelerates one's spiritual progress. The exercise teaches you quickly that you have a soul. After a few days of fasting, your physical systems slow down, and your "I" separates from your body and emotions and floats over them. Hunger is felt not as "I am hungry" but as "My body is hungry," much as you would observe your pet dog being hungry or trying to get your attention at mealtime. If someone stimulates you to anger, you feel as if he has goaded your emotional being, and you recognize a distinct time lag between the stimulus and your reaction, during which time you think about your normal reflex reaction and whether you want to react at all. Fasting therefore helps you recognize the different components of your being (body, emotional being, mind, and "I," the locus of the soul). By the end of the month your will has been strengthened; you feel that you are capable of far more than you thought, and you are less susceptible to the "I can't help myself" syndrome. Hopefully, you will be ready to progress even more upon your spiritual journey.

5. *Performing pilgrimage* (hajj) *once in one's lifetime,* contingent on one's ability to afford it financially and being in good enough physical health. The hajj consists of a trip to Mecca sometime before the ninth of Dhul-Hijjah (the twelfth month of the Islamic calendar). This day is called the Standing at (the Plain of) Arafat, about a twenty-minute drive from Mecca when there's no traffic but a two-hour drive when two million pilgrims are jamming the roads to Arafat. If you catch this day you've caught the hajj, and if you missed it, you've missed the hajj that year. Most pilgrims like to arrive in Mecca no later than the sixth of the month and spend at least three days in Mina, a suburb of Mecca, before going on to Arafat. All men wear only two pieces of unsewn white cotton cloth, one around the waist and the other around the shoulder, so as to emphasize the equality of humankind before God. Female pilgrims are fully dressed, leaving only their faces and hands exposed. Various rituals are performed during these days, the most dramatic of them being walking seven times around (*tawaf*) the cubical structure draped with a black cloth called the Ka'bah, originally built by Abraham and his son Ishmael.

This annual pilgrimage was begun by Abraham when he was commanded to build the Ka'bah, the first structure devoted to the worship of only one God (Quran 2:125–27, also 22:26–33). God commanded Abraham, "Proclaim among people the pilgrimage: they will respond, on foot, and on every means of transport, coming from every remote place" (Quran 22:26). This annual ritual of pilgrimage to Mecca today attracts over two million from all over the globe. The pilgrimage reenacts some of the rituals of Abraham. His willingness to sacrifice his son is remembered by performing a sacrifice, usually of a sheep. Hagar's running to and fro between the two hillocks known as Safa and Marwah, adjacent to the Ka'bah, is enacted by seven quick walks between the hillocks following the circling of the Ka'bah. To sit in front of the Ka'bah and just gaze at it is a serene experience.

The hajj is a visit to God's house, and the pilgrim returns transformed. Part of the reason is that the pilgrimage comes about through more than just an individual decision. More than any of the other four ritual acts of worship—with the possible exception of the *shahadah*—the experience of deciding to go on hajj makes the Muslim feel invited by God. No matter how recently before the hajj the decision was made, a vortex of activities carries the pilgrim on the journey to Mecca in time for the hajj. Financial impediments may be removed, familial or professional obligations covered, or visa restrictions lifted, so the pilgrim becomes the recipient of a string of small miracles that make the trip possible. The process seems strangely effortless. Yet once the pilgrim arrives, the stark geography of the desert landscape and the arduous nature of the journey ensure in the pilgrim's mind that this trip was not made for physical pleasure and comfort; this is no Club Med experience. If one imagines the power of divine revelation descending upon the Prophet in Mecca and Medina, as it did upon Moses in nearby Sinai, one intuitively feels that the land, not to mention the vegetation and animal life, could not withstand divine revelation's blinding power. One makes this trip purely for God's pleasure; there is no mistake about that. The pilgrim's mind is filled with such contemplations.

For centuries, the pilgrimage used to be the annual Islamic Convention before annual conventions became the norm. People from all over the world got to know each other, learned from each other, and exchanged ideas and products. Even till recently one would go on pilgrimage and perhaps acquire a fine Persian carpet from an Iranian pilgrim or frankincense from an Omani. Globalization has now changed us: almost all the prayer rugs, prayer beads, and clocks that call out the prayer times are made in China, even the "Persian" carpets.

In making the hajj, the pilgrims are drawing close to the Ka'bah, the place where Abraham initiated rites to the one God, and the place toward which five times each day they bow in prayer. In every prayer they recite the invocation (*salat*) upon the Prophet: "O God! Bestow your blessings upon Muhammad and the family [and descendants] of Muhammad as you have bestowed your blessings upon Abraham and the family [and descendants] of Abraham." A Muslim who prays only the five-time obligatory (*fard*) prayer mentions Abraham's name four times in each prayer, equaling twenty times every day. If we include the nonobligatory prayers, a Muslim invokes Abraham's name as many as fifty-two times a day. The ritual acts of prayer and the pilgrimage reveal Islam as an Abrahamic faith.

MUHAMMAD'S MESSAGE, PART 2:
SEEKING GOD'S TRUTH WITH YOUR MIND

Right knowledge of God (*iman*) is embodied in what we called the core beliefs or creed. Theologians call this the "orthodoxy" of a religion, those things that you must believe if you are to be considered a member of the faith.

Right Belief: The Five Items of Faith

The Prophet taught that right belief consists of five items of faith (*iman*):

1. *A firm belief in God, that God is one, single, unique, beyond likeness to anything in creation.* Although God in His essence is unknowable, He is described by some ninety-nine "Beautiful Names of God," which are descriptive attributes of God. Among these names, which Muslims are invited to call upon Him with, are the Merciful, the Compassionate, the King, the Holy, the Almighty, the Omnipotent, the All-Hearing, the All-Seeing, the All-Knowing, the Kind, the Loving and Tender to Creation, the Generous, the Forgiver, the Glorious, Owner of the Day of Judgment, the Avenger of wrongs. These divine names describe how God relates to humankind and the rest of creation.

The upshot of this is that we have to maintain a proper regard for God. Thinking wrongly about or attributing falsehood to God is a sin. To say that God is weak, unable to do such and such a thing, is considered by Muslims deeply sacrilegious. God is absolute, infinite. As the Creator, Originator, and Sustainer of the universe, God upholds all that exists; anything not sustained by God cannot continue to exist. Natural laws are merely the courses set by God for the operation of the material world. The series of causes that operate the world, and operate on the world, are finite in time and place. God is eternal, the prime cause, the true cause, the cause of causes. He acts but is not acted upon, sees but is not seen, causes movement but does not move, creates time and space but is beyond time and space. And yet God can be "perceived" and "known."

We are often surprised when we get to know a co-worker on the job and after some time get invited to his or her home to meet the family. We see a different person relating to spouse and children and wonder whether that was the same person we've worked with all those years. When a human is confronted with an attribute of God, say the All-Compassionate, and then with another, say the Avenger, it is hard for the human soul to recognize that these are aspects of the same God. Many humans have refused to see that and are convinced that they are dealing with a different God. A hadith suggests that on Judgment Day God will display all His attributes, and people will submit to those attributes they recognized and submitted to during their lives on earth and be unable to bow before those they had not submitted to; the most blessed would be those who submitted in this life to all the attributes of God. A common mistake we make in this life is to make separate gods out of God's different attributes and not see the One Who interacts with creation in multiple ways.

2. *Belief in the existence of the angels.* Angels are beings created of light for the express purpose of fulfilling divine commands, the most important being Gabriel (Jibril in Arabic), whose task was to communicate between God and the Prophet-Messengers. It was Gabriel who announced to Mary that she would have a son without having been intimate with a man,[6] who embraced Muhammad and announced to him that he would be a Prophet, and who spoke to him the first verses of the Quran. Other angels are 'Azra'il, the angel of death, whose task is to collect all souls at the moment of death, and Mika'il (Michael), whose task will be to blow the trumpet that will arouse the souls from their death stupor on the Day of Resurrection. We have mentioned the countless angels eternally worshiping God in the various positions of standing, bowing, prostrating, and sitting, which became the model of the Islamic choreography of prayer, and others who see to the smooth functioning of the universe.

There are angels who watch over us and record our good and bad deeds and angels who interrogate us after our death and accompany us to where we will be. Finally, there are the angels who watch over Paradise and Hell, admitting human souls into these places and executing God's command in them.

3. *Belief that God has communicated to humankind through scriptures, sent through several messengers.* The four scriptures the Quran mentions are the Torah, sent through Moses; the Psalms, revealed to David; the Evangel, revealed to Jesus; and the Quran, revealed to Muhammad. Also mentioned are the scrolls of Abraham and Moses (Quran 87:19). Muslims believe these books were authored by God and revealed through a particular prophet. Muslims believe that the similarities found in these scriptures and the Quran's references to the others are due to the fact that they all had the same author. Because some secular scholars of religion entirely reject the idea of God and some Jewish and Christian scholars of Islam reject the idea of Muhammad, they are forced to conclude that Jesus copied ideas from the Old Testament or that Muhammad copied ideas from the Old and New Testaments. Such positions have contributed to the animosity between the Abrahamic faith communities. The Muslim position is that the Quran confirms the truths revealed in all the scriptures and that although they were revealed to each messenger in the language of his people, and some variations in details of worship exist, God sent these scriptures for one broad theme: right belief regarding God and right ethics for the benefit of humankind.

4. *Belief in the Prophet-Messengers.* The Quran names twenty-five Messengers, beginning with Adam and including Noah, Abraham, Ishmael, Isaac, Jacob, Joseph, David, Solomon, Moses, Aaron, Job, Jonah, John the Baptist, Jesus Christ, and ending with Muhammad. The Quran states that although some of the Messengers have been named, many have not been named (Quran 4:163–64, 40:78), also that God sent to every community a Messenger.[7] Prophets are windows through whom people get a powerful sense of God's presence and exemplars whose pattern of behavior ordinary folk can emulate. Prophets are human, and they do err, although Muslims believe that their prophethood is protected (*ma'sum*) by God from their errors. Their errors enable us to relate to them and give us hope that we too can achieve the highest spiritual status.

Islamic theology differentiates between a prophet and a messenger. A prophet is one to whom God sent a revelation; a messenger is a prophet who was mandated to preach to his community. Thus some scholars regard Mary, mother of Jesus, as a prophet since Gabriel visited her and revealed to her that she would have a son, but she was not a messenger since she was not mandated to preach. Her son Jesus did preach and is regarded by Muslims as a prophet and a messenger, and one of the very greatest messengers of all time.

5. *Belief in the hereafter, sometimes called by Muslims the Last Day.* The hereafter is a compound concept for Muslims. It means that creation will come to an end (a kind of reverse of the Big Bang idea of creation—a big implosion), followed by a Day of Resurrection when all souls will be resurrected, followed by a Day of Judgment when souls will be judged. This is the moment when we are held accountable for our ethical actions. Those who lived a righteous life will gain divine approval and enter the bliss of Paradise while those who lived unethically will gain divine disapproval and taste the burn of their evil actions in Hell. We experience hell on earth when those we love and respect (especially our spouses, our parents, or our bosses) are upset with us, and heaven when those we love and respect are happy with us. It stands to reason that when the Creator of the universe, who is the Absolute, is pleased with us, we experience eternal Heaven, and Hell is just what we naturally experience when the Creator is disappointed with us. The philosophical underpinning of the idea of the Last Day is human accountability. We will be held accountable for our actions and will experience pleasure at our good deeds, deeds of kindness and mercy, and experience enormous pain at our evil deeds, deeds of oppression and unkindness.

These events are potently described in several places in the Quran, of which the following is one example:

When the heaven splits
When the stars disperse
When the rivers overflow
When the graves scatter
Reaps every soul its sowings and restraints
O man! What deceived you from your generous Lord—
Who created you, completed you, set you aright—
Cast you in any shape He pleased?

Yet you deny Judgment
While upon you are keepers—
Honorable recorders—
Alert to what you do
The righteous are in bliss
The wicked in Fire
Burning in it on Judgment Day
Not from it withdrawn
How will you recognize Judgment Day?
Again, how will you recognize Judgment Day?
That day when a soul controls nothing of another
And the command is God's (alone). (Quran 82:1–19)

"Righteousness," the Quran adds, "is not that you turn your faces east or west [following the details of worship without an inner ethical sense]; but righteous are those secure in their belief in God, the Hereafter, the angels, the Scripture and the Prophets; who give wealth lovingly for the love of God to relatives, orphans, the poor, travelers, petitioners, and who set slaves free; who keep the prayer and pay the *zakah*; who fulfill their promises when they make a promise, who are patiently constant during distress and affliction and in times of conflict. These are the truthful; these are the pious" (Quran 2:177).

The Quran differentiates between outer expression of belief (called *islam*) and inner faith (*iman*), instructing the Prophet to "inform those of the Arabs who assert 'we believe' that they had not yet believed, but to say 'we submit' [*aslamna*, we have become muslim], for belief has not yet penetrated your hearts" (Quran 49:14).[8] This suggests that faith is also an act of the heart.

Muslims throughout the world accept the above beliefs and practices. One cannot pick and choose among the above beliefs and practices and consider oneself Muslim. As mentioned above, wherever one goes in the Muslim world, on entering a mosque and standing next to a fellow Muslim and beginning the prayer with "God is Most Great" (*al-lahu akbar*), Muslims enter into a felt sense of being united bondsmen and bondswomen before God. That the prayer is conducted in Arabic all over the world unites Muslims in a way that perhaps only Catholics nostalgic for the Latin mass can comprehend. We may speak different languages, wear different clothes, and have different cultures and politics, but before the Creator in worship we are one.

Muslims strongly believe they know how to live religiously, to fulfill the commandment Jesus called the greatest of the laws of Moses. After commanding the children of Israel to heed the truth that "the Lord our God, the Lord is One," and to love the Lord our God with all our heart, mind, soul, and strength, Moses adds, "And you must commit yourselves wholeheartedly to these commands I am giving you today. Repeat them again and again to your children. Talk about them when you are at home and when you are away on a journey, when you are lying down and when you are getting up again. Tie them to your hands as a reminder, and wear them on your forehead. Write them on the doorposts of your houses and on your gates" (Deuteronomy 6:4–9).

Reading this verse of Deuteronomy made it clear to me that this is in fact what Muslims do. Muslim children are firmly reminded by their parents not to forget God, that God is one, and that they must live in accordance with His commands. Muslims have developed a whole art of calligraphy in which the expressions *Allah* (God), *La ilaha illallah* (there is no god but God), and other Quranic phrases are written down and practically hung "on the doorposts of their houses and on their gates." Muslims will place a piece of calligraphy above the door as a blessing. Muslim women will often adorn themselves with calligraphic necklaces and bracelets with the "Throne verse" (*ayat al-kursi*) written on it.[9] There is hardly a mosque where such calligraphy is absent, and you will find Muslims delighting in decorating their homes, their cars, and today their computers and laptops with pieces of calligraphy that mention God's name and His Oneness. Many a Muslim-owned store and restaurant you might walk into in the United States is adorned with a rug hung on the wall with some Quranic calligraphy on it, and I've even seen Muslim hot dog vendors on the corners of New York City sporting a calligraphic plate on the sides of their pushcarts.

These beliefs and practices became rapidly institutionalized in Muslim society. In mosques, usually run by a central government authority, people performed the five-times-daily prayer and attended the weekly Friday prayer preceded by a sermon. In the larger cities, some mosques had scholars devoted to the study of religious law, theology, and religious sciences. Gathering under a master, who would sit on a chair lecturing to a crowd of students, these groups of scholars developed into schools of thought.[10] Students who traveled to learn from these masters usually stayed in or just adjacent to these mosques, and in time the *madrasa* (school) next to the Mosque became a common fixture. Some mosques, such as al-Azhar in Cairo, Egypt, became leading centers of Islamic learning. Thus from the beginning the mosque was associated with learning, and the cleft between science and religion that occurred in the West did not happen in Islam. In large part this was because the Quran did not say anything about the nature of creation or the physical sciences that has been disproved by science.[11]

MUHAMMAD'S MESSAGE, PART 3: LOVE AND COMMUNION WITH GOD

It is possible to act right and believe right and yet be spiritually dead, practicing the correct rituals but not enlivened by spiritual life at our core. The Quran refers to this when it commanded the Prophet to reject the (Bedouin) Arabs' assertion that they had become believers (*mu'mins*) and to inform them that they were merely submitted (*muslim*), "for faith has not yet penetrated into your hearts" (Quran 49:14).

We can practice our faith externally, described as the level of submission (*islam*), and be absent or dead internally, which is the level of faith (*iman*). Moreover, we can be religious even in these two senses but lacking in religious beauty and virtuosity (*ihsan*).

Ihsan connotes beauty, mastery, proficiency; it is achieved by maintaining a keen awareness of seeing and being seen by God. *Ihsan* means right virtue, which encompasses two states: a state of loving God with all your heart, and a state of being close to or intimate with God, of living in connection with God.

Right Virtue: Loving God with All Your Heart

Essential to developing *ihsan* or right virtue is purifying the soul from sicknesses of the soul such as egotism, greed, lust, gossip, and envy. These are all diseases that the Prophet taught erode the value of a believer's ritual acts of worship. A famous hadith reads,

The Prophet Muhammad once asked his companions, Do you know who the bankrupt person is? The Prophet's Companions said: A bankrupt man amongst us is one who has no money or wealth. He [the Prophet] said: The bankrupt of my community is the one who comes on the Day of Resurrection with many prayers and fasts and charity. But since he hurled abuses upon others, brought calumny against others, unlawfully consumed the wealth of others, shed the blood of others and beat others, his virtues [of prayers, fasts, and charity] would be transferred to the account of those [who suffered at his hand]. And if his good deeds fall short to compensate the accounts of all those he hurt, then their sins would be transferred into his account, and he would be thrown in hell fire.[12]

This hadith teaches that even if one zealously performs the rituals of religion, one may still fail to be saved if one's ethics violate the rights of others. To be a *successful* worshiper, then, means to *submit* to the divine call, to hear and thus heed that God is one and single, and to exhibit this understanding in one's philosophy and in one's ethics. And a *successful* society is one in which both commandments, loving God and loving fellow human beings, are simultaneously fulfilled. At an individual level, Muslims therefore regard the Prophet Muhammad as the perfected human, an exemplar whose behavior is studied and emulated. At the societal level, Muslims regard the Prophet's community in Medina as the ideal society and seek to emulate its standards at a communal level.

Throughout religious history, Muslim history included, people have asked, what is the meaning of religious or spiritual mastery, and what is the process by which humans become spiritual virtuosos? And if virtue means living in such a way that we "see God," how do we achieve this?

Most of us have had some kind of transpersonal experience that made us aware that there is more to life than just drudgery. In such moments the boundaries of our self dissolve, and we feel a joyful oneness with the universe and with God. At that moment the reality of God surfaces, emerging out of our subconscious into our consciousness, and we *know* with an absolute conviction that God exists and that God is compassionate, just, almighty, and all-knowing, with everything just as it should be. This experience feels like God tapping you on the shoulder, informing you that He does indeed exist.

If, as the Prophet taught, spiritual virtuosity is worshiping God as if one sees Him, the natural question is, can such an experience be elicited for those who have not had it yet, and repeated for the benefit of those who have, with the clarity with which we see the sun or the moon?[13]

Those who have the good fortune of living in the company of a prophet are blessed by being in the charismatic presence of one through whom God speaks to humanity. The Prophet's companions felt the spiritual power, the presence and energy that coursed through the Prophet, and thereby they perceived the presence of God. In a hadith, a companion complained to the Prophet that when he was in his company and the Prophet spoke about the Hereafter, it was as if he could see it with his own eyes, but when he returned to his work and his family, he lost that feeling, and he was therefore concerned that he had regressed into hypocrisy, a major sin in Islam. The Prophet assured him that if he and others could maintain the state that they had in the Prophet's company, angels would descend upon them and greet them in public and in private (literally, in the streets and in their bedchambers).[14]

This is the state of being that many souls wish to elicit, one that evokes a prophet's company. Muslim spiritual seekers (Sufis) call this a state of "heightened consciousness" or "enlivened presence," attained by divine remembrance (*dhikr*, repeating God's names and other Quranic verses). The Quran addresses the believers: "O you who have believed: respond to God and to the Messenger [that is, the Prophet Muhammad] when they invite you to what *enlivens* you. And know that God instates [that God creates states of consciousness, and communicates] between a man and his own heart" (Quran 8:24).

The Prophet Muhammad was initiated into this state of divine presence when in deep contemplation one day in the year 610 CE, in the cave of Hira on the outskirts of Mecca. The archangel Gabriel entered into his presence, embraced him three times with increasing tightness, and revealed to him the first few verses of the Quran. Each embrace discharged so much spiritual power into Muhammad that he ran home shaking, believing he had fallen mad. Such can be the effect of the initial initiation of receiving spiritual energy. In successive revelations, the power and energy contained in each was such that the Prophet would be drenched in perspiration, even on a cold day. The Quran affirms this spiritual power: "Had We sent this Quran down upon a mountain, you would have seen it [the mountain] fall down and split asunder out of fear of God" (Quran 59:21).

By his voice, by his direct company and enlivening presence, and by using the sounds of the Quran, the Prophet taught his companions to chant certain Quranic phrases and thus to effect in themselves a similar experience. The first time this takes place, it is experienced as the initiation process that bypasses the intellect and operates directly on the soul. Done on subsequent occasions, it admits the soul into a state of divine presence, in which we commune with God and our acts of worship feel alive. The human will may not be involved the first time, for such an experience often happens serendipitously. But we can train our wills and enter consciously into a state of connection with God.

After a prophet dies, succeeding generations jostle for power, and the few intimates of the prophet who learned to carry the living presence of God are usually overwhelmed by those who desire power over others in the name of the religion. Those who retain the ability to reflect the living presence of God are regarded as saints, "God's friends" in Arabic (*waliyullah* or, in the plural, *awliya'ullah*). The definition of such a friend is given by the *hadith qudsi* (a hadith in which the Prophet Muhammad quotes God, although the words are not actually part of the Quran), describing the perfected soul, as we saw above, the soul for which God "becomes the ear by which he hears, the eye by which he sees, the hand by which he grasps, the foot by which he walks, and the heart by which he comprehends."[15] Such a soul perceives God continually and acts by God's commands. While not all humans want to be loved by God in such a way that their perceptions and actions are God-determined, there are many who do. How can these embark upon the journey and walk the spiritual walk that leads toward sainthood?

The technology of this journey is what Sufism is essentially about, and it consists of two components. The first is *remembering God*, called in Arabic *dhikrullah*, or *dhikr* for short, done best through chanting God's names or select Quranic phrases: *Allah* (God), *La ilaha illallah* (there is no god but God), and others. *Dhikr* is soul food and nourishment, and the spiritual masters are the inheritors of the Prophet's role in spiritually feeding the community. Remembrance is a powerful source of self-discovery, through which come knowledge and strength. Without knowledge, strength may be misguided and imperfect, and without strength to withstand the vicissitudes of life and combat them, no one can achieve much worth achieving. The sounds given to the Prophet and recited to him (and collectively known as the Quran) comprise the primary component of *dhikr*, God's *dhikr* coming down to humankind.

Second is the *need for a spiritual teacher*. If *dhikr* is analogous to music, and the seeker a player in an orchestra, the Teacher is analogous to the maestro, who leads and guides the orchestra. For *dhikr* to be effective, it requires a conveyer of *dhikr*, or in Arabic a *mudhakkir*, a "remembrancier," to transmit and convey the *dhikr* in the form of the Quran as well as to initiate the *dhikr* process in the hearts of those who feel moved by the *dhikr*. This was the primary role of the Prophet, who is called in the Quran a *mudhakkir:* "So remind [that is, transmit the *dhikr*], you are but a remembrancier; you are not an enforcer [that is, you do not compel them to accept God's truth and believe]" (Quran 88:21). This is the primary role of a prophet or, more specifically, a messenger.

The Prophet accomplished his role as *mudhakkir* in two ways, reflecting the two ways he received the *dhikr:* first, by appealing to the mind and convincing people, and second—and no less powerful—by teaching his companions how to inject the *dhikr* directly into their souls, to receive the divine transmission.

As the Prophet recited the Quran to his companions, its ideas and concepts appealed to their minds and intellects. Finding its teachings intellectually appealing, they then applied their will to modify their behavior in accord with its teachings. *Dhikr* in this context is called *dhikr* of the mind (*fikr* in Arabic), namely, intellectual contemplation, thinking, and so forth. This is the most common and obvious sense in which the term *dhikr* is understood by the majority of Muslims.

Sufis, however, speak of the *dhikr* of different "limbs": the *dhikr* of the tongue is repeating the divine names, *dhikr* of the heart is love of God and working to eliminate from our own heart its sicknesses of egoism, jealousy, anger, envy, lust, greed, love of gossip, and slander and to maintain correct behavior and courtesy (*adab*) before God and humankind.

Dhikr of the soul is a spiritual submission and heightened consciousness, awareness, and mindfulness of God, an intimacy or presence
(*ma'iyyah*) with God and the Teacher. *Dhikr* of the body consists of the
rituals of worship: the sacramental five-times-daily prayer preceded by
ablution, charity, fasting the month of Ramadan, and the pilgrimage.
Dhikr of the will is right choice and avoidance of sins, defined as disobedience to God. All aspects of *dhikr* work cooperatively and syner-
gistically together.

The spiritual master Ali Abu al-Hasan ash-Shadhili, founder of the
order that goes by his name, the Shadhili Order, informs us that spiritual teachers and guides (he calls them "callers," *du'ah*) are of two types:
those who make their call from within the realm of common understanding (*idhn 'am*), and those who call from the sphere of deep spiritual insight (*basirah*), with a special call and divine mandate (*idhn*, in
Arabic).

Teachers licensed to call are those who have engaged in the deep
inner struggle with their unpurified selves until their selves became
obedient, disciplined, and enlightened. They cannot achieve anything,
much less do anything, without divine permission. These callers who
possess divine license invite others to God through their entire being.
Even their silence (*samt*) is a call to God because their innermost self
"sings of God," a resonant vibration that invites others to God. Those
who respond quickly to them do so in accord with the degree of goodness and amount of faith in their hearts.

A common feature of human life is suffering, whose primary cause
is, as Sufis call it, the state of being separated from God. The thirteenth-
century Sufi poet Rumi begins his magnum opus, the *Mathnawi*, by
making an analogy between a human being cut off from God and a
reed that does not sound before being cut off from its origin and
shaped into a wind instrument:

> Listen to the reed how it tells a tale, complaining of separation—
> Saying, "Ever since I was parted from the reed-bed, my lament has
>   caused man and woman to moan."[16]

The sounds of human life, the songs we sing and the prayerful
supplications we make, even the ambitions we harbor, all express our

desire to be reconnected to God. All human suffering arises from being cut off from God, and all human joy comes from glimpses of divinity. Sufis are taught to expect worldly life to be one of suffering, to learn how to suffer so as to remain unaffected by suffering (even to die before they die so as to embrace immortality), to know how to achieve and detach so as not to be affected by the acquisition or loss of possessions. These are the main directives of a truly submitted way of life.

The most difficult challenge on the spiritual path is that of the ego. And the most difficult lesson to learn, and to keep practicing, is to ensure that one's ethical actions are dominated by the higher self and not the lower self. In a story about the Prophet's cousin, Ali was fighting an unbeliever during one of the battles that the Muslims waged against the Meccans and was about to overwhelm him when the latter spat in Ali's face. To the surprise of his opponent, Ali sheathed his sword, and when asked why, Ali replied, "I was fighting you for the sake of God. But when you spat in my face I became angry, and did not wish to strike you out of my [personal] anger." These are the standards that govern the decision-making process of an ethics based on faith.

The Greatest Love of All

In one hadith, or saying from the Prophet, God, the Creator of the heavens and the earth, announced, "I was a hidden treasure and desired [or loved] to be known, so I created the Creation, and through Me they knew Me."[17] God created the universe for the purpose of divine Self-disclosure and Self-Love.

When God finalized the creation of Adam from clay, He breathed into the earthly form a breath from His Divine Spirit (Quran 15:29 and 38:72). Therefore, between us and the Creator of the universe lies a most special relationship and a unique reciprocity. Our spirit, having been created from a divine breath, has a divine origin and all the characteristics of the Supreme Being, just as a drop of water has all the characteristics of the primeval sea surrounding the earth and therefore yearns to join with It. This is the Quranic rendering of the biblical statement that God created humankind in the divine image.[18] Our being microcosmically maps the cosmos, and in a unique sense it maps

God. Therefore our greatest love is when our love is aligned with one of the pathways of Divinity loving Itself.

The common human perspective we have of ourselves is the view of modern science. It defines a human being from an earth-centered viewpoint, as a creature evolved out of the sea, physiologically a warm-blooded mammal, related to the apes but with a thinking and creative mind; a social, gregarious animal, needing to live in communities. This definition is primarily physical, biological, and sociological, lacking in existential purpose other than to eat and drink, sleep and reproduce, like the rest of the creatures. Those governed by this definition regard the worldly life as all there is, their be-all and end-all. But this definition tells only half the story.

The other half of the story is the divine point of view, in which humans are indeed earthly creatures, but ones who are the container and repository of the Divine Spirit (*ruh*), given a special highly exalted trust and mandate by Divinity Itself (the Quranic *amanah*, Quran 33:72). When we adopt this God-centered description as our worldview, it precipitates a significant shift, focusing us on our purpose and intent. The difference is remarkable, not only in the philosophical sense, but also experientially. When we meet a person who knows himself or herself only in the human sense, that person's impact upon us is at best worldly. When we meet someone who knows himself or herself in the divine sense, that person's impact is transformative.

Right Loving: Love Your Jesus and Not His Donkey

Rumi says that the relationship between the human soul and the human body is like Jesus riding a donkey. Those whose viewpoint are merely worldly and ignore their souls are like those who "listen to the moaning of the donkey, and pity comes over them." Don't they know, he asks, that "the donkey commands you to be asinine?" Rumi advises us to "Have pity on Jesus [the soul created in the divine image within you that is riding your body] and have no pity on the donkey [your physical self]."[19] Personally I find having no pity on the donkey hard to do; I love my latte coffee and smoked-salmon-on-seven-grain-bread breakfasts. But what I do find is that by taking care of my donkey, my "inner Jesus" rides much faster. The donkey that knows it is carrying a Jesus rather than a bale of hay is a far happier and more fulfilled one.

Rumi's point is an important one. Human exaltedness lies in our spirituality—the deepest root of our psychology—not in our physiology; it is our spirituality that makes us God's stewards (*khalifah*, literally, "vicegerents of God," also servants of God) in accord with the examples of the Prophets and saints. As an exalted form of creation, we are the most developed locus where Divinity manifests its attributes, including its desire to be known. If one has to choose to prefer one at the expense of the other, we should honor our soul at the expense of our body, and not vice versa. This is Rumi's advice.

The correspondences between our spirit and God results in our very human psychology: our tendency to regard ourselves as potential hidden treasures "desiring to be known." Our struggles in life take us on journeys of self-discovery reflecting this. We seek to know and discover the purpose of our existence. But unless we reciprocate God's creation of us by conceiving of God's existence within our consciousness, we are doomed to an infinite cycle of working hard for a desired objective and, after achieving it, tiring of it quickly, just as when we were children we got bored by toys. Just as God created us in order for Him to be known, we too develop the consciousness of God within ourselves in order to be known.

Therefore self-discovery leads to God-discovery, and it is no less true that God-discovery leads to greater and truer self-discovery. We get to know God when we know who and what we are. Ironically, it is no less true that we get to know ourselves when we know God. This is succinctly expressed in a hadith of Sayyidina 'Ali, "He who knows himself knows his Lord."

Our Greatest Gift to God:
Polishing Our Mirror

Humanity has been called to perfection in the divine plan. This means not only that we must destroy all that is bad and unworthy in ourselves, but also that we must develop higher and more refined skills. One of the images Sufis use to describe the task of traversing the path is to polish his or her mirror to become the best, most accurate, and transparent divine reflector possible, which is the best way to love God back. What better offering can we offer God other than be the best possible mirror in which He sees Himself reflected? What better meaning can we give to being created in the divine image than to recognize that we are mere mirrors, and seek to perfect the divine image within us?

We can attain spiritual maturity by following a path that gradually ascends, but we can also opt to climb more quickly up a steep, narrow, and invariably more challenging path. This path lies through the way of initiation, called the *tariqah* in Arabic.

Not all souls are driven to take this path of initiation. The ones who do are the chosen, to quote Jesus, the "intimate ones" (*al-muqarrabun*) in the Quran, also called "the elite" in some Muslim writings (*al-khawass*). These souls wish to attain the goal faster not only for their own benefit, but also in order to help others forward. Like all humans, they lead just as difficult a life, full of life's sadness, tests, and problems, but are deeply enriched by insights and silent joy, because their tests in life furnish them insight. In one lifetime, they experience the content of many lives, for they wish to go on, even at that price. These chosen ones have been called by God and have heard and responded to His call. They are the ones who wish to know, who seek the fullest answer to the question: "Where do we come from and where are we going?" Prepared to subject themselves to tests and to undergo trials, they reach spiritual maturity sooner than others and find peace and joy even in this life through giving help, support, comfort, service, care, and love.

The strongest among these attain the level of sainthood (Friend of God, *waliyyullah*). Friends of God can detect the hidden motives existing in others' hearts, and they lament the negative and untoward consequences of these motives for the present as well as the future. They often seem surrounded by an ambiance of miracles, which in reality is the invisible hand of God channeling through these beloved souls that which God wishes to reveal.

Every human soul can and should begin to traverse this path, although to reach the level of sainthood requires a commitment to be pure of heart and intent, clear of speech and action, accompanied by a preparation to work for years, often in silence and loneliness, so as to achieve what is possible for human understanding.

The Quran asserts that all human souls were arraigned before God in a previous existence and asked not to forget Him during our temporary sojourn in this world. Why do we not remember this covenant with the Lord, the day when God asked us, "Am I not your Lord?" (*alastu birabbikum*) (Quran 7:172). Because there are boundaries (*barzakh*) between the different realms, veiled in such a way that they cover the consciousness of mortals when they move from one realm to another. Just as we awaken from a dream and its contents recede from our memory, so we drink from a stream of oblivion that obliterates our awareness of the experience, although the memory is imprinted in our subconscious. The task is to learn how to lift the veils and to remember in the conscious realm what we have seen and done in others.

God Made Me Fast, and When I Run, I Feel His Pleasure

The purpose of morality and ethics is to take us to God and help us keep that divine presence with us, or perhaps more correctly, to keep us with God. This is called "togetherness with God," or "togetherness" for short (*ma'iyyah* in Arabic).[20]

In the commentary to the *Risala fi't-Tawhid* of Shaykh Wali Raslan, Shaikh Ali al-Hamawi recommends that we give togetherness with God its due and always be on our best behavior for His sake. If we succeed in being present with God and allow our reality to be the theater where God's infinity and splendor intersects our nothingness, He will screen our poverty with His affluence, our weakness with His strength, our incapacity with His power, our ignorance with His knowledge and wisdom, and our abject humility with His glory, our contingent and relative nonbeing with His Being, and will display His splendor on our canvas.[21] In the words of the runner in the movie *Chariots of Fire*, "God made me fast, and when I run, I feel His pleasure."

In a similar way, God made us into many things: great artists and writers who when doing our art feel His pleasure, great farmers who when farming feel His pleasure, great parents who when parenting feel His pleasure, and so forth. But most of all, God made us worshipful beings, and our greatest pleasure actually is in contemplating God.

Muslims believe, as do many in other religious traditions, that worshiping God properly and devotedly is necessary for the community's well-being. The Prophet Muhammad came to reiterate the Abrahamic message, that there is no god but God, whom Muslims are urged to "remember frequently" (Quran 33:41) and to do so "standing, seated and lying down" (3:190). In chanting and repeating God's names, Muslims find deep solace and a palpable, tangible connection with God, for as the Quran asserts, "Surely hearts are comforted by the remembrance of God" (13:28). Devoted Muslims happily prostrate on their faces five times daily in prayerful submission to God and find that particular act the high point of the prayer rite. They avidly look forward to fasting the whole of the month of Ramadan, the ninth month of the lunar calendar, and do not regard fasting as a hardship but as deeply pleasurable and spiritually rewarding.

Before he became a Trappist monk, the young French lieutenant Christian de Cherge was powerfully attracted to the Algerian Muslims, who he said were "infused with a sense of the divine." He could talk "unselfconsciously with them about God, unlike in France, where God talk made people uncomfortable."[22] Christian monks found the Algerian Muslims "living the Christian life of devotion," while their Muslim neighbors found the monks "living an authentically Islamic life." Religion is not the label we attach to our actions, but the quality of our actions expressing devotion to God and ethical behavior to our fellow human beings.

The Sufi Way:
Al-Ghazali and the Road Less Traveled

The most important religious development since 1258 in the Muslim world was arguably the institutionalization and spread of Sufi orders. Although Sufis existed from the beginning of Islamic history, Sufi wisdom was more the treasure of a small minority, an elite of the pious withdrawn from the mainstream of Islamic political advance. Often misunderstood and maligned, Sufis were accused of excesses in matters of worship.

What made the difference was the work of one man, Abu Hamid al-Ghazali (1058–1111 CE), known in the West as Algazel. He lived in a time of political agitation and turmoil, a time when, according to the historian Abu'l-Fida', "The Abbasid Caliphate was in a state of abasement and decline, the Arab rule in Baghdad had passed away, or nearly passed away. Spain was revolting against its Muslim rulers, Peter the Hermit was summoning men to the Crusades, men were divided into Shiites and Sunnis by religious and political differences, and Ash'arism [the Scholastic philosophy in Islam] with the support of the Seljuk Turks, were opposing the Mu'tazilites [the rationalists]." Professor H. A. R. Gibb regards Ghazali as "a man who stands on a level with Augustine and Luther in religious insight and intellectual vigor."[23]

Most religious people go through a time of crisis, what St. Augustine called the dark night of the soul. An existential crisis is the equivalent of living through an earthquake. The very foundation of all that we thought was firm and that supported our worldview and identity crumbles—and yet we still live! Having arrived at the apex of his career, a well-known, extremely well connected and famous theologian, scholar, philosopher, and jurist, Ghazali went through an existential crisis, admitting to himself that at his core he was empty.

An honored and respected friend of the Seljuk minister and later ruler Nizam al-Mulk, Ghazali suffered his existential crisis in his midforties, in the early 1090s. According to one of his biographers, his character at the time was overpowered by "the devil of frivolity and of seeking leadership and fame." Ghazali delighted in putting people down "out of haughtiness and arrogance and being dazzled by his own endowment of skill in speech and thought and expression, and his quest of glory and high status." Ghazali's crisis became compounded by an overwhelming personal fear that made him unable to teach, even to speak. He "became certain that he was on the brink of a crumbling bank and already on the verge of falling into the Fire, unless he set about mending his ways."[24]

When he couldn't take this fear anymore, Ghazali decided on a course of action. He took a leave of absence from his teaching position, arranged his personal affairs, told people he was going on hajj to Mecca, and set out for Syria. After spending ten years studying with Sufis, doing his hajj as well during this time, he returned to his hometown a transformed human being and wrote his magnum opus, *Revival of the Religious Sciences* (*ihya' 'ulum id-din*). He also wrote a classic autobiographical work, which describes his spiritual crisis, what brought it about, and how he found his faith in the methodology of the Sufis.

The *Ihya'* is a "how to be a good believer" book, taking the reader from an understanding of faith to performing prayers, almsgiving, fasting, and pilgrimage. It also deals with proper behavior toward friends, spouses, and families and what the heart's maladies are and how to cure them. Finally, he talks about those things that lead to salvation: repentance, patience, gratitude, fear of God, hope, poverty, love, intimacy with God, purity of intention, spiritual mindfulness and watchfulness over oneself, remembering God (*dhikr*) and how to perform such remembrance, and meditating on death and the afterlife. The *Ihya'* continues to be a fairly complete guide for devout Muslims in every aspect of life: from religious life and worship, devotional practices, and social conduct to purification of the heart and advancement along the spiritual path.

The late Jesuit scholar Richard J. McCarthy reminds us that Ghazali's importance lay not, as we have said, in blazing a new path, but in entering on a path already blazed (but a road less traveled) and "ma[king] it the common highway." Indeed, other men were keener logicians, more learned theologians and jurists, more gifted saints; but through his personal experiences, he "attained so overpowering a sense of the divine realities that the force of his character—once combative and restless, now narrow and intense—swept all before it," ushering Islam into "a new era of its existence."[25]

What fascinates Western scholars about Ghazali is not only his profound influence upon Muslims but also his profound influence upon non-Muslims of his time and his continued influence upon non-Muslims till this day. The Jesuit father Vincenzo Poggi pointed out that Ghazali's other works were already known to the Scholastics from the second half of the twelfth century.[26] Other Christian scholars believe that Ghazali influenced St. Thomas Aquinas (1225–1274), who studied the Arab writers and admitted his indebtedness to them.[27] Poggi goes on to show that some Christian writers even plagiarized Ghazali's ideas, making them their own without giving him the credit. He also explores the influence of Ghazali's *Munqidh* on the famed Jewish philosopher Maimonides (1135–1204 CE), especially the *Guide of the Perplexed* of Maimonides, which was translated from Arabic (Maimonides wrote in Arabic) into Hebrew by Samuel Ibn Tibbon as *Moreh Nebukim*. R. J. McCarthy, Jesuit priest and Islamic scholar, suggests that Maimonides modeled himself in some respects along the lines of Ghazali, writing an apology for his faith and thus "render[ing] to the religion of his people the precious service which Ghazali had rendered to Islam."[28]

Perhaps Poggi's most important and intriguing question is, What has been the cause of the *ongoing* special interest in Ghazali shown by non-Muslim and especially Christian ecclesiastics, both Protestant and Catholic? Dismissing the possibility of simple coincidence, he suggests that it has to do with "something real which draws to Ghazali the attention of those who, though not belonging to his religion, *have however at heart the defense of the rights of God and have confidence in a religious renovation of humanity* [italics mine]."[29]

In simple words, Ghazali is required reading for all those who believe religion has a role to play in our individual and collective lives and has to be brought into the public square. This is surely significant for those of us working in the interfaith arena today.

Shedding his previous arrogant qualities, Ghazali was transformed into a character serene of soul and noble of qualities. He criticized servile conformism (*taqlid* of the worst variety), recognized the truth and validity of every field of knowledge, from philosophy to the physical sciences to religion and spirituality, acknowledging the viability of each but also recognizing the limits of each. His relentless focus on grasping the truth, and on the truth being important above all, led him to apply the rule "Do not know the truth by men, but rather, know the truth and you will know its adherents."[30] His open-mindedness to those of other faiths combined with his aversion to cheap accusations of heresy make him an important figure in any discussion on bridging the Muslim world and the West.

Overcoming Pretense

R. J. McCarthy asks rhetorically: Does Ghazali, across the gulf of more than nine hundred years, have anything to say to us? Does his *Munqidh* have anything to offer to the men and women of today? Perhaps more than anything else, it is about helping us to be spiritually honest with ourselves, which defines the religious problem that most of us have.

What is this religious problem? Most people are conformists: we conform to fashion in matters of clothing as well as in matters of ideas.

It's hard to avoid conformism, even in the matter of our beliefs, our ideas, and our values. But blind conformism in religious practice leads to a specific and unique religious problem: pretense.

Pretension is natural to the religion business, where people pretend to know but in fact don't know. This is hypocrisy, which the Quran pointedly criticizes and for which the Prophet's companions were always on the lookout, deeply concerned that they might have fallen into it. The Quran calls hypocrisy one of the diseases of the heart (Quran 47:29), adding that while God can show us hypocrites by "marks on their faces" (Quran 47:30), we can certainly recognize them by the "melody[31] of their speech."

Ghazali felt that in the hands of the *ulama'* of his day the purpose of religious knowledge had become corrupted, used for worldly advancement, whereas religion's real purpose was the attainment of salvation in the world to come. Comparably, Martin Luther preached against the church and the corruption of religious knowledge when used for worldly advancement. Such corruption is endemic to the religious condition, and its seed has to be recognized and uprooted from individuals and movements if one wants to be genuinely religious. Otherwise religious knowledge is used for evil ends.

Ghazali stated that *thinking* or knowing a lot about God compared to having a loving experience of God, technically called an "unveiling" (*kashf*), is analogous to knowing all about drunkenness but never having been drunk.[32] Fake religiosity is like the doctor who knows all about health but is not willing to take the medicine that makes one healthy. The right path is therefore one of making the seeker drink from the cup of unveiling, of spiritual health, the results of which are not only an interior knowledge and awareness of God, but an outer working on oneself to purify one's being from all the spiritual diseases, of which hypocrisy, egoism, and self-delusion are the worst—and the vices Ghazali himself possessed before he undertook his own spiritual journey.

By speaking to his readers in terms of the highest thought of his time, and in the simplest terms accessible to common people, Ghazali was able to fire up much real piety, piety that exists universally in the hearts of ordinary people, despite the failure and corruption of their political, intellectual, and even religious leaders. Ghazali was perhaps the greatest leader in the religious encounter of Muslims with Greek philosophy, and he brought orthodoxy and mysticism into closer contact. As a result of his work, theologians were more ready to accept and respect mystics, and mystics became more careful in remaining within the bounds of orthodoxy. By probing the essence of the religious experience, Ghazali made Islam a universal religion relevant to human reality and less an Arab religion associated with Arab culture. His service was invaluable in a time when the Arab character of the Islamic world was waning, with political power moving toward non-Arab Asian societies.

Ghazali's message to us today suggests how Muslims must rise to meet the challenge the West poses. Muslims must dismiss neither the West nor their own tradition but instead study and understand both, in order to value what can be admired and discard what is not relevant and to demonstrate and debate our position in simple and clear language accessible to all. There is much in the Muslim experience that is as valuable to itself as it can be to the West, as there is much in the Western experience that is valuable to Muslims. Muslims today are in need of a revival of the religious sciences that speaks as profoundly to the eternal as to the contemporary human condition, and most of all, Muslims must do this with honesty, attention to truth, and beauty of character.

CHAPTER 3

What's Right with America

Those who work and live at the points of intersection between America and the Muslim world have no higher calling than to heal the relationship between them. America and the Muslim world seem locked today in a dysfunctional can't-live-with-them-and-can't-live-without-them embrace. We must remember that at bottom, we're all just people: people with similar dreams, similar aspirations, similar frustrations, and similar needs. And as in human relationships, it's about what each side wants from the other and how to structure a working arrangement that gives each party what it wants.

If there is any quarrel Muslims have with America, it is that the United States does not always live up to its own ideal of ethics and values. To use the Reverend William Sloane Coffin's phrase, Muslims see our disagreements as a lover's quarrel in our joint efforts to claim a brighter future between America and the Muslim world. "American Christians should live *at loving odds* with their country and the world," he advised, "much as the biblical prophets and Jesus himself lived at dangerous odds with the Israel and the world of their day." It is advice that American Muslims also would do well to heed. "Christians should never think," added the Reverend Coffin, "they honor the greater truth they find in Christ by ignoring truths found elsewhere."[1]

American Muslims too should not ignore truths found outside their faith tradition. The Prophet in a hadith urged the Muslims to seek knowledge even if it's in China, and scholars have taken this to mean that there are truths to be found in other cultures and traditions—advice that the Muslim world avidly acted on during the first six centuries after the Prophet's time. The ninth-century Islamic scholar al-Kindi advises with a voice twelve hundred years old, "We should never be ashamed to approve truth and acquire it no matter what its source might be, even if it might have come from foreign peoples and alien nations far removed from us. . . . For indeed truth abases none and ennobles all."[2]

Muslims admire and love a lot about America. What I now aim to demonstrate may surprise readers, namely, that America is substantively an "Islamic" country, by which I mean a country whose systems remarkably embody the principles that Islamic law requires of a government. From a different perspective, it means that Muslims around the world believe in the principles that undergird American governance and want these principles upheld in their own societies. Their gripe is that America has historically acted in a way that gives the strong impression that America seeks to deprive Muslims of their inalienable rights in their native lands.

WEST WING VERSUS DYNASTY

Like Mecca in the Quranic narrative, and the Promised Land in the biblical narrative, America was forged in religiosity. Its immigrants hailed from Europe, braving the Atlantic Ocean to find and establish their religious liberty and freedoms. On emigrating to America, the Pilgrims saw in the Israelites' forty-year passage through the wilderness their own story, America their Promised Land, and their community a New Israel crossing over from a life of religious slavery. America, in a profound sense, continues the story of establishing the good society attempted by Abraham, by the prophets of the children of Israel, and by the Prophet Muhammad and his four successors in Medina. It offers a theory of governance that has best institutionalized the ethical principles of the Abrahamic ethic and the two greatest commandments common to the Abrahamic faith traditions.

Although the Abrahamic ethic sowed the conceptual seeds of democratic governance, democracy as we know it today did not truly take root and flower until a few millennia later, with the advent of the American Revolution. With the exceptions of some truly benign caliphs, only the period of rule of the Prophet in Medina, followed by that of those known as the Orthodox Caliphs, also based in Medina, a period that extended from 622 to 656 CE, is considered by Muslims as that era when governance was most in accord with the Abrahamic ethic.

The model of governance that historically prevailed in most of the known world was the dynastic empire, and with the rise of the Umayyads in Damascus in 656 CE, the Muslims succumbed to dynastic rule, a paradigm of governance that did not display Islamic religious values. Although still called caliphates, all succeeding governments were in effect monarchies, in which one man held all the power and passed the rule to a successor, usually his son. This was true of all the caliphates, from the immediate successors to the Umayyads, the Abbasids, who established their capital in Baghdad (750–1258 CE) to the Moguls in India (1526–1858 CE), the Safavids in Iran (1501–1732 CE), and finally the Ottomans in Turkey (1281–1924 CE). Dynastic and autocratic rulers always sought to prevent the rise of institutional forms of power that could act as a check and balance on their rule.

Muhammad Asad, a Polish journalist who lived in Saudi Arabia, converted to Islam, and participated in shaping the state of Pakistan at its birth in 1948, laments, "There has never existed a truly *Islamic* state after the time of the Prophet and of the Medina Caliphate headed by the Prophet's immediate successors. . . . Whatever forms of state and government came into being in Muslim countries after that first, earliest period were vitiated, in a lesser or higher degree, by ideological deviations from the erstwhile simplicity and clarity of Islamic Law, or even by outright, deliberate attempts on the part of the rulers concerned to deform and obscure that Law in their own interests."[3]

As we shall see, many Muslims regard the form of government that the American founders established a little over two centuries ago as the form of governance that best expresses Islam's original values and principles.

In 1776, a century and a half after the Pilgrims landed in the New World, America's founders gathered in Philadelphia and drafted the Declaration of Independence, which dissolved the political ties that had bound the American people to Great Britain. Eleven years later, many of the same founders met again to draft a plan for governing the new nation, the Constitution of the United States. Whereas the Declaration outlined the founders' moral vision and the government it implied, the Constitution amplified and worked out the system of government that expressed the values of the Declaration. These two documents together describe the supreme values and fundamental law of

America. As such they are the set of overall beliefs, creed, or "religion" under which all Americans operate.

The Declaration sets forth what constitutes legitimate government, then proceeds to show how far English rule had strayed from that ideal. For Muslims, this description of legitimate government is consistent with the principles of Islamic law. The "repeated injuries and usurpations" that English rule had inflicted upon the Americans are injuries as well under Islamic law.

Grounding itself in reason, just as the Quran and the Abrahamic ethic did in asserting the self-evident oneness of God, the Declaration opens with the most important line in the document: "We hold these Truths to be self-evident."[4] The language evokes the long tradition of natural law, which holds that there is a higher law of right and wrong from which to derive human law and against which human laws may be—and ought to be—measured. It is not political will but moral reasoning accessible to all that is the foundation of the American political system.

But "nature," at least in the eyes of believers in God, is just another word for "God's creation," and thus natural law must mean "the laws that God established and structured creation on." These span the spectrum from the laws of the physical sciences such as mathematics, physics, biology, and chemistry to the sociological and psychological laws that govern human relationships, all of which are knowable to humans through reason. Thus the first paragraph of the Declaration of Independence opens with the words "When . . . it becomes necessary for one People . . . to assume . . . the separate and equal Station to which the *Laws of Nature and of Nature's God* entitle them" (italics added).

To Muslims, the law decreed by God is called the Shariah, and therefore the "Laws of Nature and of Nature's God" are by definition Shariah law. It is a law that has to appeal to human reason and be in accord with human nature, informing us that "a community based on ideas held in common is a far more advanced manifestation of human life than a community resulting from race or language or geographical location."[5]

In 1775, a year before the American Revolution began, Alexander Hamilton wrote, "The sacred rights of mankind are not to be rummaged for among old parchments or musty records. They are written as with a sunbeam, in the whole volume of human nature, by the hand of Divinity itself, and can never be erased or obscured by mortal power."[6] Almost fifty years later, in 1824, Thomas Jefferson noted in reminiscing about the drafting of the Declaration of Independence, "We had no occasion to search into musty records, to hunt up royal parchments, or to investigate the laws and institutions of a semi-barbarous ancestry. We appealed to those of nature, and found them engraved on our hearts."[7] Could the Abrahamic ethic as *natural religion*—Muslims' *din al-fitrah* as the core definition of Islam—be any more lucidly and evidently expressed?

What's right about America is its Declaration of Independence, for it embodies and restates the core values of the Abrahamic, and thus also the Islamic, ethic. Since human liberty is one of its aims, and reason the method by which we justify our political order, then the cardinal moral truths from the Declaration of Independence that flesh out the Abrahamic ethic are:

> That all Men are created equal, that they are endowed by their Creator with certain unalienable Rights, that among these are Life, Liberty and the Pursuit of Happiness—that to secure these Rights, Governments are instituted among Men, deriving their just Powers from the Consent of the Governed.

As defined by our rights, we are equal; no one human being has rights superior to those of another human. We are born with these rights; we do not get them from anyone or any government. Indeed, the opposite is the case: whatever rights government has come from us, the governed, by our consent. And our right to the pursuit of happiness implies that each one of us has the right to live our lives as we wish—to pursue happiness as we think best—provided only that we respect the equal rights of others to do the same and do not infringe on their rights in this regard. America's founders thus outlined the moral foundations of a free society—and in the process, an *Abrahamic* society. These beliefs are fundamental to all Americans and may be said to constitute the American "religion" or creed that all Americans subscribe to and believe in. They are also beliefs fundamental to all Muslims, who regard these beliefs as essential to Islam.

THE AMERICAN "RELIGION" THAT EVEN
ATHEISTS BELIEVE IN

Religious practice consists of two parts: one part concerns humans' relationship to God, how we worship, what happens after death, and so forth. Our Christian friends call this the "vertical dimension" of religious practice, embodied in the first commandment to love God with all our heart, mind, soul, and strength. The second is the sociological part, which relates to our social life and how we interact with the world around us, what our Christian friends call the "horizontal dimension" of religious practice. This is embodied in the second commandment, to love for our neighbors what we love for ourselves. While all Americans recognize the first part as religious practice, most Americans do not think of the second as religious. Muslims do, which is why Muslims do not see the separation of church and state in the same way that Americans see it.

No community of people can function, let alone pursue happiness, unless and until it achieves a high degree of unanimity on what is right and what is wrong in human affairs, and no such unanimity is possible unless the community agrees on a moral obligation arising from a permanent, absolute moral law. On the basis of such an agreement, the group accepts a set of rules that constitutes a moral obligation binding on all members of that group. This set of rules expresses and fleshes out the horizontal dimension of the group's religion. *It fleshes out the details of how the second commandment is to be expressed.* And this set of rules flows of necessity from the vertical dimension or is at least related to it. These normative values give the community its sense of meaning.

What we call the American way of life can also be called the American religion in that it provides all Americans with a structure of ideas and ideals, of aspirations and values, of beliefs and standards, synthesizing all that commends itself to Americans as the right, the good, and the true in life. This does not necessarily mean that these values are scrupulously observed in daily practice; just like any religious people who sin, Americans frequently violate these standards. But violated or not, these values are felt to be normative and relevant to business and politics and daily life in a way that the formal tenets of official liturgical or "vertical" religion are not.

Democracy and liberty, in a peculiarly American way, provide a manifestation of the Abrahamic ethic. Politically, the American creed expresses itself in the values and rights enumerated in the Declaration of Independence and the Constitution; economically, this worldview manifests as free enterprise and a free market economy; socially, it means an egalitarianism and a concern for vulnerable members of society. Together, these components imply vigorous economic competition and high social mobility. The American way of life is individualistic, dynamic, pragmatic, affirming the supreme value and dignity of the individual, who is striving to get ahead and wants to be judged by achievement: deeds are what count. Although some see in this American horizontal dimension of religion a kind of secularized Puritanism, a creed shaped by American Protestantism, we can equally assert that at its core this expresses the Abrahamic, *and equally the Islamic*, ethic.[8]

By the twentieth century, these ideas had reshaped the historic faiths of Christianity and Judaism on American soil. Historian of American religion Perry Miller observes, "As many noticed, the Protestant churches in America, even though brought from Europe, showed more qualities in common than any one retained with its European stem. And they felt that in America, the synagogue was no longer an alien. Even the Catholic Church in America acquired a tone unlike Catholicism in Europe."[9] While *theologically* the American Catholic Church regarded itself as the one true church, in actual *social* attitudes many American Catholics as well as American Protestants and American Jews tended eventually to think of their religious groups as existing side by side in a pluralistic harmony that was somehow of the texture of American life.

Fully in keeping with the principles of the Abrahamic ethic, American religious pluralism was not merely a historical or political fact; it became, in the mind of the American, the primordial condition of things, a self-evident and essential aspect of the American way of life and therefore in itself an aspect of the American creed. Pluralism of religions and churches is something quite axiomatic to Americans, and it is the foundation of the American understanding of the doctrine of separation of church and state—the idea that government may not do anything suggesting the preeminence or superior legitimacy of one church or religious doctrine over another. Until the last third of the twentieth century, pluralism of religions and houses of worship was just as axiomatic to Muslims in their lands, and for Muslims this pluralism flowed out of Quranic injunctions.

AMERICA:
A SHARIAH-COMPLIANT STATE

Many American Muslims regard America as a better "Muslim" country than their native homelands. This may sound surprising if not absurd to many Americans, and Muslims outside America, but it is founded on the argument that the American Constitution and system of governance uphold the core principles of Islamic law.

Muslim legal scholars have defined five areas of life that Islamic law must protect and further. These are life, mind (that is, mental well-being or sanity), religion, property (or wealth), and family (or lineage and progeny). Any system of rule that upholds, protects, and furthers these rights is therefore legally "Islamic," or Shariah compliant, in its substance. Because these rights are God-given, they are inalienable and cannot be deprived of any man or woman without depriving them of their essential humanity.

What I am demonstrating is that the American political structure is Shariah compliant, for "a state inhabited predominantly by Muslims neither defines nor makes it synonymous with an Islamic state. It can become truly Islamic only by virtue of a conscious application of the sociopolitical tenets of Islam to the life of the nation, and by an incorporation of those tenets in the basic constitution of the country."[10] By the same token, a state that does incorporate such sociopolitical tenets has become de facto an Islamic state even if there are no Muslims in name living there, for it expresses the ideals of the good society according to Islamic principles. For America to score even higher on the "Islamic" or "Shariah Compliance" scale, America would need to do two things: invite the voices of all religions to join the dialogue in shaping the nation's practical life, and allow religious communities more leeway to judge among themselves according to their own laws.

The Declaration holds certain truths as self-evident, which links with the Quranic notion of natural religion (din al-fitrah), beliefs embedded in the human heart. Because the Quran asserts that humanity was created from one man and one woman, we are therefore of one family and equal in the eyes of God, differentiated only by our piety and ethical nature. The founders initially enumerated the inalienable rights as life, liberty, and property, replacing the word *property* with the phrase *the pursuit of happiness.* Comparing the Declaration's list of rights to the Shariah's list of rights, we find *life* common to both, while we may say that the Declaration's *liberty* and *pursuit of happiness* embrace the Shariah's items *mental well-being, family, property,* and *religion.* Aren't our happiness and personal fulfillment found when we are mentally well, enjoying time with our family, tending to our homes, serving humanity and freely practicing the religion of our choice?

The founders then turned to government. Governments exist, the Declaration says, to secure these inalienable rights so that citizens may live the lives they choose. The powers that the government may need to achieve this objective must be derived from the consent of the governed if they are to be just. And if "any Form of Government becomes destructive of these Ends, it is the Right of the People to alter or abolish it, and to institute new Government, laying its Foundation on such Principles, and organizing its Powers in such Form, as to them shall seem most likely to effect their Safety and Happiness." So the Declaration maintains—all fully consistent with and expressive of Islamic law's requirements.

The Shariah's intent is to satisfy both elements of the Abrahamic ethic. As the early fourteenth-century Hanbali theologian and legal scholar Ibn al-Qayyim al-Jawziyyah stated,

> The foundation of the Shariah is wisdom and the safeguarding of people's interests in this world and the next. In its entirety it is justice, mercy, and wisdom. Every rule that transcends justice to tyranny, mercy to its opposite, the good to the evil, and wisdom to triviality does not belong to the Shariah although it might have been introduced therein by implication. The Shariah is God's justice and mercy among His people. Life, nutrition, medicine, light, recuperation, and virtue are made possible by it. Every good that exists is derived from it, and every deficiency in being results from its loss and dissipation. . . . For the Shari'ah, which God entrusted His prophet to transmit, is

the pillar of the world and the key to success and happiness in
this world and the next.[11]

That the American ideals of good governance also emanate from
the Abrahamic ethic as part of natural religion deeply embedded in the
human heart, a natural religion grounded in reason, brings out how
much the American ideal expresses the common ground of Judaism,
Christianity, and Islam.

THE IMPORTANCE OF "BUY-IN" (*BAY'AH*) BY THE PEOPLE

Consent of the governed is called *bay'ah* by Muslims. The Arabic term,
which literally means "a sale," was used to denote the act by which the
caliph was elected (or "bought into") by the community, proclaimed
and recognized as the leader of the Muslim community. Originating in
the ancient Arab custom of sealing an agreement with a handclasp, it
became established in the Muslim community after the Prophet tried
to make a pilgrimage in 628 CE and was denied entry into Mecca. A
false rumor had gone around that his emissary, 'Uthman bin 'Affan,
who had gone into Mecca to negotiate with the Meccans, had been
murdered. The atmosphere got tense, and the Prophet asked his followers to pledge their allegiance to him, showing that they would follow the Prophet in whatever he decided. This they did.[12]

After the Prophet's death in June 632, the *bay'ah* was also used as
the means by which his successor and the first caliph, Abu Bakr, was
elected and designated caliph by the assembly at Medina. Ali, the
Prophet's cousin and son-in-law, did not give him the pledge until a
few months later, and Sa'd Ibn 'Ubadah, leader of the tribe of Bani
Sa'idah, who had sought the office himself, refused to acknowledge
Abu Bakr as caliph and eventually migrated to Syria.

On accepting the *bay'ah* from the people, Abu Bakr praised and
lauded God, then addressed the congregation in the following words:

I have been given the authority over you, and I am not the best
of you. If I do well, help me; and if I do wrong, set me right.
Sincere regard for truth is loyalty and disregard for truth is
treachery. The weak amongst you shall be strong with me until

I have secured his rights, God willing; and the strong amongst you shall be weak with me until I have wrested from him the rights of others, God willing. Obey me as long as I obey God and His Messenger.[13] But if I disobey God and His Messenger, you owe me no obedience. Arise for prayer, may God have mercy upon you![14]

On Abu Bakr's death, he nominated as his successor 'Umar bin al-Khattab, and the community pledged their allegiance to him. Thus the *bay'ah* served as a confirmation process for the caliph.

After the Umayyads established themselves as a dynasty in Damascus in 656 CE, thirty-four years after the Prophet's death, the Muslim community was forced to pledge allegiance to rulers they did not particularly like or approve of. Imam Malik ibn Anas (713–795 CE), who was born in Medina and lived there all his life, and who founded the school of jurisprudence that goes by his name (the Maliki *madhhab*), issued a fatwa that the *bay'ah* would be illegal if obtained by duress. For acting in a sense like an independent judiciary, Imam Malik was ordered whipped by the governor of Medina, Ja'far ibn Sulayman.[15] His fatwa restraining the Umayyads represents an early expression of support for representative governance.

These precedents demonstrate that under Islamic law the *bay'ah* was neither necessarily unanimous nor could it be forced upon the community but was intended to be a voluntary act that involved the general public. Many opinions have been issued on the number of electors required (*ahl al-ikhtiyar*) for the procedure to be valid: from all "the upright men of the whole empire" to what we may call a representative quorum. But in later centuries, when pre-Islamic forms of governance reemerged based on the rule of an upper class, the *bay'ah* became a process less of election than of simple homage to the one appointed.

Muslim jurists extracted a number of principles of right governance from the community's *bay'ah* to the Prophet and from incidents in the Prophet's own life in which he took the better advice of his companions. Regarding these principles in light of Abu Bakr's acceptance speech, above, and the opinions of the earliest jurists, like the sample fatwa above of Imam Malik, Muslim jurists concluded that these principles must be in place for the *bay'ah* to be valid:

- The government is not legitimate without consent of the governed.

- Consent of the governed may not be coerced or obtained under duress.

- The ruler must remain faithful to the divine prescriptions. If the ruler does not abide by these prescriptions, then those who have performed the *bay'ah* in his favor are released from their obligations.

- The person elected to be the leader does not have to be "the best" person according to a set of spiritual or religious criteria but a person who is able to maintain the government's legitimacy by securing, protecting, and furthering the inalienable rights of the governed.

- Abu Bakr's statement "if I do wrong, set me right" means that a legitimate government must allow itself to be checked, for human beings err, and the presumption that a government is inerrant or infallible is inconsistent with Islamic principles and law.

- The government is not legitimate unless it treats a regard for truth as loyalty and a disregard for truth as treachery, protects the rights of the weak from being trampled by the strong in society, and abides by divine prescriptions (which is the meaning of obeying God and obeying His messenger).

Only a government that abides by the above principles of *bay'ah* is deemed invested with God's authority and protection or, in popular language, Islamically legitimate. The Quran addresses the Prophet's companions who pledged their allegiance to him in Hudaybiyah that "they have pledged their allegiance [as well] to God. God's Hand is upon their hands. Whoever breaks [his pledge], has done this to his soul's injury; whereas whoever fulfills his covenant with God, He will grant him a mighty reward" (Quran 48:10).

SMART FOUNDING FATHERS: SEPARATING THE POWERS

We can see that in both Islamic and American ideals of government, a legitimate government allows a system of checks and balances on its rule. When the founders focused on drafting the new Constitution in 1787, they wanted a government strong enough to secure Americans' rights against domestic and foreign oppression but not so powerful as to be itself oppressive. To this end, they authorized a central federal government and gave it specific powers, then checked and balanced these powers through a series of extraordinarily thoughtful measures.

It's helpful to remember that in 1789 most power was held by the states, and the newly born federal government had little power. It would not be an exaggeration to say that the influence of Washington, D.C., two hundred years ago compared to that of the states was more like that of Brussels today, as headquarters of the European Union.

The Preamble to the Constitution starts by reminding the reader that power comes from the people: "We the People of the United States . . . do ordain and establish this Constitution." But the power the people agreed to give to the government, to exercise on their behalf, is strictly limited. These powers were then enumerated in the Constitution, with the rest reserved to the states (or to the people), never having been granted to either level of government. In common parlance, this means that "we the people" are giving "you the government" specific x and y powers, but remember, we retain the overall power and can withdraw it from you when we want.

The enumeration of power is intended to limit power. Congress was not granted unlimited power but *just* that power necessary for government to execute the enumerated powers. The founders intended the doctrine of enumerated powers to be the principal defense against oppressive government because the government could not abuse a power it did not have in the first place. But knowing how humans tend to be power hungry and may abuse power when they get it, they added other defenses in addition to dividing power between the national and the state governments. They separated the powers of the national government among three branches: the presidency (the executive branch), Congress (the legislative branch), and the courts (the judiciary or legal branch), with checks and balances between them. The checks and balances would ensure that the right distance remained between the various powers.

The founders felt there was a "right distance" or balance between the centers of power, neither too much distance nor too little. The balance of powers between the judiciary and the other two branches, for example, does not mean that there is a firewall of separation, with the judiciary acting completely independently. Neither does it mean that the president or any member of Congress is or can be above the law or that the president and Congress have nothing at all to do with the courts. In fact, the separation between the branches describes specific relationships between them that put the right distance or balance between each branch of power, allowing it its independence and at the same time balancing and checking that power by the other branches.

Separation of powers certainly means that each branch is independent of the other two in discharging its daily work. The president's power over the courts is demonstrated by his right to nominate judges to the court. But to provide checks and balances over the president, Congress has the right to approve or disapprove his nominations, a process that can be arduous for a Supreme Court justice nominee. But once the judge is on the bench, neither the president nor the legislature can force him to judge a case in a particular way or seek to penalize him for having judged that way—although Congress can impeach and remove judges. In deciding cases or controversies before them, the courts may exercise their judicial checks by reviewing the actions of congressional legislation and executive acts to ensure that they do not exceed the limits imposed by the Constitution.[16] This is how the courts exercise a balancing power to the executive and legislative branches, and this is how America defined just the right balance between the judiciary and the other two branches.

The separation of powers doctrine in the history of American governance is about ensuring that too much power does not coalesce in any one branch, for that can adversely affect the liberties of the people. After Franklin Roosevelt was elected for his fourth presidential term, Congress realized that so much time in power could cause power to increase in the executive branch to a degree that exceeded the balance recommended by the principle of separation of powers, and it corrected this imbalance by ratifying the Twenty-Second Amendment to the Constitution in February 1951, limiting the president to a maximum of two four-year terms. This was in spite of the country's president not even having the power to call in the military or the National

Guard to arrest members of Congress who don't agree with him on matters of policy. As powerful as he is, the American president is circumscribed in how he may use his powers—an essential aspect of our separation of powers doctrine. Americans recognize that right government, government that adheres most closely to the Abrahamic ethic of human freedom, liberty, and human happiness, is very much about balancing power between the various centers that possess and wield it.

What in 1790 was an infant federal government has grown into the most powerful government in the world, having vastly outgrown its "parents," the states. While the executive, judicial, and legislative branches remain the main three branches of government, they are no longer the only federal institutions that possess truly mind-boggling power. I suggest that we add some other centers of power to this discussion, in order to better compare the centers of power in the United States with those in other countries. In addition to the above three branches of American government, we may add two power centers that report to the government: the military and the Central Bank (called in America the Federal Reserve). The national economy and the media are two other centers of power that are independent of the government in the United States although they have to abide by certain government regulations.

The U.S. military, the most powerful military in the world today, barely existed when the Constitution was drafted and ratified. In fiscal 2004, its budget is $399.1 billion, equal to the next twenty countries' combined military budgets.[17]

With its funds appropriated by Congress, the American military's relationship to the federal government is like that of an employee of a civilian government, and it is deliberately kept that way. There is a "right distance" between the American government and the American military. As powerful as it is, the military has no say institutionally in the affairs of governance and cannot throw its weight on the side of or against a particular candidate running for political office, although military personnel certainly do vote. It is none of the military's concern if taxes are raised or lowered by Congress, if the courts rule that abortion is permitted or illegal, or how the Federal Reserve should set the money supply. Although a tool of foreign policy, the military cannot involve itself in deciding foreign policy, neither can it declare war or rise up against the presidency. It cannot even refuse to go to war if asked to, claiming that this is not a war it believes is necessary for our defense. It cannot raise its own money to pay for military personnel salaries, military armament, and other equipment required but instead must apply to Congress, which then decides how much it ought to pay and appropriates the requisite funds. Americans do not normally think of the military when they think of the separations of power, but from the perspective of populations living under military regimes, it is a significant separation or balance of power that Americans enjoy.

To provide an analogy, consider the following fictitious scenario: imagine Colin Powell, when still Twelfth Chairman of the Joint Chiefs of Staff, the highest military position in the Department of Defense during the Clinton administration, discussing with other generals in the Pentagon's dining room the scandals erupting in the administration. Embarrassed for their country with the messy way things are run, as they usually are in a democracy, they decide that they could run the country better than those on the other side of the Potomac River in the White House and Congress.

The generals hatch a coup and march tanks on Washington, and Powell takes over as president. With tanks in downtown Washington and Wall Street, the military takes over offices of the *Washington Post*, *New York Times*, and other television, radio, and print media. The generals then proceed to nationalize the American oil industry and other major industries, force the judiciary to make abortion legal (or illegal), and compel the Federal Reserve to print more dollars so as to increase the wealth of the nation.

This probably wouldn't be accepted by the American people—although if you have tanks in Times Square and on Wall Street and soldiers eyeing you with machine guns on key corners, what could the average American do? Imagine the chagrin that Americans would feel if foreigners said to them, "If you don't like General Powell's military rule, why don't you throw him out of office?" With such a concentration of power, the generals could bend opinion leaders to their will, and if they didn't like it and resigned, would the generals have difficulty finding replacements to endorse their ideas and preferences?

In a nutshell, this is what happened to Egypt in 1952 when Gamal Abdel Nasser, who was not even a general but a lieutenant-colonel, with a number of military officers took over power in a revolutionary coup. Egypt, very much at the time a pluralistic society of Muslims, Copts (Christians of the Coptic Church), and Jews, with significant immigrant Greek and Italian populations, was struggling forward under the continued shadow of British military presence to become a democratic nation. Since 1923 it had had a multiparty political system, the first one established in 1919, the Wafd party, including on its platform Egyptian Copts, Jews, and Muslims. But in 1953 Nasser outlawed all political parties and established Egypt as a dictatorship under his one-man authoritarian rule, to the detriment of Egypt. This example is not an isolated one, nor is this scenario limited to countries in the Muslim world.

What makes Muslims living under such authoritarian regimes grind their teeth in frustration is when Americans who ought to know better tell them, "Well, if you don't like Saddam Hussein's military rule, why don't you overthrow him?" What adds insult to injury is that his military rule was supported some years ago by the United States itself for its own foreign policy purposes. Just after the first Gulf War, President George H. W. Bush announced that if the Iraqis would rise up against Saddam Hussein, the United States would support them. They took him at his word, rose up against Saddam Hussein—and Bush withdrew his support, allowing Saddam Hussein to use his helicopters to massacre tens of thousand of Iraqis. There's a German proverb that says, "He who holds the ladder is as bad as the thief," and in the Muslim mind, the United States was complicit in the massacre. The unfortunate message this sent to the Muslim world was, "We don't want you to enjoy the freedoms we have in the West." This was not an isolated example, and the pattern has continued to feed rage against the United States.

In much of the Muslim world today these separations of power don't exist the way we enjoy them in the United States and western Europe, where they are commonly, and erroneously, thought to be a natural or automatic adjunct to democracy. Democratic rule does not necessarily imply proper governance. Democracy takes place at the ballot box; it is *presumably* a system whereby the electorate can peacefully change the ruling administration if or when it is dissatisfied with the rule. The caveat *presumably* is necessary because the people can do so only if government officials respect their oaths to uphold the Constitution and not deprive the people of their rights. Because rulers are held accountable in this way by the people, rulers—who almost always want to hold on to their rule—have a strong incentive to improve the quality of governance. But if the government usurps the power from the people and uses the police force against them, there is often little the people can do, especially if supported by major foreign powers.[18]

We have mentioned the American central bank, called the Federal Reserve Bank (the Fed for short). The Fed is sometimes considered a fourth branch of the American government because it is made up of a powerful group of national policymakers freed from the usual restrictions of day-to-day administration oversight.[19] Its board of governors is appointed by the president but is formally and operationally independent of the executive branch and protected by tenure well beyond the president's. Relatively free from partisan political pressures, the Fed must report frequently to the Congress on the conduct of monetary policy. The Fed is essential to Americans' Constitutional right to pursuit of happiness, which is part of the Abrahamic ethic, for our relative prosperity is unimaginable without the existence of the Fed and the vital roles it plays in assuring American economic health. Established in 1914 to help the American banking system respond flexibly to business cycles and the economic crises often accompanied by collapse of the monetary system, the Fed, when it takes action, has a significant effect on the American economy through its control of interest rates and, subsequently, on stock, bond, and other financial markets. Serving as the banker to both the banking community and the government, the Fed also issues the national currency, conducts monetary policy, and plays a major role in supervising and regulating banks and bank-holding companies.

Compare this to the banking system of Iraq under Saddam Hussein or Indonesia under Suharto, in which the ruling family regarded the banking system as its private bank—clearly an example of too little distance between the leaders and the very heart and lifeblood of the economy. We can't imagine our American president dipping into the U.S. Treasury to build his presidential library, much less to pay for a family home in the Bahamas. While these may have been the most egregious examples of misgovernance in the Muslim world, the relative health of the banking systems in much of the Muslim world is not as robust as it should or could be. If the richest Americans decided to park the equivalent of 10 percent of America's funds in Swiss banks because they were not secure about the health of American banks, what would that do to the robustness of the American monetary system? This is one of the challenges facing the Muslim world in building a healthy economy. With banking systems not up to par with that of the U.S. banking system under the eye of its Federal Reserve board of governors, many a foreign banking and monetary system does not have the right distance from state leaders to be independent and healthy.

The picture that emerges from this review of the separation of powers is that the relationship between each power center and one or more branches of government is not a wall of separation but a highly nuanced set of relationships that defines the mandate of the power center, its duties and responsibilities, and the limits of its authorized power. At all times these centers of power must operate to protect and advance the interests of the general citizenry and not the interests of certain segments of society over others, nor even of itself.

CAN I SPEAK MY MIND AND WORSHIP ANY WAY I WANT?

Fearful that the government might attempt to coopt some of the people's rights, the American founders specifically excluded a number of rights, which they enumerated in the First Amendment of the Constitution: "Congress shall make no law respecting an establishment of religion, or prohibiting the free exercise thereof; or abridging the freedom of speech, or of the press, or the right of the people peaceably to assemble, and to petition the Government for a redress of grievances."

This amendment has become known as "the establishment clause," and it was needed to protect an essential right of the Abrahamic ethic, namely human liberty to worship freely, as well as the rights to be educated and informed on government actions and to critique the government if need be.

These rights are organically linked to each other. We assemble in our various houses of worship—churches, synagogues, mosques, temples, gurdwaras—and pray, sing hymns, and recite our scriptures. To do this requires two rights: to freely assemble and to freely speak. In a situation in which the state decides that only one religion is correct and others heresies, then these rights are nonexistent.

The freedom of the press is also organically linked to freedom of speech. The media's role in informing the public on how well the elected government is adhering to its mandate and not depriving the people of their rights is one of its most important functions in ensuring proper governance.

Evidently the founders did not want government to co-opt the power of institutional religion (the "church") or the power of the media. No state-owned church is therefore constitutional. Americans are free to practice any religious belief they choose unmolested by the government, whose task if any is to protect this right to any American, as long as their belief does not infringe on the rights of another. Neither are the forces of power, the military or the police, or even the judiciary, available to the government to be used to coerce any citizen to or against a religious belief. This was the core meaning of separation of church and state, defining the right distance between the state and the religious power centers.

Essential to right governance is a free press, defined as independence of the communications media—newspapers, books, magazines, radio, and television—and its immunity from government control or censorship. Freedom of the press is regarded as fundamental to individual rights, human dignity, self-respect, and personal responsibility, core aspects of the Abrahamic ethic (values protected by the Declaration). At the core of this amendment's concerns is the protection of expression that might be critical of government policies. The media's role is in part to inform and educate the people on what is happening in their world, and, by recognizing the right to dissent, the U.S. Constitution ensured that its emerging republic encouraged peaceful and orderly social and political change.

Taken as a whole, the media can be regarded as one of the centers of power, for it influences and shapes public opinion. We can therefore rightly regard this as another power center categorized under the "separation of powers" umbrella. In the United States, the major media is not generally state owned,[20] and therefore its freedom and independence is popularly assumed and taken for granted. But it is possible to have a state-owned media that is free. In Britain, for example, the

British Broadcasting Corporation (BBC) is state owned but independent and free to report as it sees fit—as evidenced by the furor that erupted when the BBC revealed alleged attempts by the government to falsely show that Saddam Hussein had weapons of mass destruction. The BBC's relationship to the British government is like that of the Federal Reserve's to the U.S. federal government, in that the Fed is a government-established institution performing a particular task but is free to do its job as it sees fit.

An independent media must be free to report on anything, especially on the government, and to comment on what it sees as right or wrong. We are accustomed in America to regularly hear reports of how the president or members of Congress were angry at the media for portraying them in ways they didn't like or for criticizing their policies. This provides the population the freedom to discuss government policies and the options available to them, resulting hopefully in a more maturely thinking population. A democratic society requires an educated society, and part of the media's role is to educate society in this regard. Americans are usually suspicious of any media outlet that toes the government line.

In several Muslim nations, the press and media are state owned and not free, and therefore they function more like cheerleaders for the government and its policies. This is changing with the likes of al-Jazeera TV, and it explains this channel's popularity in the Muslim world. In this day and age, however, with dish antennas and the Internet, more Muslims are aware of what their options ought to be, which feeds the frustration of the young regarding the status quo. They see the freedoms others enjoy in the United States and Europe and do not understand why they can't have this too.

Freedom of speech has its limits, however. Any expression that constitutes libel, slander, obscenity, sedition, or criminal conduct leads to infringement on the rights of others. It has long been recognized that restraints on liberty of utterance are therefore necessary. The nature and extent of such restraints—how they are to be imposed and the means by which they are enforced—have constituted important questions in law and government.

Islamic law prohibits Muslims from making libelous statements against unbelievers and those who reject their faith, a law based on the

Quranic commandment: "Do not curse the [false] gods that they [the polytheists] call upon [in worship] lest they in turn curse God in enmity [to you] out of their [understandable] ignorance" (Quran 6:107–9).

WHO SAYS AVOCADOS ARE ALWAYS IN THE VEGETABLE SECTION?

Americans take for granted these very important separations of power but often presume that they are part and parcel of democracy. Americans go to a country where elections were held and see a state-owned media, relatively poor degree of economic privatization, no effective central bank, and a dysfunctional civil society and think to themselves, "There's no democracy here!" But perhaps that's analogous to coming from a supermarket in a tropical climate, where you find mangos, papayas, avocados, and coconuts in the fruit section. Then you go to a supermarket in a temperate climate and see mangos that never get ripe, no papayas, avocados in the vegetable section, and the only coconut available is dried shredded coconut in the dessert section, and you say to yourself, "There's no fruit here!"

Just as avocados are in the vegetable section of the grocery store because we put them there, separation of powers exists in our democracy because we put them there. Separation of powers does not automatically follow from democracy. There certainly was democracy in the first draft of the Constitution, if by that we mean the power of the people to elect the government. But the separation of powers and the freedoms we enjoy, such as free speech, separation of church and state, the abolishing of slavery, the granting of suffrage to women, and the term limits on the presidency, were all added to the American Constitution later, in the amendments. They were not automatically in place just because we elected our rulers democratically.

A democracy that lacks separation of powers and good governance is what *Newsweek International* editor and *ABC News* political analyst Fareed Zakaria describes as an "illiberal democracy." These are typically "democratically elected regimes, often re-elected or reaffirmed through referenda, but who routinely ignore constitutional limits on their power and deprive their citizens of basic rights."[21] Examples he gives of this would be Ghana, Peru, the Palestinian Authority, and Venezuela.

The word *democracy* is an arrow that can point to different kinds of political realities. Until we recognize that the separations of power and respect for human rights do not automatically follow from democracy, we are in danger of believing that a good society resembling ours is created simply by giving people the right to vote. This is why it is good to define our terms and understand them well. As a case in point, look at the situations in Afghanistan and Iraq. We err when we focus exclusively on democracy and presume that good governance automatically follows.

Good governance is much more than free elections. It includes a separation of powers, especially an independent judiciary; a rule of law that respects human liberties and protects the rights of minorities against the tyranny of the majority; social safety nets to protect those in need; an economic infrastructure that generates a healthy economy; and a system for peacefully dismissing those in power who are not doing a good job. By evicting those in power in a nonviolent way, the electorate exercises its power to grade the ruling regime and to change its leadership as society evolves and matures. Allowing a fresh crop of people the opportunity to rule allows the country to adjust itself to stresses that, when not addressed, build up into pressures that result in political revolutions. It's like rebooting your computer; certain operational bugs get flushed out of the system.

The above judicial, economic, military, and legislative separations of power and protection of human rights—all in harmony with Islamic law—are more urgently needed in the Muslim world than popular elections.

LIVE WELL AUTOCRATICALLY OR LIVE POOR DEMOCRATICALLY?

If people had to choose between an affluent society lacking in freedom or a democratic but economically poor society, which would people choose? Most people seek the best possible material quality of life for themselves and their families. They are happiest when materially comfortable. For most people, peace of mind is less about whom to elect to the government than about their ability to secure a good living. That's why so many Muslims risk their lives to emigrate from their countries to western Europe and the United States, where they find happiness easier to pursue. And even my South African friends, who suffered under apartheid, confide to me that they would prefer financial freedom under a slightly authoritarian regime, such as that of Singapore, which canes naughty children who scratch people's cars, over a purer democracy that remains mired in hunger and poverty.

In building a nation, it's better to focus first on economy building and helping all citizens get a slice of the pie than on giving them the vote in a feeble economy. What does democracy mean to a poor and hungry person? During the Great Depression in the 1930s, many Americans began to wonder about democracy, and some flirted with socialism and communism. Living under the relatively strict Singapore government, which focuses on the economic well-being of its people, gives Singaporeans a better quality of life. BCCI, the bank that failed in the 1980s under a lot of scandal, had branches all over the world, including the United States, but could not obtain a banking license in Singapore because of its strict banking regulations. Some governments, such as those of Singapore, Malaysia, and other Asian countries such as South Korea and China, are less enamored of democracy in a pure sense than they are of trying to establish governance that improves the material quality of life of their populations.

CHURCH AND STATE IN AMERICA: SEPARATED OR DIVORCED?

Having examined a number of separations of power, we now come to the separation of church and state. What did it originally mean in America, and has the historical understanding of it evolved in America over these two centuries? What explains the apparent differences between Muslims and Westerners on this issue? To find our similarities, which I believe are significant, we need to look at the original intent of this idea, both in the Constitution and in the texts of the Quran and the hadith, and how the ideas of the relationship between religion and state evolved historically.

Remember when we discussed the separation of powers, we pointed out that it was about adjusting the right distance or balance between the centers of power, neither too much nor too little. Muslims view the church-state relationship as it exists now in America as one of too much distance (more like a divorce); Americans regard what Muslims want as too little distance (a marriage).

One difference between Muslim and Western perceptions on this issue is that each is also talking about slightly different things when they use the word *religion*. Separation of *church* and state is not identical to separation of *religion* and state. Because Muslims do not have a church in the organizational sense, they generally do not register a difference between these two statements: they generally presume that separation of church and state implies a separation of religion and state. Remember too that Muslims regard the command to treat each other as we want ourselves treated as a religious commandment, the second greatest commandment.

Above we spoke of the American way of life, based on the Declaration of Independence and Constitution, which modern Americans do not regard as a religion, although some have rightly called it the "American Creed."[22] It bears repeating: *Muslims do regard American values as a religion*. The American way of life as expressed in the Declaration and Constitution is itself an essential part—*although not all*—of what Muslims include in their notion of religion and religious law. If we accept that this American Creed manifests its own religious quality, then we can begin to understand the Muslim position that religion and state can never be truly separate. Those ethics, moral values, "natural laws," and "self-evident truths" that define a society are its de facto religion. When Muslims hear "separation of church and state," they think, "separation of the truth (that all are created equal) from the state, and separation of those rights, that derive from the laws of nature and of nature's God, from the state," ideas that to Muslims are incoherent.

This very point has given rise to unnecessary disputes between Muslims and non-Muslims, who feel threatened when they hear Muslims say that we all have to live "under Islam." The concepts included in the American creed are all "Islamic" in the sense that they are fully consistent and in accord with Islamic law and principles. If they weren't, Muslims could not live freely as equals in America. As we pointed out, the overarching American religion that all Americans live under is "Islamic" in the sense that it is fully compliant with and expresses the Islamic Shariah. (I am referring here to the ideals of the Declaration and Constitution and not necessarily to the reality or gaps between ideals and reality in the United States, either historically or at present.)

WHAT THE FOUNDERS ESTABLISHED: A RELIGIOUS STATE WITH A STATE RELIGION THAT ALLOWED ALL RELIGIONS

What were the founders' concerns that motivated them to draft the establishment clause, the first section of the First Amendment, which reads, "Congress shall make no law respecting an establishment of religion, or prohibiting the free exercise thereof"?

Having come to America for religious liberty, the founders were concerned that the powers of state might be used to further one religion above any other, to enforce one religious set, doctrine, or interpretation over another, or to harm a religious establishment. The separation of church and state was intended to mean that the state may not prejudicially side for or against any one religion or church, must equally allow all religions the freedom and liberty to practice, and must not involve itself in any differences of opinion even within one religious tradition.

Pluralism of religions and churches is the foundation of the establishment clause. This is similar to the Islamic injunction in the Quran: "Say: O disbelievers: To you your religion, and to me mine" (Quran 109:6). This verse and others together demonstrate that pluralism *of* religions is a fundamental human right under Islamic law.

Pluralism *within* religion developed in the field of Islamic law as Muslim scholars recognized that differing interpretations on a number of issues could be maintained while still adhering to the letter and spirit of the Quranic and Prophetic legal injunctions and their core prescriptions.[23] All the Muslim schools of law (*madhhabs*) recognized each other as equally valid. An ideal Muslim society, therefore, was one in which such pluralistic interpretations within Islamic jurisprudence had to be admitted.[24]

The intentions of America's founders matched the Islamic idea, namely, a nation "under God." The authors of the Declaration and the Constitution focused especially on the social aspects of the Abrahamic ethic, the rights and liberties of individuals and their freedom to practice their religion, or practice no religion at all, as their consciences dictated, unimpaired by the state. These rights flow from the Abrahamic ethic, from the second commandment to treat one's fellow human beings the way one wants to be treated. But the founders generally believed in one God, God the Creator of everything, thus of nature. Their concept of such a God was very much the Abrahamic concept, the one all-powerful providential Creator, a concept of God that can be accepted by all Abrahamic religions.

Scholar of Islam Murray Titus shows that until the time of Christ, the phrase "kingdom of God" was understood in Judaism to mean exclusively the temporal kingdom of the Jewish people, whose real ruler was Jehovah—God. The Israelite prophets directed their messages toward the children of Israel, and the Old Testament notion of the kingdom of God was intended for one nation only. Muhammad, however, came with a message directed toward gentiles as well as the children of Israel. Islam was intended as a religion for all of humankind; therefore its ideal of a kingdom of God had to be one that embraced within its purview all of humankind, "as Allah was the ruler of all men." Titus points out that Muhammad broadened the meaning of the idea of the kingdom of God and that "Muhammad gave to Allah a *universal* significance, and to His rule world-wide implications which made Islam a universal religion from the start." The Islamic ideal, he says, "therefore holds that human society should be so organized as to acknowledge Allah as its supreme ruler" yet be a pluralistic society that accords with the Abrahamic ethic.[25]

Muslims do not regard any state as authentically Islamic other than that established by the Prophet in Medina, followed by his successors, known as the four Rightly Guided Caliphs. The principles of rule laid down by the Prophet and his four successors show that the Islamic conception of state is not one in which Islam *in the liturgical sense* has to be held as the state religion but rather that the state must be *a religious state*, in which God is the ultimate ruler. This is consistent with the understanding expressed in the American Constitutional worldview.

Writing in May 2002, Supreme Court justice Antonin Scalia adds that even if we define *government* in the most limited way, as "lawfully constituted authority" or "lawfully constituted authority that rules justly," such government *"derives its moral authority from God"* (italics mine). He regards it a "mistaken tendency to believe that a democratic government [is] nothing more than the composite will of its individual citizens [and] has no more moral power or authority than [the citizens] do as individuals." Citing the apostle Paul in Romans 13:1–5 (but making a point that Muslims and people of most religions subscribe to), he says that every human soul is subject to the powers ordained by God and that to resist them is to resist the ordinance of God. We are subject to right government for conscience' sake. "The reaction of people of faith to this tendency of democracy to obscure the divine authority behind government should not be resignation to it, but the resolution to combat it as effectively as possible," says Justice Scalia. "We have done that in this country (and continental Europe has not) by preserving in our public life many visible reminders that—in the words of a Supreme Court opinion from the 1940s—'we are a religious people, whose institutions presuppose a Supreme Being.' These reminders include: 'In God we trust' on our coins, 'one nation under God' in our Pledge of Allegiance, the opening of sessions of our legislatures with a prayer, the opening of sessions of my Court with 'God save the United States and this Honorable Court,' annual Thanksgiving proclamations issued by our President at the direction of Congress, and constant invocations of divine support in the speeches of our political leaders, which often conclude, 'God bless America.'"[26]

In other words, the founders intended America to be a religious society and nation, a society whose ethics emanate from our religious beliefs. Their intentions were not that the president and people working in government had to be atheist or irreligious or that the president could not attend church, synagogue, mosque, or temple. All this is delightfully consistent with Islamic law.

Our government's moral authority derives from the Constitution, whose moral basis is God's law—another way of saying, as Thomas Jefferson did, the "Laws of Nature and Nature's God." As long as the government officials who have sworn an oath to uphold the Constitution and its laws act accordingly, they have moral—and divine—authority; when they violate it, they have lost that moral and divine authority.

The Quran speaks to this when it says, "Say: O God, Lord of Sovereignty! You invest sovereignty in whom You please, and divest sovereignty from whom You please" (Quran 3:26), and, "Obey God and obey the messenger and those in authority from among you" (Quran 4:59). Because the principles of the Declaration and Constitution are consistent with divine ordinance, the particular method of government and a particular scheme of sociopolitical cooperation that follow from it are thereby invested with divine sovereignty and command an authority that comes from God.

The power of the community is of a vicarious kind, being held, as it were, in trust from God. A Shariah-compliant state owes its existence to the will of the people and is subject to control by them, although it derives its ultimate authority from God. Three sayings of the Prophet found in the hadith speak to this point: "My community will not come to consensus on a wrong, and if you disagree, follow the largest group";[27] "It is your duty to stand by the united community and the majority";[28] and "the hand of God is upon the majority."[29] These sayings together have led Muslim jurists to conclude that, as Muhammad Asad put it, "When the majority of the community has decided to entrust the government to a particular leader, every Muslim citizen must consider himself morally bound by that decision even if it goes against his personal preferences."[30] This is precisely what we do in America, although we may not have voted for our president; once the election results are in, we owe him the respect that is due the office of the presidency.

Many traditional American phrases evoke Quranic expressions:

For the phrase "In God we trust," compare "Our Lord, we have indeed heard a Crier calling to faith, saying 'Trust in your Lord, so we have trusted . . .'" (Quran 3:193) or "[The messenger and the believers] all trust in God, in His Angels, His Scriptures, His Books and His Messengers . . ." (Quran 2:285).

For the phrase "one nation under God," compare, "Surely this community of yours is one community, and I am your Lord, so be dutiful to Me" (Quran 23:52). The context of this verse speaks of numerous messengers, implying that in spite of the diversity of religious expressions, the human community is still one community, or nation, under God. Muslims are thereby Quranically urged to regard all humanity—and at the minimum certainly the Abrahamic faiths—as one pluralistic community under God: *e pluribus unum*.

For asking that God bless our community, our land, compare the following Quranic verses: "We made the people who were deemed weak to inherit the eastern and western lands which We had blessed. And the good word of your Lord was fulfilled upon the Children of Israel because of their patience. And we destroyed what Pharaoh and his people had wrought and what they had built" (Quran 7:137; see 34:18 for towns that God had blessed). On calling God's blessing on ourselves, Muslims are commanded to "Greet each other with God's salutations, blessings, and good things" (Quran 24:61).

WHAT MIGHT JUST THE RIGHT DISTANCE BETWEEN CHURCH AND STATE LOOK LIKE?

In his farewell address, George Washington summed up the role of religion in America: "*And let us with caution indulge the supposition, that morality can be maintained without religion. Whatever may be conceded to the influence of refined education on minds of peculiar structure, reason and experience both forbid us to expect that National morality can prevail in exclusion of religious principle*" (italics mine).[31] Clearly, the founders of this country, like devout Muslims, intended to build a society that was moral in character and that founded its morals on a religious ethic. Americans have always been a religious society, and are mighty proud of that. If the distance between religion and society in America is, as Muslims see it, too great, how might we imagine a proper separation between religion and state in America—one that is neither a divorce nor a marriage?

Muslims and Americans can agree that separation of church and state is substantively different from separation of religion and state. We can agree also that this means that state powers should not be used to further one religion or religious belief over any other but to encourage and protect people of any and all religions to practice their faith freely. To this end,

1. Each religion shall be independent of state intrusion. The state shall not get involved in making any statements about the correctness of religious belief or practice.

2. Religious discrimination, and the inciting of hate crimes, should be prohibited.

How might a religiously pluralistic state structure its court system so as to accommodate religious communities' desire for greater religious liberty and fulfillment?

Islamic law divides laws into two broad categories pertaining to human actions: ritual acts (*'ibadat*) and worldly acts (*mu'amalat*). Laws pertaining to rites of worship such as prayers and fasting deal with when prayers and fasting should be done, who is exempt from these acts and when, prerequisites to ritual acts, and so forth.

Laws pertaining to worldly acts are further subdivided into three groups: (1) family law or laws of personal status, dealing with issues such as marriage, divorce, alimony, child custody, and inheritance; (2) transactions—property rights, contracts, rules of sale, hire, gift, loans and debts, deposits, partnerships and damage to property; and (3) criminal law, pertaining to murder, theft, libel, and so forth.[32]

It is easy to see that the American courts have no overlap with Islamic laws pertaining to acts of worship (*'ibadat*). For example, they have no jurisdiction over when Ramadan starts—that is, when American Muslims must start fasting. This has more to do with ritual and liturgical practice, which American law grants every religious group its freedom to decide. Because of these freedoms, Muslims in America might celebrate the beginning and end of Ramadan on different days, according to their individual interpretations of when the crescent of the new moon can actually be sighted.

Now let's take a case from family law. If an American Muslim couple decides to divorce, and their preference is to judge their case according to Islamic law, and their case involves issues of child custody and support, this is likely to bump up against the U.S. courts' interpretation of how to deal with such cases. The same can happen with a Jewish or Christian couple, who may prefer to have the issue decided according to their laws.

Separation of church and state, as described above, will not be violated if we establish separate Muslim, Jewish, or Christian personal status courts to render judgments for Muslim, Jewish, or Christian couples seeking to have their case heard under such laws and to have these decisions ratified by the secular state courts. To a limited degree, this is already happening.

For example, I am licensed by the State of New York to conduct weddings according to Islamic law. The state recognizes weddings I conduct as legally valid and does not regard this as a violation of church-state separation. But if a couple comes to me for a divorce, while I may divorce them according to Islamic law, this divorce will not be recognized by the state courts. And I have no means of making this divorce legally binding according to American law. If one or both members of the couple decides to violate the provisions of the divorce ruling—as they might, since people have a tendency to be contemptuous of rulings that do not go in their favor—I cannot issue a contempt-of-court ruling or call in the state's institutional powers, such as the police, to enforce the legal decision.

Or, for another example, Islamic law prohibits a deceased Muslim from disinheriting certain beneficiaries: every member of the immediate family shares in the estate, and no bequest can be made that exceeds one-third of the estate. But an American Muslim who dies in this country without a will is going to have his or her estate divided according to American law, which will give the estate to the next of kin only, not to all members of the immediate family, and so certain beneficiaries may be disinherited according to American law that would have been mandatory in Islamic law. It would not be a violation of church-state separation if American Muslims dying intestate would have their estates automatically disbursed according to Islamic law.

From the above examples, we see how it may be possible in America to develop further our ability to fulfill religious communities' needs for laws that reflect their belief systems without violating the important principles embodied in a correct understanding of what separation of church and state means.

We mentioned above that in the American model of separation of powers, the checks and balances feature permits the courts to exercise their power to judicially review acts of Congress or the president to ensure that they are constitutional. It also would not be a violation of church-state separation to have a subsidiary entity within the judiciary that employs religious jurists from diverse religious backgrounds to comment on the compliance of certain decisions with their religious laws and to provide guidance to their religious communities on how kosher or Shariah compliant these decisions are. Most decisions would not change, but those few that intersect matters of religion would provide American religious communities with much greater clarity and much greater guidance on those issues that affect their religious belief and practice. It would also make America a great example to the world of how God centered it is. More important, it would provide the United States with a moral rudder and guidance to ensure that its policies are in keeping with religious ethical values and the principles that lie at the core of our Declaration of Independence and Constitution.

CHAPTER 4

Where the Devil Got in the Details

A good forty years ago, the late professor Wilfred Cantwell Smith, for a decade head of Harvard's Center for the Study of World Religions, wrote about getting us to clean up our use of the word *religion*. A lot of conflict has been spawned by the profound ways in which our understanding of this term has changed.[1]

As we have seen, the word *islam* in the Quran means "the act of submission." As Professor Smith liked to say, Judaism, Islam, and Christianity are in reality verbs, not nouns. He explained, "Islam is a verbal noun: the name of an action, not of an institution; of a personal decision, not a social system."[2] In the Quranic verse (49:17) where God commands the Prophet to inform the Bedouin Arabs, "Don't favor me with your *islam (islamakum)*," the term means "your personal commitment to heed God's words."

In the Semitic languages (and classical Japanese) the verb is primary. Studying Arabic, a Semitic language, starts with studying verbs and their varieties. Even adjectives are considered a variety of verb in Arabic, because they express the way a noun "acts" or "projects" itself to the observer, whether an apple, for example, projects itself as red or green. The Indo-European languages, especially Greek, gave the noun a much higher rank, "so that ever since in Western thought *reality has tended to be conceived in terms of entities, while in the Old Testament, it is conceived primarily in terms of events* (italics mine)."[3]

Now if we interpret the word *islam* as a personal commitment in Quran 5:3, which states, "*inna-ddina 'inda-llahi-l-islam,*" we get, "Certainly religion with God [that is, in God's eyes] is the personal act of [human] submission" (Quran 5:3). This translation, as Smith points out, is "virtually identical" to the definition of religion given by the

Catholic Encyclopedia: "Religion . . . means the voluntary subjection of oneself to God."[4] This definition from the *Catholic Encyclopedia,* translated into Arabic, would restate the Quranic verse! Now imagine some modern Arab perusing this Arabic translation in Cairo and reading the definition, "Religion is Islam to God." He or she might say, "*Alhamdulillah!* [God be praised]! The Catholics have seen the light of Islam!"

When we interpret Quranic occurrences of the word *islam* to mean "a religious system" instead of "a personal act," the meaning can become highly sectarian and explosive. Quran 3:85 reads: "Whoever seeks other than self-surrender (*islam*) as religion, it shall not be accepted from him." If what is meant here is that God will not accept an act of religiousness that is done without submission to God, any pious Jew or Christian would agree. But if interpreted, as many erroneously do today, "Whoever seeks anything other than the religious system of Islam, it shall not be accepted of him," the verse has sectarian implications that contradict the unambiguous meaning of Quranic verses such as 2:62 and 5:69: "Surely those who believe, the Jews, the Christians, and the Sabians, whoever believes in God and the Last Day and does good, they have their reward with God; they shall not fear, nor shall they grieve." Defining *Islam* as a religious system rather than a universal act of submission is dangerous and has fed Islamic triumphalism and fueled modern Islamic militancy and sectarian violence.

The use of terms such as *Judaism, Christianity,* and *Islam* to refer to systems of observances and beliefs—of an institutionalized historical tradition—is a modern one that did not appear until the seventeenth century and really took hold in the nineteenth century, says Smith. Through a study of Muslim book titles through the centuries, he noticed that "since the latter part of the nineteenth century, there has demonstrably been a sudden and almost complete shift to a use of the term *Islam* to name a religion."[5] The tragedy is that Muslims themselves have had their paradigms of thinking—their conceptual framework—shaped by the West, in this case to the detriment of both.

Smith suggests that this happened as a result of European scholars traveling through greater regions of the world in their study of foreign religious practices. He compares them "to flies crawling on the outside of a goldfish bowl, making accurate and complete observations on the fish inside, measuring their scales meticulously, and indeed contributing much to a knowledge of the subject, but never asking themselves, and never finding out, how it feels to be a goldfish."[6] As a Muslim, I am grateful to Professor Smith for explaining exactly how Muslims were made to feel by Orientalists, who treated Muslims like biological curiosities preserved in triethylene chloride. The work of these scholars, fueled by Western Enlightenment values, led to the notion of religions as disembodied belief systems rather than acts of human piety.

I would add to Smith's thesis that this usage is also one of the unfortunate by-products of the invention of the corporation, which created artificial "persons." Around the same time that the use of the word *religion* was undergoing change, cities were incorporated, investment ventures were incorporated, and religion, which once referred to acting piously, became known instead as an identity. Religion changed from something you *did* into something that you *were*. Instead of you owning your religion (as an act that you do) and being responsible for your religion (your acts of religiosity), you instead belonged to your religion; it became something that owns you. A whole complex of subtle psychological shifts takes place between people and religion: by the end of this shift, Religion, Inc., owns people, and religion becomes responsible for people instead of the other way around. Such is the power of language over how we think and therefore how we act.

WHAT DO *JEWISH, CHRISTIAN, MUSLIM* REALLY MEAN?

Why so much talk about the pitfalls of language? As we shall see later in this book, these types of language pitfalls have presented major stumbling blocks to Westerners and Muslims understanding each other. One way in which language has confused Muslims and non-Muslims is what I call imposing a "presumption of similarity" by using the same adjective to describe vastly divergent nouns in a way that implies a common set of values.

For example, what does the word *American* signify in the following usages: American religion, American law, American history, American state, American art, American architecture, American furniture, American fashion (of clothing and dressing style), American banking, American name, and American food? And what can we say about foreign universities studying American studies, American religious fundamentalisms, and American foreign policy? How can we possibly define the common denominator of *American* in all these instances?

How then can we presume that a coherent meaning exists for the word *Islamic* in Islamic religion, Islamic law, Islamic history, Islamic state, Islamic art, Islamic architecture, Islamic dress, Islamic name, Islamic banking, and Islamic food? Not to mention, in many Western universities, Departments of Islamic Studies, Islamic Knowledge, or Islamic Sciences. How can we define *Islam* and *Islamic* in a coherent way in all these instances?

Does eating American food (steak and potatoes) or wearing American fashions inform us about how one might be accepting the ideals of American constitutional law? What does American banking or American foreign policy tell us about American ideals?

In the same vein, are Muslims sinning if not living in an Islamic state? Is eating Jewish food un-Islamic? Is it Islamically acceptable to celebrate Thanksgiving and eat turkey? Does a Muslim woman violate her religion if she doesn't cover her head? Is it a sin to do business with a bank?

The danger with labels is that they begin to own us rather than the other way around. Peripheral issues become the definition of the essential. Non-Muslims then regard "Islamic militancy" as something that emanates from Islamic theology rather than as something that certain people calling themselves Muslim have done, usually for political purposes. And Muslims can adopt Islamic dress and an Islamic name to demonstrate Islamic credentials while being unaware, because uninformed on Islamic theology, doctrine, and law, where they may be violating important norms of Islamic ethical behavior.

The use of the new term *Islamism* to refer to militancy done ostensibly in the name of Islam is a particularly pernicious use of language. It merges the faith of Islam with modern political movements in such a way as to make non-Muslims think that Islam itself is the source of the militancy. When we use language in such a way that it creates relationships that do not exist in reality, the results are not only confusing but dangerous, because people can and do act upon their misunderstandings.

The Romans called the early disciples at Antioch *Christianoi*, which originally meant "Jews (and later anyone) who believed that the messiah had come." (By this definition, Muslims are also Christian because they accept Jesus as the Messiah.)[7] As Smith points out, members of the church at first resisted this appellation—they were embarrassed by it—because it meant being Messiah-like (*Christ* is the Greek word for *Messiah*) or Christ-ish.[8] Imagine being asked, "Are you Christlike or of a Messiah nature?" which is what they understood if asked "Are you Christian?" But by the nineteenth century the word *Christian* came almost exclusively to mean "pertaining to Christians; or to the institution of Christianity." The same shift occurred in the use of the word *islam* by Muslims. The Quran, the Prophet, and his contemporaries and later generations used the word *muslim* to mean "someone submitted to God." Devout Christians and Jews were therefore regarded as "muslim." But by the nineteenth century the word *muslim* came almost exclusively to mean "pertaining to the practice of the Prophet Muhammad." This difference in meaning and significance is huge.

WHAT'S THE CONFLICT REALLY ABOUT?

Does religion cause conflicts? This is an idea popularly expressed, and it deserves to be explored at some length.

Ultimately, the root cause of conflict is nearly always the loss of an asset, a thing of really high value. An asset can be anything—an idea, like losing your honor, the right to teach your children creationism instead of evolution, or something real and tangible, such as your inheritance. Our beliefs are among our most treasured assets, and our religion, being a major subset of our beliefs, is thus a deeply prized asset, as are our freedom and liberty. An employee might become angry because he feels denied his rightful share of a bonus, a child might take legal action for being left out of her parents' estate, countries might fight over agricultural water from a border river, or two men might fight for the love of a woman. People become incensed when they feel that an asset has been taken from them wrongfully, whether it was by theft or unlawful seizure or even when they suspect they paid too much for it (as when they exclaim, "We were robbed!").

The other root cause of conflict is issues of power—who gets to control decisions. A husband and wife can argue about the color of a new carpet, where to go for vacation, or who does the dishes. Over time, a buildup of such disagreements can lead to such acrimony that the relationship becomes untenable. While disagreements on these relatively insignificant issues are often considered the source of the conflict, they are not really, for when the couple patches things up, they usually wonder in amazement, "We were fighting over this?"

In reality, they were fighting over power, over who gets to decide what about what. The anger is not primarily over the choice of carpet color but over the right to control the decision. This is why we often end up blurting out, "Don't tell me what to do!" We cherish the right to make our own decisions, even to commit our own mistakes.

These two root causes, the power to control decisions and how assets are distributed, make up the root causes of almost all conflicts. Issues become triggers of violence if they translate into loss of power or tangible assets.

Once an argument is kindled, a psychological pattern develops in which we look at what differentiates us from the other side and often wrongfully attribute the conflict to that difference. This difference then contributes to the otherness of our opponent and feeds the righteousness of our cause. So if the argument is between a man and a woman, in our anger we blurt out, "Women! They're so emotional!" or "Men! Such insensitive brutes!" We attribute the cause to gender difference, and in time a gender war breaks out. Generations pass, and eventually books are written on how men are from Mars and women from Venus; and since we can live neither with nor without them, a two-state solution of sorts is worked out, whereby women have domain over certain areas of life and men over others.

If the difference is one of skin color or race, we attribute the cause of disagreement to that, and in time we have an ethnic or racial conflict; if the difference is religion, we have a religious conflict. After a generation or two, people are taught to think about these differences in such a way that they genuinely begin to believe that women are not capable of being highly educated, much less of becoming leaders, that educating women in the hard sciences will addle their brains, that Arabs or Muslims "cannot handle democracy," that Arabs and Jews have hated each other since Ishmael and Isaac, that Hindus have always hated Muslims, that Sunni Muslims and Shiite Muslims can never get along, that blacks are genetically inferior to whites, that northerners are superior to southerners and city dwellers better than suburbanites—the list of prejudices goes on. In time these differences become deep-seated beliefs that continue to fuel the conflict and that may take generations to correct.

Those traits that have historically been used to prevent groups of people from sharing in power and economic assets are in reality secondary causes and should more accurately be regarded as identity tags, which we find useful for labeling the other in any given conflict. We can create any number of such identity tags, including those of gender, skin coloring, tribal affiliation, class or family, and, of course, religion. What we call the glass ceiling in the United States is an example of gender differentiation; the massacres in Rwanda between Hutus and Tutsis are an example of tribal conflict; the tensions in India are about religion and (within Hinduism) caste (class) differentiation; while the Irish troubles represent a conflict between subgroups of the same religion (Protestants versus Catholics). Each of these differences is not the root cause of the conflict but rather the identity tag used to separate one group from another with regard to the real root causes of the conflict, namely, power and economics.

For proof that religion is not a root cause, study Protestant and Catholic theology and you will be hard-pressed to discover the cause of the conflict in Belfast. Moreover, in January 2002, the chief rabbi of Israel, the chief mufti of Egypt, and the archbishop of Westminster could agree on the joint Alexandria Declaration calling for peace between Jews, Christians, and Muslims, yet this would do nothing to reduce the death toll in the Arab-Israeli conflict. The United Nations Millennium Summit convened over a thousand religious representatives, who made sincere and lofty pronouncements about the need for peace between religions, but their calls had no effect on the second intifada in Palestine or on the nuclear tension between India and Pakistan because the religious leaders lacked the means to address the root issues of power and economics.

The Taliban considered themselves good, devout Muslims. The Pakistanis consider themselves devout Muslims. The Iranians consider themselves devout Muslims. Yet in the 1990s, Iran almost went to war against the Taliban when the Taliban killed ten Iranian diplomats and journalists. The Taliban also massacred many Shiites, the predominate Iranian group, and Shiites have been attacked in Pakistan. These conflicts have less to do with teaching and theological principles than they do with real or perceived infringements on assets.

When a conflict drags on for years, people tend to forget its true source and attribute it instead to the differentiating secondary causes. Thus the Irish believe that Catholics and Protestants are naturally disposed to violence against each other, Jews and Arabs are taught to feel that their hostility is fundamental to their Jewishness or Arabness, and many Sunni and Shiite people believe they are fated to fight each other. In reality, however, these differences are only secondary identity tags by which we define the other, whom we are taught to demonize.

What makes this misunderstanding even more pernicious is that it's not hard to find causes for conflict that go far back in history. It's easy to find incidents from the Prophet Muhammad's time or verses from the Quran and Bible to justify the position that Jews and Muslims must be enemies. In the process, centuries of warm relationships that prove the opposite are steadfastly ignored and forgotten.

Based on my own observation of conflict, I disagree with the thesis that religion is the root of many conflicts. It is certainly one of the many trigger points or secondary causes of conflict, and a volatile one at that, but it is rarely the root or primary cause. Rather, as I said above, violent conflict is nearly always related to perceived injustice in the distribution of power and assets.

The Hindu-Muslim conflict between India and Pakistan today is primarily fueled by the dispute over who owns Kashmir (an economic asset). The conflict that led to the partition of India into India and Pakistan sprang from the fear of a disparity between Hindus and Muslims in the governing structure (a power dispute). Though the original power issue was resolved by that partition of the subcontinent, the unresolved Kashmir issue (the economic asset) still continues to feed the conflict. Thus while India and Pakistan have nuclear weapons targeted against each other, India has no weapons targeted at Bangladesh—or Malaysia or Egypt or any other countries with majority Muslim populations. Neither Bangladesh, originally part of the 1948 partition and known as East Pakistan, nor Egypt, which has excellent diplomatic relations with India, has a territorial interest in Kashmir.

Religion is clearly not the root cause of the Hindu-Muslim conflict. If it were, then India would have equally tense relations with Bangladesh and Egypt. Remove or address the root cause, namely, power or assets, and the identity tag fades as a basis for violence. Resolve the Kashmir issue, and India and Pakistan will likely be each other's largest trading partner.

The Palestinian-Israeli conflict, for example, was fundamentally about how the land of Palestine (an economic asset) was acquired. Resolve this issue, and it is likely that Jewish-Muslim relations will rapidly improve. (Again, Israel and Palestine will likely be each other's largest trading partner.)

The Sunni-Shiite divide was originally about power, namely, who would rule over the Muslim community after the Prophet: those who were his family descendants or those who were considered best qualified. Today, things have become so bad in Pakistan that Sunnis have killed Shiites during the Friday prayer in their mosques—an absurd and tragic situation that violates the core principles of the Quran and the Prophet Muhammad's teachings!

IS THE BEEF ABOUT BELIEF?

Beliefs are powerful for two reasons:

1. They can affect our power or economic status.

2. They constitute an asset of their own.

Rabbi David Hartman, founder of the Shalom Hartman Institute in Jerusalem, was asked in the summer of 2002 at New York's Chautauqua Institution, "Would Jews be happier if Christians gave up their belief that Jesus is divine?" Without hesitation, Rabbi Hartman responded; "I don't care what you believe—as long as the difference between your beliefs and mine don't get me kicked out of the party. . . ." By *party* he meant the opportunity to participate fully in the greater community of global society—sharing in the available power and economic benefits with fellow citizens—and getting excluded from this is precisely what Palestinians see has happened to them.

Many of us value ideas such as our philosophy of life, our world-view, or the social compact that binds us to others and determines how we interact with them. I suggest that for most people, atheists and ag-nostics included, the most important of these values are those that, when violated or infringed, invoke the fight-or-flight syndrome. Most of us do have a set of core beliefs that determine how we relate to the world around us; and therefore, in this sense, I would like to suggest that we are all "religious." The questions then remain: What is our re-ligion? How does it differ from the other major religions? And how can we all get along?

Beliefs are among our most deeply prized "possessions," and they are especially cherished by those whose identities are wrapped up in their beliefs on a particular matter. It doesn't often matter what the be-lief is. What matters is your psychological attachment to the impor-tance of the belief, especially as it affects you personally.

I'll never forget when my maternal grandfather purchased some fresh lamb liver from the village butcher and requested that it be mar-inated in a mixture of onion juice and fresh lime juice before being fried. He completely blew a gasket when my mother and her step-mother failed to abide by his instructions. I never saw him become so emotional over anything as he was over this. Now I understand: his re-quest had been vetoed (a power issue, particularly important for a tra-ditional Arab male in his home); and his asset (the delicious lamb liver he was anticipating, the freshest one in the butcher shop) had in his eyes just been destroyed.

The challenge to anyone involved in conflict resolution is always how to map the core, underlying issues of power and assets, which often are not obvious on the surface. What keeps violence going, illog-ical though it nearly always is, is the powerful set of emotional attach-ments on each side, which completely override the normal needs of daily living.

One requires no advanced degree in economics or political science to recognize that chaotic, systemic violence is unhealthy for society. People don't feel safe, financial markets are upset, and life becomes severely interrupted when violence erupts. Look at what has happened to Israelis and Palestinians over the past few years. The vicious cycle of the second intifada with its suicide bombings against Israelis, targeted assassinations of Palestinians, and the destruction of homes and the turmoil over illegal settlements have resulted in a downward economic spiral for both sides. While the Palestinians were suffering malnutrition, the Israeli economy was in free fall, and both sides continue to feel terribly insecure.

AGGRESSIVE FUNDAMENTALISTS: THE DEFENSE TEAM

Konrad Lorenz, author of the important work *On Aggression*, posits that "aggression, the effects of which are frequently equated with those of the death wish, is an instinct like any other and in natural conditions it helps just as much as any other to ensure the survival of the individual and the species."[9] When a group feels under attack, then, in order to ensure its survival, a certain amount of aggression in its name is bound to evolve. I believe that this defensive instinct is what leads to the rise of all religious fundamentalist movements, and it certainly has been the case with Islam.

The first aggressive militancy in the name of Islam arose with the Kharijites, literally, "seceders." This occurred during the caliphate of the much loved and respected fourth Caliph Ali, first cousin and son-in-law of the Prophet, who was challenged by the governor of Damascus, Mu'awiyah,[10] in a bid for political power. Ali had intended to dismiss a number of governors, including Mu'awiyah, because they did not rule in accord with Islamic rules of justice. This precipitated a rebellion against Ali that led to the Battle of Siffin between Mu'awiyah and Ali. In that battle, Ali was on the verge of winning when one of Mu'awiyah's men hatched a clever ploy: hanging sheets of the Quran from their lances, meaning "let's make the Quran decide between us." This caused Ali's men to stop fighting, brought a lull in the battle, and eventually precipitated an arbitration from which no clear victor emerged. As a result, some of Ali's strongest warriors were angered that Ali was too soft on his challengers in defending the *ummah* (community) from this challenge to its right.

Before being labeled "seceders," the Kharijites were merely warriors frustrated by being held back from fighting the enemy—the governor

Mu'awiyah, who in their eyes was destroying the faith of Islam. In the end, however, this group made history by tragically fighting Ali, their own leader, all because of a passionate difference of opinion.

The Kharijites seceded from Ali and ultimately even assassinated him. While Mu'awiyah certainly carried out aggression against Ali, he did not do so in the name of Islam. His battle was about power and control. The Kharijites, on the other hand, saw themselves defending Islam by fighting for the rightful leader of the community, and they believed that the rightful leader of the community had to fight and protect his people. If not, he forfeited his right to be the leader of the community. They even developed a theory of the caliphate and the qualifications of the imam (the leader of the Muslim community) based upon their ideas.

This situation is somewhat reminiscent of General George Patton at the end of World War II. Patton believed strongly that the United States should have continued its march through Germany and challenged the Soviets as well. Instead, he was overruled by President Harry Truman. Now imagine if Patton, regarding Truman's decision as accommodation of the Soviets, had "seceded" from Truman and fought him because he wasn't aggressive enough against the enemy of the United States. Patton would then have been in the position of the Kharijites. In a sense, what we'll call the Kharijite phenomenon is somewhat like Patton going all the way, or being holier than the pope in aggressively defending the community from its enemies.

Lorenz's thesis is that this kind of aggression in defense of the community evolved biologically for the protection of the species. The "species" being protected could be racial, tribal, or religious. For example, the violent Black Panther movement in the 1960s represented this kind of aggression in the context of the civil rights movement, seeking the defense of American blacks against white people who had imposed the historical injustice of slavery (and later discrimination) upon them. But after President Lyndon Johnson pushed through civil rights legislation, and American blacks made progress in their battle for civil rights, legal and voting barriers fell, affirmative action plans were created, and racial discrimination against blacks became a violation of law. As all this occurred, black militancy inevitably waned.

While this does not explain all the causes of religious aggression, or aggression committed in the name of religion, I believe that a significant portion of religious fundamentalism of the twentieth century (Muslim, Christian, Jewish, Hindu, Sikh) was a result of this defensive reaction against perceived attacks. The fundamentalists are Kharijite-style Lorenzian aggressors intent on defending their religious group against attacks from whatever source: Jewish fundamentalists against secular Jews; Sikh fundamentalists reacting to Indira Gandhi's physical attack on their sacred site, the Golden Temple; or Muslims reacting to modernization and its perceived militant secularism.

Geneticist Richard Dawkins, in his book *The Selfish Gene*, offers some interesting ideas on aggression that complement Lorenz's theory. Among his insights are that if we expect help from our biological nature to build a society in which individuals can cooperate generously and unselfishly toward a common good, then we should know how our nonconscious biology operates.[11]

Among the behaviors we observe in the animal kingdom, he notes the stinging behavior of worker bees in defense of the hive. The worker bee dies as a result, since in the act of stinging, vital internal organs are torn out of the body. Her "suicide aggression" against the invader had as its purpose saving the colony, but she herself is not around to reap the benefits. Biologists do not believe that the bee performed this as a martyr seeking eternal life in bee heaven, and they naturally ask, how was this nonconscious, altruistic, aggressive behavior *genetically* determined?

What he proposes is that the spectrum of behavior in the animal kingdom, from parental altruism to aggression against others, which might look to us either as examples of conscious individual selfishness or individual altruism, can be explained by applying a branch of mathematics called game theory, in which the payoffs for a variety of different behavioral traits are computed. Because payoffs appear to benefit less the well-being of the individual organism than the well-being of the gene and appear to bypass our conscious behavior, which is rooted in our sense of will and values, he calls this idea "gene selfishness."

He observes that there is something called an *evolutionary stable strategy*. When a group experiences aggression against it as a result of some desire to obtain a benefit at its expense, patterns of mutually aggressive behavior develop that express stable configurations. While mutual cooperation provides greater payoff for both sides, aggression is likely to take over for the purpose of some short-term gain.

The upshot of Dawkins's analysis is that human beings are *"built as gene machines . . . but we have the power to turn against our creators. We, alone on earth, can rebel against the tyranny of the selfish replicators* (italics mine)."[12] To the extent that human behavior is biologically and genetically determined, Dawkins's theory explains why humans will fight for their nation, for tribal or regional solidarity, for family solidarity, and, within the family, ultimately for oneself. It also explains to some extent the role of suicide in human behavior, when it is done as part of a payoff for one's group. It is reasonable to conclude that just as bees evolved to commit an act of suicide aggression to ward off the attack against their biological species, so, to the extent that human groups follow evolutionary behavior, *suicide aggression will develop as one means of responding to what is viewed as an attack against the group.*

Surrendering to "the tyranny of the selfish replicators" means to me what happens when we allow ourselves to succumb to the evolutionary stable strategies of violence and aggression demonstrated by game theory calculations. "Rebelling against our replicators" is when we recognize that a greater social payoff can be obtained by cooperating with each other in building a harmonious, pluralistic civil society. Evolutionary stable strategies of aggressive and violent human behavior are likely to take over when the social rules of cooperation are destroyed or attenuated, as we have seen in Afghanistan and Iraq. Game theory suggests that the benefits to society of cooperation are far greater than the evolutionary stable payoff, where aggressive behavior is allowed to occur. The natural question is, how can we apply our conscious foresight to *artificially stabilize* the greater payoff of cooperation?

The short answer is by structuring the governance of society in such a way that the most stable strategy is one that maximizes the payoff, and severe penalties are imposed for those upsetting that configuration. We call this "democratic rule," where government operates "by consent of the governed." In such a society everyone is concerned about his or her "payoff" (however one defines life, liberty, and the pursuit of happiness) and seeks to maximize it. When a population finds a way to hold its government responsible for the maximum payoff, game theory indicates that such a society would pull the evolutionary stable strategy point toward nonviolence.[13]

Our religious and ethical teachings, and especially the principle of the second commandment, namely, "Do unto others what you love done to yourself, and avoid hurting others the way you want to avoid hurt yourself," by urging us to cooperate and rein in our aggressive tendencies, are intended to provide society with a greater overall payoff—even without the extra payoff that religious people expect in an eternal afterlife.

WHAT'S BEHIND RELIGIOUS VIOLENCE?

Professor Ashutosh Varshney, who studied Hindu-Muslim conflict and violence in Indian cities, demonstrated that personal relationships, and the quality of those relationships, can consistently prevent outbreaks of violence across the religious divide.[14]

The puzzling issue he probes is why, "despite ethnic diversity, some places—regions, nations, towns or villages—manage to remain peaceful, whereas others experience enduring patterns of violence." And why do "some societies, after maintaining a veritable record of ethnic peace, explode in ways that surprise the observer and very often the scholar as well?"[15]

Professor Varshney observed two categories of civic intercommunal relationships and engagement: *associational* and *everyday*. By *associational* he means political parties, business associations, trade unions, professional associations, reading clubs, film clubs, sports clubs, festival organizations, and the like. By *everyday*, he means routine interactions of life such as Hindu and Muslim families living in the same neighborhoods and visiting each other, eating together, jointly participating in festivals, and allowing their children to play together in the neighborhood.

While both categories of relationships are healthy and help to attenuate tensions, the associational relationships are far better at withstanding strong shocks. In urban settings, personal relationships tend to be fewer, which explains why Hindu-Muslim violence tends to be primarily an urban, rather than a village, phenomenon. The presence of associational relationships prevented violence in cities with the same Hindu-Muslim demographics as those where violence occurred but where such associational relationships were absent.

Looking at the nature of the associational relationships, we see immediately why they are binding. Issues of money and power tend to be concentrated in associational forms of civic engagement rather than in relationships of the everyday category. Business associations, trade unions, and political parties represent money and power connections, while reading, film, and sports clubs allow the formation of personal identity and common-interest bonds. In cities where networks of such social bonds, economic links, and power sharing relationships have existed across religious lines, these relationships dissipate the tensions that in other places percolate to the point of exploding. And in cases where violence has appeared imminent, Hindu and Muslim community leaders were able to keep it from erupting. They had vested interests to protect; the boundaries that separated "us" from the "other" were dissolved by the bonds of self-interest.

How might we apply this information to heal conflict, say between Israel and Palestine? One approach is to find ways to make the political and opinion leaders across the divide personal partners in each other's direct losses and gains. This example may sound simplistic, but if we could create a workable formula by which every time a Palestinian is killed by Israelis, the Israeli leadership personally loses a painfully large sum of money, and every time an Israeli is killed by Palestinians, the Palestinian leadership personally loses a painfully large sum of money, pressure would quickly be brought to bear at the highest levels to reduce the violence. This is the idea behind the blood money reparations, which are paid, under Islamic law, to the family of the victim by the assailant. Another application of this principle took place in older times, when binding ties were forged by marrying the king or prince to a princess from the other side. Today, we cannot expect to see Ariel Sharon's son marry Yasir Arafat's daughter, but you get the point. In today's world, the solution requires a critical mass of associational ties across the divide, including a wide variety of business, civic, and social ventures.

EXCUSE ME, BUT WHICH GOD ARE YOU FIGHTING FOR?

Contrary to popular opinion, the Quran, as the latest iteration of the Abrahamic ethic, expressly and unambiguously prohibits the use of coercion in faith because coercion would violate a fundamental human right—the right to a free conscience. A different belief system is not deemed a legitimate cause for violence or war under Islamic law. The Quran is categorical on this: "There shall be no compulsion in religion" (2:256); "Say to the disbelievers [that is, atheists or polytheists, namely those who reject God]: ... 'To you your beliefs, and to me mine'" (109:1–6).

Let us investigate these issues further. People will fight for what they value personally. I'm far more likely to become emotionally involved if someone throws a rock through my window than through a stranger's living room window across town. When our personal territory is transgressed, our buttons of aggressive and defensive instinct are pressed. This is an application of the late House Speaker Tip O'Neill's well-known observation that "all politics is local."

We are hardwired this way, to defend values that are dear to us— just as a mother elephant will fight to the death to protect her baby elephant, whom she values highly. A mother elephant may fight for another elephant's baby, although likely with less passion, but she certainly won't fight for a lioness's baby. We humans have an unfortunate tendency to regard people of different religions, races, or ethnic origins as almost a different species and therefore to be valued and treated differently from ourselves!

In fighting for something, people will always justify their position in terms of their deepest values: namely, justice, truth, honor, freedom, national pride, or the protection of a loved one. For some, God is the All-being Creator, in whom is anchored their understanding of absolute justice, absolute truth, absolute love, absolute freedom. Atheists and agnostics, who do not share the idea of a Being-Creator and may indeed consider that belief to be silly, nevertheless will often fight for ideals like justice, truth, honor, and democracy. Thus it is perfectly logical and natural that people will fight—and sometimes to the death—in the name of their "God," whether a personal God or something that represents their deepest-held human values.

As noted previously, the Quran does not allow aggression against others *just because* of their beliefs. In a particularly instructive verse, the Quran goes further and *even forbids aggression against those who reject God*, instructing Muslims to be pluralist and open to other's belief systems:

> Follow that which is revealed to you from your Lord—there is no god but He; and turn away from the polytheists [meaning, "leave them alone"]. Had God willed, they would not have set up others [other gods to be worshiped]. We haven't appointed you over them as a protector, nor are you their guardian [meaning, you aren't responsible for their disbelief in God]. Do not curse the gods that they call upon [in worship] lest they in turn curse God in enmity [to you] out of their [understandable] ignorance. Thus have We made every people think their actions are beautiful. But then they will return to God, Who will inform them about what they really did. (Quran 6:107–9)

In a highly instructive teaching, the Prophet showed how being unkind to others can reflect unkindness upon ourselves: "One of the most heinous acts is for a person to curse his parents," to which someone asked, "O Messenger of God, how could a person [stoop so low as to] curse his parents?" He replied: "He curses the father of another man and in retort the other person curses his own father and mother."[16] Muslim jurists have taken this to mean that we are responsible for others' hostility toward us if it results from their own ignorance and as a response to our aggression against their values.

The Quran allows fighting only in defense—when we are attacked or thrown from our homes or denied our basic rights because of what we choose to believe:

> God does not forbid you from acting well and justly to those [who do not believe in God] who do not fight you because of your religion, nor expel you from your homes; God loves the just. God only forbids you from patronizing those who fight you because of your [choice of] religion, and expel you from

your homes, and aid others in your expulsion. Those trusting them are wrongdoers. (Quran 60:8–9)

But even in those cases where fighting is allowed, the Quran never allows the killing of innocent people and instructs the Muslims to lay down arms as soon as the other side sues for peace: "And if they incline [or sue] for peace, you also [must] incline to it, and trust in God" (Quran 8:61). Spontaneous aggression is strictly prohibited: "If they [unbelievers] leave you alone, do not fight you and offer you peace, God does not permit you any excuse [literally, allows you no way] to be against them [that is, to be aggressive toward them]" (Quran 4:90).

These Quranic principles are extremely important, and Muslim leaders, as well as leaders of all faiths, should take the time to understand them. Non-Muslims should use these verses in their discussions with Muslims. What these Quranic verses mean is not only that humans are free to believe the way we wish to but also, and perhaps more important, that differences in beliefs should not be the basis of denying anyone their human and civil rights or their full participation in the social and economic worlds in which they live. This is the core condition of pluralism, a fundamental Islamic ethic strongly supported in the Quran.

DON'T BE MESSING WITH OUR CHERISHED BELIEFS!

The following section of the Quran points out the emotional ties that bind us to our beliefs and traditions, and how, in spite of our conviction that we are logical and right-minded, we find beliefs and traditions extremely difficult to alter:

And they swear with the strongest oaths that if God sent down a sign [meaning some miracle] that they would then believe. Say to them: Signs belong to God [miracles, in other words, are up to God]. And what makes you think that if We sent down miracles they would believe? . . . But even if We sent angels down to them, made the dead speak to them, and brought all kinds of things to them, they still wouldn't believe unless God willed them to; but most of them are ignorant of that. (Quran 6:110, 112)

What God is saying here is, "Been there, done that." Human attachment to dogmatic ideas and traditional beliefs, even when wrong, is proverbial. There is a wonderful Jewish story that makes this point well. At a gathering of rabbis the wise men were debating a section of Holy Law, and one of them found himself at odds with the rest of the group on a point of interpretation. Knowing he was right, he called upon God to intercede. "Please, God, if I am right, let the streams of Israel flow uphill," the rabbi prayed. Immediately the waters of the land changed direction. Unfortunately, his adversaries were unmoved. "Please, God, if I am right may the trees bend to the ground." And they did. But still his fellows were intransigent. "Dear God, may you speak aloud and support me," he begged. The clouds promptly parted and a great voice from heaven boomed forth: "My friends, I have to tell you, you are wrong and he is right. This is what I intended." The lone elder smiled in triumph, but the group remained unimpressed. "Oh, we pay no attention to heavenly voices," they said, "because the correct answer on this point was written down and determined long ago." And you still wonder why even prophets with miracles were rejected?

Trying to convince people purely by the logic of your argument is an uphill battle. You're better off appealing to their emotions. If people are emotionally attracted to your idea, then they are more likely to generate their own arguments in support of it. Changing long-held and cherished beliefs, even when they are clearly mistaken, is extremely difficult. This is why the role of clear-sighted and clear-thinking mainstream religious leaders—from all faith traditions—is so critically important.

YOU SURE GOD TOLD YOU TO DO IT?

Returning to the issue of when the use of force is justified, let us look at the importance of the *intent* on the part of the actor. Humans are highly sensitive to disingenuousness and insincerity of intention. Women upset with their husbands will blurt "Don't 'sweetheart' me!" when the apparently contrite husband tries to sweet-talk her. It isn't that she doesn't approve of his sweet words, it's that she sees just action not matching intention. We understandably question people's intentions, especially when they claim to fight for a certain cause. The furor against Prime Minister Tony Blair in Great Britain and in the United States because no weapons of mass destruction were found in Iraq arose because it looked like the true motive for the war was in fact something else. People hate being fooled, and many wondered if Iraq would have been invaded had it lacked oil. This is why, in a court of law, intention is critical. We don't judge it murder when someone's car slips on an icy road and slams into a pedestrian. We judge it as accidental homicide, very different from premeditated homicide; that is murder.

The very first hadith in Imam Bukhari's collection quotes the Prophet saying, "Actions are judged by intention."[17] Imam Shafi'i, founder of the school of jurisprudence in Islamic law that goes by his name, believed that this one hadith contained one-third of all wisdom. And Islamic spiritual teachers never tire of warning us to watch and guard our intention and to purify the intentions with which we perform our spiritual and religious practice. This is no less true of political or military intentions.

When people want to do something and they seek your support in their action, they invariably proffer reasons that they know will resonate with you. What better reason to cite than *your* most deeply held values? So many people claim to be doing something "for God." The following well-known story about two men in adjacent beds in a psychiatric ward makes this very point. The doctor asks the first why he did what he did, and the patient answers, "God asked me to do it," to which the other man retorts, "No, I didn't." But this humorously begs the question, Do we accept what others are ostensibly doing in God's name as *really* being done in God's name?

Let's take as an example the Aum Shinrikyo group, whose members in March 1995 released poisonous sarin gas in the Tokyo subway system, killing several commuters and injuring thousands. Historian of religion Mark Juergensmeyer considers them "an offshoot of Japanese Buddhism" and asks, "Why would religion, much less Buddhism, lead to such a thing?"[18]

Juergensmeyer interviewed Takeshi Nakamura, one of Aum's members, who joined because he was looking for something personally transformative and socially prophetic, not like most forms of (Japanese) Buddhism, which, to him, were "for scholars or existed solely to facilitate funerary rites." He regarded Japanese society as hierarchical and powerful, one that did not adequately exemplify the principles of justice, fairness, and freedom, a society that could not easily change. Aum's leader, Shoko Asahara, offered through his movement "not only a mystical personal experience [which Juergensmeyer says was achieved by having the initiates sip a beverage from a glass laced with LSD] but also an egalitarian community and a vision of a transformed social order that greatly appealed to Nakamura's social concerns." It becomes clear that Asahara is motivated as much by an internal rage against Japanese society as by an internal desire for power, to "be like a king," and "to be like Christ."[19] An old expression goes, "Buddha and the devil are never more than a hair's breadth apart."[20] If we fail to recognize this hair's breadth of difference, we risk confusing right expressions of religiousness with wrong expressions, and in the process, we may do wrong to others. This is why sincere Buddhists do not regard Aum Shinrikyo as a genuine expression of Buddhism, any more than sincere Muslims regard September 11 as a genuine expression of Islam. In the words of another old saying, "Every man has been given a set of keys, which can open the gates of heaven. The same keys however, can also open the gates of hell."

Spiritual seekers seek to be religious in the sense of being pious. But they can easily come under the influence of those whose intentions are about power or wealth—two "gods" to whose seductive powers few humans are completely immune. All authentic spiritual traditions teach the importance of making sure that we are not fooled, a matter that is not as easy as we might think. As the great Sufi master Jalaluddin Rumi said, "Fool's gold exists because there is real gold."

When people kill in the name of God, they are usually really doing so in the name of their ego, their struggle for power, or their desire to obtain some other asset. This asset may even be their desire for justice, which is easily couched in religious terms. Juergensmeyer shows that some Buddhists are just as susceptible to couching their desire for justice in religious arguments by reminding the reader that Sri Lanka's prime minister in 1959, W. R. D. Bandaranaike, was killed by a Buddhist monk. Since Buddhists believe in the law of karma, Juergensmeyer explains that "politicians who were ruthless and were seen as enemies of religion could reasonably expect bloodshed as a sort of karmic revenge for their actions."[21]

Aum's leader Asahara misinterpreted the Tibetan Buddhist concept of *phoa*—transferring consciousness from the living to the dead to elevate their spiritual merit in reincarnation—to conclude that in some cases he was helping people by killing them. Juergensmeyer explains: "If the persons killed are scoundrels, or are enmeshed in social systems so evil that further existence in this life will result in even greater negative karmic debt, then those who kill are doing their victims a favor by enabling them to die early. Their early deaths would be a kind of mercy killing, allowing their souls to move to a higher plane (or more accurately *prevent* them from descending to a lower plane) than they would otherwise have been able to achieve."[22] This is not so different from Islamic militants who believe that innocent victims of their militancy automatically get into Paradise so they are being done a favor.

Imam Shadhili, sheikh of the Shadhili Sufi order, warns spiritual seekers: "Be familiar with the Whisperer [Satan's] conveying something resembling knowledge that has come presumably by way of inspiration and unveiling." He advises the spiritual traveler to ignore this if it violates "the decisive truth from Scripture and the Prophet's teachings."[23]

If we eliminate the usual, common sources of conflict, namely, perceived injustice in power and economics, and if we create a society in which people of all religious persuasions participate together in their collective governance and have equal access to the material fruits of society—a society that exemplifies the principles of justice, fairness, and freedom—we shall have eliminated most of the underlying reasons why people kill in the name of God.

AREN'T MUSLIMS REQUIRED TO WAGE JIHAD?

Jihad means "struggle." While Muslims use the term *lesser jihad* to refer to what Christians call a "just war," the term *greater jihad* refers to the psychological war we wage within ourselves to establish the kingdom of God in our behavior and to build a lifestyle that reflects God's commandments, both in our individual life and in our collective communal lives. Jihad is about building what Western philosophers would call "the good society."[24]

Muslims are strongly encouraged to follow the practice, or precedent, of the Prophet, called his *sunnah*. At an individual level, we try to emulate him in our spirituality, in how we deal with our family, friends, and colleagues. To provide guidance in complex situations, many American Christians now ask in a given situation, "What would Jesus do?" Muslims have been asking, "What would the Prophet do?" ever since the Prophet's time. A collection of the Prophet's sayings and actions, called the Hadith, is used not only as a guide for Muslims' behavior but also as a primary source of Islamic law after the Quran.

At a collective level, all Muslims have a dream that they will someday live in a society that governs itself like the Prophet's did in Medina from 622 to his death in 632 CE. This is the Muslims' equivalent of the biblical kingdom of God, and Muslims have always had a strong desire to find ways to reestablish the basis of such a society.

Sometimes this desire has led to expressions of returning to a past ideal, to the times of the "pious predecessors" (*as-salaf as-salih* in Arabic). For example, in the late nineteenth century neoorthodox reformers began a group in Egypt calling themselves *salafis*, aiming to regenerate Islam by a return to the tradition represented by the "pious forefathers." They, like other similar Muslim groups, are trying to recreate an ideal.

This is not all that different from American constitutional lawyers who speak about the original intent of the founders and the nation's need to respect constitutional provisions written two centuries ago. This doesn't mean that these constitutionalists want to return to life in the late 1770s. But the struggle to maintain a democratic society that respects our Bill of Rights is analogous to the struggle to establish a just society that is part of the Muslim "group jihad." In some ways, the "group jihad" is the struggle to wage a constitutional society in the Islamic understanding of that term.

Rutgers University scholar Benjamin Barber, in his book *Jihad vs. McWorld*, describes two fronts in America's war against terrorism since September 11 that reflect and well describe this Muslim understanding. The lesser jihad for Americans would be the deployment of our professional military, intelligence, and diplomatic resources to combat terrorism and perceived threats to U.S. security. Applying this idea to American efforts to deal with the Saddam Hussein regime, the lesser jihad would be the war that ousted him militarily.

The greater jihad is "winning the peace" in Iraq—and in the rest of the Middle East. This is what Barber calls "the second front," which must engage "every citizen with a stake in democracy and social justice, both within nation-states and in the relations between them. It transforms anxious and passive spectators into resolute and engaged participants—the perfect antidote to fear."[25]

While the lesser jihad is usually advanced in the name of retributive justice and parochial (in our case secular) interests, it must be followed by the greater jihad, advanced in the name of distributive justice and religious and social pluralism.[26] This is the Jihad of Peace—conducted on behalf of all humankind.

The first Quranic verse allowing the Prophet and his followers to fight those who had unjustly aggressed against the Muslims, expelling them from their homes because of their religion, reads as follows:

> Permission [to fight] is given to those against whom war is wrongfully waged, and have been oppressed—and God is indeed able to aid them—those who have been unjustly expelled from their homes for no other cause than they say "Our Lord is God." And had God not repelled some people by others, it is certain that cloisters and churches and synagogues and mosques, in which God's name is much extolled, would have been destroyed. (Quran 22:39–40)

The Quranic mention of cloisters, churches, synagogues, and mosques clearly proves that the objective of fighting must be, first, defensive and, second, to establish a pluralistic religious society, where God's name is extolled in all languages. Jihad is therefore legitimate only to further the Abrahamic ethic, to further political and religious freedom and justice.

The Quran adds,

> God does not forbid you respecting those who do not fight you on the basis of religion, nor expel you from your homes, that you be kind and deal justly with them. God indeed loves those who deal justly. God only forbids you regarding those who fight you on the basis of your religion, who expel you from your homes, and aid others in your expulsion—that you

ally with them. Whoever allies with them are unjust. (Quran 60:9–10)

It urged the Muslims to "fight in the way of God those who fight against you, but do not yourselves commit aggression: God does not love the aggressors" (Quran 2:190); "Expel them from where they expelled you" (Quran 2:191); "Fight them until there is no more persecution, and people are free to worship God [literally, 'and all religion is for God's sake']. But if they desist, then all hostility shall cease except against the oppressors" (Quran 2:190).

Jihad is not limited to the military sphere. The Prophet said, "The most excellent jihad is to speak up for truth [meaning to stand up for what is right and just] in the face of a tyrannical authority."[27]

Islamic jurisprudence thus contains the concept of a just war, as does Western law and jurisprudence. This concept of just war addresses a variety of questions. When are we permitted to conduct war? Under what circumstances? How do we decide? Muslims also have a detailed understanding and description of who is to be considered a legitimate target and who is not. It is noteworthy that Islamic jurists ruled clearly that the attacks of September 11 were not allowed under Islamic law. Those acts of terror were not within the norms of a just war. A number of the Islamic world's greatest jurists stated this publicly, but unfortunately, this fact received little attention in American news media.[28]

DYING TO KILL

While we have seen that jihad, a just, defensive war, is sanctioned under Islamic law, suicide no matter to what end is expressly forbidden. The strongest prohibitions are in the Hadith, where the Prophet made explicit statements such as "Whosoever shall kill himself shall suffer in the fire of hell"[29] and "shall be excluded from heaven forever."[30] It is also related that the Prophet refused the funeral rites to a person who committed suicide.[31] A particularly poignant story is given by the Prophet describing an occupant of hell. This was a man who fought on the Prophet's side, was wounded in battle, and, unable to stand the pain of his injury, fell on his sword.[32] The Prophet remarks in a version of this hadith that "a man may appear to people as performing the acts of an inhabitant of Paradise while he is [in the Hereafter] an occupant of Hell, and a man may appear to people as performing the acts of an inhabitant of Hell while he is an occupant of Paradise."

There is not a single incident under any circumstances, no matter how extenuating, in which the Prophet permitted suicide. The strongest Quranic prohibition on taking one's life is given by the following particularly compassionate set of verses:

> God desires to be merciful to you, . . . to make light your burdens, for man is created weak. . . . Do not kill yourselves; certainly God is Ever Merciful to you. And whoever commits this aggressively and unjustly, We shall cast him into the Fire; and this is easy for God. (Quran 4:27–30)

While the majority of exegetes have interpreted the phrase "do not kill yourselves" to mean "do not kill each other," some have taken it also to be a prohibition against suicide. Why, then, have some Muslim jurists approved of suicide bombing against non-Muslims and now even against fellow Muslims? The short answer is that they gave it a different name: martyrdom operations. In this view, the perpetrators of suicide bomb attacks are willing to give up their lives for a greater cause in which they strongly believe, following the tradition of Japanese kamikaze pilots and the Tamil Tigers of Sri Lanka.

The longer answer requires two things: that I offer a mini-course in the logic of Islamic jurisprudence and that we look at the sociological aspect of suicide.

First, let's discuss the concept of "the permitted (*halal*) and forbidden (*haram*)" in Islamic law.

In Islam, all human actions can be divided into the two classes of what is permitted and what is forbidden, so that whatever is not expressly forbidden is de facto permitted. Some people try to make a list of all possible actions and then tell you that if they don't find it on their "permitted" list, it's automatically forbidden. Others do the reverse: if they don't find it on their "forbidden" list, it's automatically permitted. The latter is usually easier because the "forbidden" list is much shorter.

This question of whether a particular act is permitted or forbidden is the domain and objective of Islamic law, generally called Shariah, which Muslims regard as being God's law, covering the subject of what God has commanded. This body of law is primarily the commandments and prohibitions mentioned in the Quran, regarded by Muslims as literally the word of God, and secondarily those of the Prophet Muhammad, who amplified, explained, and interpreted the Quranic injunctions and in some cases also legislated. These two primary sources of Islamic law are often called "the texts." All other subsidiary sources of Islamic law arise from human efforts to interpret the texts or to derive new laws that are consistent, or at the very least not inconsistent, with the texts. Such secondary sources have included the consensus of opinion (*ijma'*), analogy to existing rules (*qiyas*), public interest (*maslaha*), social customs ('*urf* or '*adat*), state legislation, and judicial opinions, among others.[33]

Within the first three centuries after the Prophet's death, a number of great scholars developed the science of Islamic jurisprudence, called *fiqh* in Arabic, and recognized that, even in the case of some issues pertaining to worship commanded in the Quran and as explained by the Prophet's practice, more than one interpretation was valid.

This could happen in a number of ways. The Prophet sometimes did something differently at different times; for example, he used to pray with his hands crossed on his chest, but he also prayed with his hands straight down his sides. Thus while both schools regarded these variations as valid, one school preferred one method while another preferred the other. Or the Prophet traveled once during Ramadan, and some companions fasted, others did not, intending to make it up later after the month of Ramadan, since the Quran permitted travelers to postpone their fast; the Prophet approved both ways.

Another example of differing and evolving interpretations is given by the Quranic injunction that enjoins Muslims to leave their business at a certain time on Friday and hasten to the Friday prayer, after which they may return to their business. During the Prophet's time, the entire community did that in Medina.

But as the community grew and Islam spread to non-Muslim countries and societies, the question arose as to whether this injunction invalidated a business transaction conducted by a Muslim during the time of Friday prayer. While one school of law may interpret the Quran as forbidding such a business transaction (this is true in Saudi Arabia today, where all businesses are required to shut down even during the five-times-daily prayer), another school might say that while it is a sin for someone not to perform the Friday prayer, the business transaction is nevertheless deemed valid. If you try suing a case in a Saudi court today, claiming that during the time of the Friday prayer you skipped the prayers and instead sat behind your defendant's closed doors and agreed to a deal on which he later reneged, the judge will likely not be amused by your lack of religiosity, and he might be disinclined even to hear your case. And if you've ever been in front of a judge, you know that a judge with no appetite for your case is unlikely to be careful in his judgment. The closest equivalent in America would be a deal transacted on a Sunday in violation of the "blue law" forbidding sales on Sunday, except that the law was written commanding you to "leave your business and perform the mass," after which you could go back and do the deal.

So we see how societal questions evolved that could be interpreted in more than one way, and this eventually led to the rise of a number of schools of jurisprudence (*madhhab*, plural *madhahib*), each of which generally regarded the others' opinions as valid but less preferable to its own.[34]

Most specific issues enjoined by the Quran or the Prophet were clear, but in other areas, Muslims had to exert real effort to arrive at a sense of what would or would not be legally permissible. Whatever was finally determined to be legally consistent was deemed *shar'i*, a word that many Muslims confuse to mean "necessarily required by God."

To illustrate how easily Muslims have gotten confused on this point, let's say that on the basis of *maslaha*, the public interest, we establish a law saying that for the sake of safety, motorists cannot drive faster than fifty-five miles per hour. This law is *shar'i*, which means that it is certainly consistent with the Quran and the *sunnah* (precedents established by the Prophet), as it emanates from complying with the ethics of the Quran, which values the preservation of human life. So you can have a Muslim jurist issue a fatwa (a legal opinion) that this law is *shar'i*. But that does not mean that violating this particular law is a sin. This is where some Muslims get confused, because not all Shariah law is Quranic law, although all Quranic law is Shariah law. In fact, over fourteen hundred years, in over fifty countries, Muslim jurists have developed an entire body of Shariah law that is neither Quranic nor *sunnah.*

The above example was perhaps easy to see through, but let's look at another. While the Quran explicitly prohibits the drinking of wine (and by extension all intoxicants), no penalty was ever imposed either by the Quran or the Prophet for committing this sin. However, during the caliphate of Umar (who ruled from 634 to 644 CE), there was a Muslim fellow who when drunk uttered loud, libelous statements in the streets of Medina about members of the community. Deciding that they needed to stop this offense, Umar convened a session of experts, and Ali, later the fourth caliph, recommended that the offending person receive forty lashes, this being the penalty for libel.

This penalty effectively ended the drunk's offensive bellowing, but it later became the Shariah penalty for the sin of drinking wine. But imagine a Muslim judge in Peshawar being asked to rule on a drunk who merely fell in a stupor on the roadside but who uttered no libel and committed no other offense. If our judge checks his manuals and reads that "the Shari'ah imposes the penalty of forty lashes for the sin of drinking alcohol," and he doesn't know the foregoing bit of legal history and incorporate it into his thinking, what do you think he will do?

Prohibited acts are prohibited because we have appetites for them. God does not prohibit us from eating poisonous mushrooms and thorns because there is no need to; we know that they are bad for us. But there are things that are bad for us or for our society for which we have prodigious appetites. How many of us can resist scanning the gossipy pages of the *National Enquirer* while standing at the checkout counter at the local grocery store? How many people find illegal ways to transfer funds into their accounts? People have tastes for these sins of gossip, theft, adultery, even killing—and that is why these actions that harm society are prohibited.

While sins are prohibited, the concept of necessity (*darurah*) permits a temporary and specific lifting of the prohibited act. For example, while killing is expressly forbidden, if a rapist attacks a woman and she kills him in self-defense, we call this justifiable homicide. And although consuming alcohol is prohibited, drinking Nyquil, which is one-third alcohol, to reduce the effects of the flu is permissible because of its necessity, but only until your flu is gone. Once you've recovered, your excuse disappears.

As we saw in the previous chapter, Muslim jurists have defined five fundamental objectives or rights that the Shariah law is obliged to protect: life, religion, property, family, and sanity.[35] If application of a particular law jeopardizes any of these, it may be temporarily suspended. For this reason, when the religious police (*mutawwi'un*) prevented schoolgirls from escaping a fire in a Saudi school just because the girls weren't wearing their veils, those policemen were acting in direct violation of the core values of Shariah law. In essence, some Muslims today have forgotten the key Shariah principle that, to borrow a phrase from the teaching of Jesus, the Shariah was made for man and not man for the Shariah.

In conclusion, several explanations exist for the legal approval that some Muslim jurists have given for suicide bombing. Many of these jurists have defined for themselves a pragmatic distinction between suicide and martyrdom. This view holds that because Palestinians are victims of Israeli occupation and have suffered from illegal settlements and the loss of their homes and lands, Palestinians have a right under Islamic law to defend themselves militarily. Furthermore, because the Palestinians have no conventional military force with which to defend themselves, these jurists have used the rule of necessity to allow the use of suicide bombing ("martyrdom") against Israeli targets. Problematic as suicide bombing is theologically, it has become hailed within Palestinian circles as the only means of drawing world attention to their plight.

None of this alters the fact, however, that the Prophet himself always condemned suicide, regardless of mitigating circumstances.

A SOCIOLOGICAL VIEW OF SUICIDE BOMBING

Suicide bombing is a tragic phenomenon that strikes at us all. It takes a terrible toll of innocent lives, while it also reflects the deep despair and hopelessness of its perpetrators. It is a phenomenon that no civilized society—in the Muslim world or the West—should be content to accept. Solving a problem invariably requires understanding it; and to solve the problem of suicide bombing, it is essential that we stretch our minds around its psychological, sociological, and even biological aspects as we investigate its underlying impulses.

In his classic work, *Suicide,* sociologist Emile Durkheim makes a number of important observations about suicide. Durkheim's most counterintuitive finding is that *the suicide rate is constant for a given society.* Suicide is a function of collective or societal issues rather than individual issues, and the general suicide rate can be explained only sociologically, not individually. The individual causes for suicide are often hard to identify because those who succeed are not around to explain their act; we can only observe causes for attempted suicides that fail or learn from those who succeed and leave behind detailed explanations.[36]

Durkheim found that statistically suicide correlates less with individual phenomena than with social phenomena, such as the family, political and economic society, and religious group. These correlate within a given society to a collective inclination toward suicide, "a rate of self-homicide which is fairly constant for each society as long as the basic conditions of its existence remain the same. . . . This inclination is a reality in itself, exterior to the individual and exercising a coercive effect upon him."[37]

Durkheim divides suicides into three categories:

1. When individuals are rigidly integrated into their society and their lives are rigorously governed by custom and habit, suicide may be *altruistic.* Here the individual may take his or her own life because of higher commandments, either those of religious sacrifice or unthinking political allegiance.[38] Here the individual sacrifices himself or herself for the sake of the community.

2. Opposite to the case above, *egoistic* suicide results from the individual's lack of integration into society. This can occur when the individual, ungoverned by custom and habit, is left to his or her own resources with little family or community support. This type of suicide is infrequent in cultures that closely integrate the individual into the collective life. If in the first case society overintegrates the individual, in the second it underintegrates him or her.[39]

3. *Anomic* suicide (from the term *anomie*) occurs when the individual feels completely alienated by a sudden collapse of social stability

and standards. In this case, the individual's needs and their satisfaction were in the past regulated by society, but something fundamentally upsets this regulation, causing a profound state of psychological alienation. An example would be a person who finds sudden wealth and is unable to cope with her new opportunities or a prisoner who, upon winning parole after thirty years of a socially structured life within prison walls, is unable to cope with freedom.

Here the common social beliefs and practices that underpin the person's life make him or her the embodiment of what Durkheim calls the "collective conscience"; anomic suicide "is the reflection of society at work in the individual." In a complex society, some individuals become highly dependent upon the traditional social structure in which they live. When a sudden crisis upends this structure, anomie may manifest itself in an increasing suicide rate. And "where the rate increases rapidly, it is symptomatic of the breakdown of the collective conscience, and of a basic flaw in the social fabric."[40]

Durkheim argues that individual forms of suicide display mixed types, such as the ego-anomic, altruistic-anomic, and ego-altruistic. George Simpson, an editor of Durkheim's work, observes, "The most widely accepted view today in psychoanalysis is that suicide is most often a form of 'displacement'; that is, the desire to kill someone who has thwarted the individual is turned back upon the individual himself." In the case of anomic suicide, "the individual inflicts upon himself the result of the frustration and anger caused by the perceived unraveling of the social fabric of his world."

It is noteworthy that high-income groups have relatively high suicide rates. This is consistent with the fact, for example, that the suicide bombers who flew planes into the World Trade Center and the Pentagon came from relatively well-to-do families. Durkheim explains, "Those who suffer the most are not those who kill themselves most. . . . Life is most readily renounced at the time and among the classes where it is least harsh."[41]

Durkheim suggests that anything can serve as the occasion for suicide.[42] The private experiences usually thought to be the causes of suicide reflect the victim's moral predisposition, which itself echoes the moral state of society. An individual may feel sad, but the sadness arises not from a particular incident, argues Durkheim, but from the group to which the person belongs. Of particular importance, Durkheim also found that "suicide cannot be halted in its upward curve by education, exhortation, or repression. . . . All ameliorative measures must go to the question of social structure."

Applying Durkheim's insights to the phenomenon of suicide bombing committed in the name of Islam, and in particular the suicide bombings in Israel and those of September 11, and those in Saudi Arabia, Morocco, Kenya, and in Iraq, we can reasonably infer the following:

The conscious willfulness of the perpetrators is experienced by them as a form of extreme altruism. Imitating the Japanese kamikaze pilots of World War II and the Tamil Tigers of Sri Lanka, they feel they are sacrificing themselves for a cause that will make them heroes in their community. Simultaneously, however, at a deeper level, this conscious willfulness is fueled by profound anomie—a powerful sense of alienation caused by a deep tear in the traditional society and culture. Noting that the kamikaze and Tamil Tiger suicide operations were conducted at a time when the Japanese and the Tamil Tigers were losing their wars, we may additionally observe that suicide operations do not arise from a collective sense of success.

Robert Pape, a political scientist who studied suicide terrorism from 1980 to 2001, points out, "Religion is not the force behind suicide terrorism." He says, "The data show that there is little connection between suicide terrorism and Islamic fundamentalism, or any religion for that matter," adding that the group responsible for the highest percentage (40 percent) of all suicide attacks has been the Tamil Tigers in Sri Lanka, who are adamantly opposed to religion. Rather, he suggests, nearly all suicide terrorist campaigns are "coherent political or military campaigns," whose common objective is a specific and strategic goal, namely, to compel military forces to withdraw from their homeland. Religion is rarely the root cause, although it is used as a tool in recruiting and can be employed to serve the broader strategic objective. "From Lebanon to Israel to Sri Lanka to Kashmir to Chechnya," the objective was "to establish or maintain political self-determination."[43]

Without consciously using Durkheim's model, those Muslim jurists who have judged suicide bombings as permissible (calling them martyrdom operations) have in effect differentiated altruistic suicide from other forms of suicide and have judged it to be a justifiable sacrifice toward the greater good of their society.

Suicide bombing in the name of Islam is therefore a *sociopolitical* phenomenon, not a theological one. The group identity provided by religion provides the basis for making a statement from within the collective conscience of Islamic society, namely, that the collective anomie is crying out for correction; that the collective conscience of Muslim society has broken down; that a basic flaw exists in its current social fabric. The perpetrators' acts, which at first seem to express only their personal temperament or fanaticism, are really the external expression of a deeply rooted societal angst.

Muslim society, feeling injustice and pain, is collectively "reaching out" (in Durkheim's terms) to those viewed as causing the pain. Because the perpetrators are generally above average in education and material well-being compared to the rest of Muslim society, their willingness to commit suicide may be partly a compensation for guilt for their own situations and on behalf of the flaws in their society. To borrow Christian language, they are offering themselves up both for the sins of their community and for the sins of those whom they perceive to be acting against their community. Suicide bombing in the name of Islam[44] is an expression of rage by the Islamic collective conscience directed against those viewed as thwarting the *political* aspirations of Muslim society and exacerbating old psychic wounds and frustrations—wounds and frustrations that overshadow anything that life currently has to offer.

As one who has ministered to people in times of difficulty, such as a mother depressed over the loss of a child or a lost pregnancy or a friend suffering from terminal illness and physical pain impossible to medicate, I have found that people in such states of depression are unable to find meaning in either their liberty or their lives. People can simply be so unhappy that they can appreciate neither their freedom nor the many options remaining to them. In this state, they may consider and even attempt to terminate their own lives. Such depression can afflict societies as well as individuals. Americans have a trenchant name for committing suicide: "checking out" from life.

Any long-term solution to the problem of suicide bombing must address the pain and hopelessness felt by many in Muslim societies, and ameliorating the pain requires that we examine the social issues that contribute to it. We must address those aspects of Muslim society that feed the phenomenon of suicide bombing, and we must especially take account of Islam's strong sense of social justice, a sense that has real impact on the psychology of individual Muslims and of Muslim society as a whole.

And herein lies hope. Perceived social injustices can be corrected. Tears in a social fabric can be repaired. The collective anomie that fuels suicide bombings can be healed. Two things are needed: a deep, thorough understanding of the underlying societal pathology; and an extremely skillful, sensitive approach to its treatment. The latter will require, among other things, that the West and the Islamic world work together to find ways to improve individual lives by assimilating core principles of participatory governance into Islamic societies. Ultimately, the effort will also require a solution to the Israeli-Palestinian conflict— because for millions of Muslims, that conflict has become a metaphor for much of what is wrong between the Muslim world and the West.

Solving the Israeli-Palestinian conflict, however, may not be as impossible as it sounds. Moderates on both sides of the conflict already agree on most, if not all, of the key principles that will almost certainly be incorporated into the final settlement, whenever it comes. Even more important, polls indicate that substantial majorities on both sides of the conflict would accept these principles if they led to a just, secure, and lasting peace.[45]

In conclusion, eliminating suicide bombing will require that we address its underlying societal causes. This effort will be neither easy nor impossible—but it is absolutely essential to the future of our world. In later chapters, I will offer some specific ideas that could assist in achieving this goal.

"UNCONSTITUTIONAL" TO AMERICANS EQUALS "UN-ISLAMIC" TO MUSLIMS

Islam teaches a strong sense of social justice. Every Muslim has a personal ambition, at an individual level, to become a perfected human being, and the way we perfect ourselves is to try as much as possible to be like the Prophet. At the collective level, many in the Muslim community aspire to build a society that embodies the values established by the Prophet in Medina, when he personally ruled over that community. The first four caliphs after the Prophet were the most concerned about social justice. The caliph 'Umar, for instance, could not sleep if there was a hungry woman in Medina, and he would roam the streets at night to ensure that all were protected against the injustice of hunger. (In this way, he offered his own personal social safety net.) Unfortunately, since the time of the four "Rightly Guided" Caliphs, Muslims have lived under a good deal of injustice. Because Islam itself is felt to be rooted in justice, attempts today by Muslims to recreate a just society are often phrased in Islamic vocabulary and language.

Rational people can become violent when they see no alternative to correct an injustice. When America bombed Afghanistan in response to September 11, that was an act of violence targeted against those it believed to be perpetrators and supporters of the attack against America—justified in the name of America's deepest values.

When we Americans feel wronged on domestic issues involving our fundamental democratic values, we often blurt, "This is unconstitutional!" Even though we may not know which clause of the constitution is being violated, we just feel it in our gut. This statement, therefore, is primarily an intuitive expression, and most Americans still need the help of a constitutional lawyer to help them articulate the legal and logical arguments behind their intuitive sense of being wronged.

In a similar way, when Muslims feel violated, they may blurt out, "This is un-Islamic!" Muslims may not know which verse of the Quran or teaching of the Prophet is being violated, but their instinct tells them this. When Christians say, "This is un-Christian!" they mean that the act was uncharitable or unkind. The term *un-Islamic* to Muslims combines the meanings of *unconstitutional, unethical, wrong,* and *unkind.* Together, these add up to "sinful."

In the United States, when we want to correct a flaw in our democracy, we often address the issue in constitutional language, for that is the highest authority we can claim on our behalf. A favorite American expression when we see something wrong is "There ought to be a law against this!" If you're angry enough, you'll look for such a law and then use it to seek retribution. If we find an existing legal principle on our side, we may use it to sue and prove that the person wronging us has violated the law or the Constitution; and if we don't find the law we need, we may try to create it. In the United States, we do this by lobbying our congresswoman or senator to enact legislation.

Muslims are no different—but the authority to which they turn is religious. When wronged, Muslims rush to the Quran and Hadith collections to hunt for a verse or Prophetic teaching supporting their positions. Better yet, one might call upon the nearest mufti to obtain a fatwa on the matter. Usually Muslims can find some Quranic verse or teaching of the Prophet that justifies their sense of being wronged. "See," they conclude, "we *do* have a law against this! If only our law (Islamic Shariah law) were implemented, our sense of being wronged would be addressed!" And how can you go higher than God for authority?

The word *Shari'ah* means "road," and the implied imagery of the term is that our life is like a road in a desert, with God the oasis we seek. Thus the primary focus of Shariah law is on humankind's journey toward intimacy with our Creator, and the Shariah's purpose is to establish the links or guideposts between God and humanity. The Shariah is the body of divine guidance, its structure, format, and construct. It is important to Muslims because it is the guide by which the Muslim determines what is good or ethical. To Muslim ears, "Shariah law" means all that is constitutional, ethical, right, and compassionate—the conditions necessary for what Americans call the pursuit of happiness. This is why many Muslims seek to base their national legal systems on Shariah law, for that is the highest authority they can claim on their behalf in correcting wrongs.

Furthermore, claiming that God is on your side gains you popular support; this appears true in all cultures and religions. This is an additional reason why most of the political liberation movements in the Muslim world use Islamic religious vocabulary and give themselves names like Jema'ah Islamiyyah ("Islamic Group"), Hezbollah ("God's Party"), Lashkar Muhammad ("Muhammad's Soldiers"), and so forth. They use this religious language both because it comes naturally to Muslims when issues of fairness and justice arise and because it is the Muslim equivalent of draping oneself in the flag, to use the American expression.

Despite the Islamic names used by violent opposition groups in the

Muslim world, however, most of the support they attract in the streets is based on secular and material popular concerns. Caryle Murphy, who for many years was Middle East correspondent for the *Washington Post*, describes how Egypt's Jema'ah Islamiyyah (Islamic Group) was voicing the people's frustration and anger, "speaking on behalf of those who had no *wasta* [connections], saying out loud what they really thought of their neglectful and uncaring leaders." She quotes an Egyptian trucker who explained, "People don't sympathize with Jema'ah Islamiyyah because they love it, but because they hate the government. . . . Despair is the reason for the [Jema'ah]." Her interview with another Egyptian yields a similar analysis: "Part of the reason for the wave of Islamist violence in Egypt, was poverty and a lack of jobs. "It's economic," he said. "The solution is not to arrest people, but to find employment. But the government doesn't care about these very dangerous things."[46]

Taking Egypt as an example of the challenges facing the Muslim world—especially for those under thirty, who generally comprise substantial majorities of the population—many unemployed or underemployed people live without any light at the end of the tunnel. Murphy explains: "Egypt's problem is not terrorism but lack of democracy and respect for lawful institutions. Like the generals who aborted Algeria's 1992 election in an attempt to stop an Islamist movement from winning, the Egyptian government sent a message to its moderate Islamist opposition: The ballot box is a narrow gate through which you will not pass as long as we are in charge." Murphy's footnote to this quote is most instructive: "Ayman Zawahiri [Osama bin Laden's lieutenant] warned that the aborted 1992 Algerian election was proof that 'Western powers' and 'their clients' would never permit Islamic parties to come to power through the ballot box."[47]

The origins of so-called Islamic violence lie not in religion but in the politics and economics of the Muslim world. Without greater participation in governance and a healthy economy, scenes of unrelenting poverty and extreme frustration will continue to characterize much of the Middle East. This combination of conditions creates a fertile breeding ground for extremist philosophies and terrorism. To make matters worse, centralized economies, owned usually by the state, leave most Muslims feeling cut off from the economic wealth of the nation. They feel deprived of life, liberty, and the pursuit of happiness—rights that appear to be reserved for a tiny minority. Disenfranchised in their homelands, many Muslims cross deserts and oceans seeking these rights in Western lands, and it is only natural that they would use Islam's language of social justice to express their grievances and their aspirations for the freedoms and economic empowerment that many in the West routinely enjoy. And when a wrong goes unaddressed, people often become militant.

The critical lesson to draw from this discussion is that the popular drawing power of violent Islamist opposition groups derives not from religion, but from their ability to tap into the personal frustrations and feelings of social injustice that are felt daily by millions in the Muslim world. Violent groups have become adept at capitalizing on these frustrations and then addressing them with a religious vocabulary that inspires total commitment in their followers.

African American preachers used the vocabulary of religion in waging the civil rights struggle in the 1960s and 1970s. The Reverend Martin Luther King Jr. used the language of both the Bible and the Constitution to agitate for the correction of social wrongs. As affirmative action and civil rights programs began to improve the lives of African Americans and as they rose to become mayors, congressional representatives, generals, business leaders, Supreme Court justices, and even Secretary of State, the militancy of Black Power movements ebbed.

IS THE WAR ON TERRORISM THE NEW COLD WAR?

Since 1968, according to the RAND Corporation, the United States has been the country most frequently targeted by terrorists. The State Department's counterterrorism unit reported that during the 1990s, 40 percent of all acts of terrorism worldwide have been against American citizens and facilities.[48]

Webster's defines *terrorism* as the "use of terror and violence to intimidate, subjugate, etc., especially as a political weapon or policy; and the intimidation or subjugation so produced." In the last century we have added an additional meaning: the willingness by one side in a conflict to randomly kill innocent civilians—often including children—on the other side. The recipient society feels terrorized.

It is difficult to comprehend how any civilized society could condone the random killing of innocent civilians and children, and yet, sadly, the practice has become a fixture in today's world. Why? No easy answer exists to this terrible question, but we can gain a few clues by examining some profound cross-cultural misunderstandings. Terrorism is an extremely difficult issue to write about objectively, because no issue in my experience arouses passions that are (understandably) so inflamed and so immediate. I can only ask my reader, whether you come from a Western or a Muslim culture, to suspend your immediate judgments as you read this section and to try to put yourself in the shoes of someone from the other culture.

Dispassionate observers have noted that the term *terrorism* is almost always used to describe actions by the "other side" in a given conflict. "We" are therefore by definition never the terrorist, even when we use violent means to gain our objectives and even when innocent civilians and children are killed in the process.

Unfortunately, the word *terrorism,* highly charged as it is, is used differently in the Muslim world than in the West. My work in interfaith dialogue over the years has taught me that if we are to have any hope of solving disputes across divides, especially those between the Muslim world and the West, we must define our terms dispassionately. In doing so, we can begin to fathom both sides of the psychological divide and try to see ourselves as others see us. By using the vocabulary of our common high ground, a vocabulary that enables us to understand the psychology and viewpoint of the opposite side in the dispute, we may find ways to bridge the divide.

In the West, terrorism is usually defined by the acting party's intent to harm innocent people. If a suicide bomber intentionally takes the lives of innocent people, he is obviously guilty of terrorism. By contrast, if the United States and its coalition forces drop bombs on the wrong buildings in Baghdad (or any other city), and the bombs kill hundreds or thousands of innocent people, including many women and children, we define this as collateral damage, not terrorism. We draw this distinction because we had no intent to kill civilians. We sincerely regret the loss of civilian lives, but we consider this an unavoidable cost of attaining our greater goals, which might be freeing Iraq from Saddam Hussein, for example, or ensuring the security of the United States against attack by weapons of mass destruction.

By contrast, however, many Muslims in the Middle East look primarily at the results of our actions, not just the intent that we announce in order to justify them. Partly, this is due to the fact that a great many people in the Middle East simply do not trust what America says. As an example, many there believe that our government greatly exaggerated the scare over Iraqi weapons of mass destruction as a pretense to allow us to invade and achieve our government's true intention, which was finishing the job begun by George H. W. Bush in 1991 and strengthening America's energy security by imposing American hegemony over the Middle East. From this viewpoint, many Arabs have a hard time accepting the deaths of thousands of Iraqi civilians as mere collateral damage. The result is a common view in the Middle East that the United States is perfectly willing to kill innocent civilians when it suits America's goals.

Israelis and Palestinians usually disagree about which side is most guilty of terrorism. Israelis point with enormous, heartfelt passion to the innocent lives destroyed by Palestinian suicide bombers. To the Israeli mind, such attacks reflect a monstrous evil, and most Israelis have hardened in their view that the only way to stop such attacks is to respond with increasing violence toward organizations that direct these acts of terror. Israeli warplanes and tanks fire on homes and neighborhoods where Hamas members are suspected of hiding. Palestinian homes and whole villages are bulldozed in the name of Israeli security, while dividing walls are built through Palestinian farmlands.

In a Palestinian refugee camp in the occupied territories, however, the perspective on terrorism is quite different. Groups fighting the Israeli occupation are seen as willing to give their lives for the cause of the Palestinian people. While some Palestinians argue strongly that their fighters should restrict their attacks to Israeli military targets in and around illegal Jewish settlements, others accept the deaths of Israeli civilians in Tel Aviv as a cost of the liberation struggle.

Israelis point to the intentional, repeated killing of innocent civilians as obvious proof that the Palestinians are guilty of terrorism—and the horrible images of bomb victims cannot be denied. Palestinians, however, counter that the overall number of civilians killed is higher on their side, and they rage with equal passion against "Israeli terrorism," pointing, for example, to Israel's alleged complicity in the 1982 massacres of hundreds (or thousands) of Palestinians in the refugee camps of Sabra and Shatila. Meanwhile, the carnage on both sides continues.

The truth is that killing innocent people is always wrong—and no argument or excuse, no matter how deeply believed, can ever make it right. No religion on earth condones the killing of innocent people; no faith tradition tolerates the random killing of our brothers and sisters on this earth. God does not want us to kill each other: "Do not kill the soul which God has made sacred except by right [of justice]" (Quran 6:151). And God has certainly prohibited killing the most defenseless members of our societies.

Islamic law is clearly against terrorism, against any kind of deliberate killing of civilians or similar "collateral damage." The roots of terrorism lie not in theology but in human psychology and in the hatred born of violent conflict over politics, or power, and economic assets such as land.

In their frustration and rage, the perpetrators of what we call Islamic terrorism are telling us, as Benjamin Barber phrases it, "Your sons want to live; ours are ready to die." Our response must be this: "We will create a world in which the seductions of death hold no allure because the bounties of life are accessible to everyone."[49] This must be our collective global vision. Succeeding in this, we will have won the war on terrorism.

OSAMA BIN LADEN: A "MUSLIM ROBIN HOOD"?

I watched a 1998 taped interview in which Osama bin Laden justified his attacks on Americans with the following argument: He said that President Bill Clinton, at that time in the midst of the Monica Lewinsky scandal, had bombed Iraq to distract Americans from his personal troubles. Bin Laden cited a poll showing that more than two-thirds of the U.S. population supported the bombing, which he said did not affect the Saddam Hussein regime but merely added to the suffering of the Iraqi people. Bin Laden claimed that more than a million Iraqis had died as a result of the U.S.-led sanctions, including fatalities from cancer caused by the depleted uranium in armor piercing weapons used in the first Gulf War. Sanctions, he said, deprived the people of medical supplies and devastated the Iraqi economy. Bin Laden continued that because the American government raises its money by taxes levied against the people, American taxpayers are funding the American military and the bombs. This meant, he argued, that we, the American people, approved of the killing of innocent Iraqis, and because we paid for the weapons, we were therefore complicit in this crime against humanity, targeted against Muslims. Thus, Osama bin Laden concluded, the killing of American civilians was justified. In essence, he reasoned that in a democratic nation, a government "*of* the people and *by* the people" meant that its policies were *of* its people and *by* them. Hence we, the people, were personally responsible.

In parts of the Middle East, polls indicate that many people view Osama bin Laden in some ways like a modern-day Robin Hood.[50] Look at the parallels they see: Robin Hood was the Earl of Loxley, a nobleman; Osama is a scion of a wealthy Saudi family, the bin Ladens. Robin Hood gave up his comfortable life to support King Richard, who was fighting against Saladin, regarded by Christians as an infidel (in the Third Crusade); bin Laden gave up the option of living a comfortable life to fight the antireligious infidels, the Communists who invaded and were occupying Afghanistan.

Bin Laden was supported and trained by the Saudi and U.S. governments. When the Soviets were driven from Afghanistan and bin Laden returned home, like Robin Hood he spoke to the issues that many young Muslims were unhappy about. Particularly, many highly educated Saudis desire a greater role in the decision-making process of their country and wider participation in both the wealth and development of the nation. Had bin Laden had the opportunity to run for political office in Saudi Arabia, he might have gained elective office and would then have had the opportunity to busy himself in the effort to build his nation and shape its direction. The opportunity to participate safely in politics is a great desire and need in many Muslim countries. Thwarting this desire is perhaps one of the greatest contributing causes to violence in these countries.

The warrior bin Laden was denied the opportunity to serve his nation. It's always wise to allow former soldiers to run for elected office and to give militantly inclined people the opportunity to cut their teeth trying to build something in the real world. Frustrated, bin Laden began to focus on what he thought were Saudi society's inequities and injustices, problems from which no society in the world is immune. Like Robin Hood speaking about the wrongdoing of Prince John and the Sheriff of Nottingham, who hunted deer but didn't allow the poor to hunt them, bin Laden spoke of analogous issues in Saudi Arabia. And again, like Robin Hood living simply with his band of merry men in Sherwood Forest, bin Laden lived in caves with his band of men. In any culture, this can be a heroic image; to many frustrated people in the Muslim world, the image was irresistible.

When I came to the United States in the late 1960s to enter Columbia University, I was fascinated to see American college students from prosperous American families sporting Che Guevara posters on the walls of their dormitory rooms and singing songs about revolution. Guevara, a revolutionary fighter and friend of Fidel Castro, cut a heroic figure to many of my fellow Columbians, symbolizing the effort of one man to struggle for social justice as he saw it. Should we be surprised that bin Laden cuts a similar figure to many Muslim and non-Muslim youths today?

Bin Laden spoke to Middle Eastern issues in a manner that gained him a fair amount of support. A Pew study indicates that "solid majorities in the Palestinian Authority, Indonesia and Jordan—and nearly half of those in Morocco and Pakistan—say they have at least some confidence in Osama bin Laden to 'do the right thing regarding world affairs.' Fully 71 percent of Palestinians hold this view of bin Laden."[51] But the difficulty of running for political office in the Middle East allows bin Laden to live on the outside of society and claim to represent all Muslims. In this way, a lack of democratic governance can create stresses that, if not addressed, can crack the structure of society. As we saw earlier, most human conflicts arise over the distribution of power or assets. In bin Laden's case, it was about power.

"WE LOVE LADY LIBERTY, BUT, HEY, AMERICA— YOU TALKIN' TO ME?"

We cannot solve a dispute with our spouse without seeing our spouse's point of view. Similarly, if we cannot see why the rest of the world, Muslim or non-Muslim, is upset with us, we are likely to expand the chasm between us rather than bridge it. Because the United

States is powerful beyond the understanding of most of its citizens, we are viewed like the macho man who doesn't recognize that women find him insensitive. We wonder why much of the world is concerned by the way we project our raw power unilaterally without listening to our friends—and we are surprised to discover that much of the world actually fears us.

For half a century, our foreign policy allied itself frequently with regimes that have denied basic human rights, and we have even helped to overthrow nascent democratic governments; the 1953 CIA-assisted coup that overthrew Prime Minister Mossadegh and replaced him with the Shah in Iran is a classic example. Most Americans are unaware of this bit of history, but Iranians are worried that America may be inspired to repeat history in that fashion. We have not been assiduous about using our strength to empower the Muslim population.

It's like saying, "We have a special treasure—a liberal society that expresses the values of the Abrahamic ethic whose principles are part of our faith traditions—but it's not for you. It's for Americans and Europeans, even for Japanese, Russians, and South Africans. We'll suggest democracy for China, but we don't really care about democracy and human rights in the Muslim world. In fact, we'll even support dictators who will deprive you of your human rights." Consequently, in the minds of many in the Muslim world who have lived under dictatorial leaders supported by the United States, America is seen as complicit either in creating their problems or in maintaining a status quo of injustice. And even in situations in which we're not directly involved, because America is recognized as the world's sole superpower, capable of shaping what it wants, America is regarded as at least partly responsible.

A few weeks after September 11, Secretary of State Colin Powell made a strong statement during a speech at the United Nations in which he said that the war against terrorism required our support for democratic governments. He said that this was also a war against poverty, against human rights violations, and against a lack of education and other things holding Muslims back.

Benjamin Barber writes,

Those in the third world who seem to welcome American suffering are at worst reluctant adversaries whose principal aim is to make clear that they too suffer from violence, even if it is less visible and destroys with greater stealth and over a longer period of time than the murderous schemes of the terrorists. They want not to belittle American suffering but to use its horrors to draw attention to their own. . . . What they seek is justice, not vengeance. Their quarrel is not with modernity but with the aggressive neo-liberal ideology that has been prosecuted in its name in pursuit of a global market society more conducive to profits for some than to justice for all, . . . a betrayal of the democratic principles to which Americans claim to subscribe.

He adds, "It is finally hypocrisy rather than democracy that is the target of their rage."[52]

Illustrations abound of how the United States and the Muslim world see history differently. For example, among Muslims it is frequently asserted that the U.S.-led sanctions against Iraq between the first Gulf War and the end of the 1990s resulted in the deaths of over five hundred thousand children.[53] Americans, of course, have a completely opposite perspective. In the U.S. view, Saddam Hussein was putting billions of United Nations oil dollars into his personal bank accounts while his people were suffering. If Hussein had really wanted to end the sanctions, all he would have had to do was keep his word and live up to the terms he agreed to in his 1991 surrender documents. The sad result of this classic example of miscommunication is that many Muslims saw the Iraq sanctions as another example of American injustice, while Americans were furious that Muslims would criticize them instead of a dictator who had murdered so many thousands of his own people. And to make the situation more complex, while the United States now showcases evidence of Hussein's reign of terror upon his people, for twenty years the United States was allied with him, supporting him in his war against Iran. We even left him in power after the first Gulf War, at a cost of tens of thousand of Iraqis, who died in his poison gas attacks.

In 1953, as cited earlier, the United States helped to overthrow the Iranian prime minister, Mossadegh. And when, after more than twenty-five years of rule, the Iranians wanted to replace the Shah, we supported him against the will of his people until the very end.

An analogous situation arose with Ferdinand Marcos in the Philippines, another strongman with whom the United States had been allied. Marcos too was resented by his own people, who clearly wanted to overthrow him, a move also supported by the Filipino religious body, the Catholic Church. In the Philippines, however, the United States reacted completely differently—and far more wisely. In this case, we actively helped in the transition. We told Marcos to come and live in Hawaii, we helped Corazon Aquino rise to power, and we planted the seeds of democratic governance in the Philippines.

Had the United States done the same with the Shah and helped Ayatollah Khomeini to gain power in Iran, we might well have maintained excellent relations with Iran, and our ambassador likely would have had a choice seat at the annual independence day celebrations. Instead, the United States has had to contend with being called the "Great Satan" and hearing regular chants of "Death to America!"

While the United States has spoken loudly against human rights violations in the Communist world, in China, and in South Africa under apartheid, the deafening U.S. silence about such violations in the Muslim world was exceedingly painful to Muslims for many years. The plaintive question Muslims in the Middle East would ask us American Muslims was, "Why does the United States call for democratic governance elsewhere but suppress such efforts in the Muslim world? Are Muslims undeserving of human rights and democracy?" The feeling often expressed in the Muslim world that the United States does not care about the suffering of Muslims and non-Westerners adds to a growing mistrust and general hostility toward the West.

Added to this are other issues, such as trade. Lately, American domestic policy and European Union farm subsidies have had a debilitating impact on Third World farmers. American subsidies to cotton farmers, for example, have made it impossible for cotton growers and farmers in Egypt and Africa to make a living, for American cotton growers can afford to sell their product below what it costs African farmers to produce.

An additional major source of Muslim anger toward the United States is the Arab-Israeli dispute. A number of conflicts exist in the Muslim world today, including the Pakistan-India dispute over Kashmir and the Russia-Chechnya conflict, but the Israeli-Palestinian conflict is viewed in the Muslim world as being sustained by America. The contrast between America spending much of its time sitting on the sidelines of the Palestinian-Israeli conflict while rushing to spend over a hundred billion dollars on a war against Iraq has caused great anxiety in much of the Muslim world. As a result, comfort with our intentions and trust in our evenhandedness are both very low, as recent regional polls have demonstrated. And this anxiety over U.S. intentions is not limited to the Muslim world. Newspapers and polls taken in Europe, Russia, and many other parts of the world reveal similar questions in people's minds.

If the United States could prove that it was truly committed to implementing a successful Israeli-Palestinian peace plan, one that was fair to the long-term needs and aspirations of substantial majorities on both sides, this would mark a huge turning point in the Muslim world's attitude toward us. Many on both sides of the Israeli-Palestinian conflict believe that if we invested the same effort, time, and financial resources in Middle East peace that we have been spending on the Iraq war, we could resolve the conflict and save a great many lives.

Most important of all, in terms of those things that matter most to America—such as increasing U.S. security, reducing terrorism, and stabilizing the world economy—the benefits of investing in peace would vastly outweigh those of investing in war.

WE DON'T GET NO RESPECT!

Comedian Rodney Dangerfield's signature plaint well captures the way Muslims feel treated by Western media, and by the American media in particular. We know how annoying it can be when a spouse or parent insists on interpreting to others what we "really mean" rather than accepting what we are saying. That's the Muslim complaint. Muslims feel that the American media is like the spouse or parent who doesn't hear what the partner or child is saying. And, of course, Americans feel exactly the same about how al-Jazeera television portrays them.

My personal experience with the major American news media, especially since September 11, clearly suggests that portraying Islam and Muslims as *moderate* is a low priority. My first experience was a few weeks before the United States went to war in Afghanistan. The Muslim chaplain of the U.S. armed forces sought a fatwa as to whether it was acceptable for Muslims serving in the military to participate in hostilities against Afghanistan, since they would be fighting fellow Muslims. A fatwa was issued on September 27, 2001, by Sheikh Yusuf Qaradawi and four other signatories, pointing out that under Islamic law the events of September 11 were terrorist acts, whose perpetrators should be brought to justice, and therefore it was their duty to act accordingly (see the appendix). I was called by the *New York Times* to comment on the fatwa, and I strongly recommended that it be printed, since the *Times* then was running a special section called "A Nation Challenged." The fatwa would have made valuable reading for the *Times*'s Muslim and non-Muslim readers alike and would have helped amplify the Muslim moderate voice. Unfortunately, the fatwa was not published, and the article describing it was buried on the bottom of an inside page.

My most recent experience of this was in December 2003. After many months of work on an initiative to encourage the U.S. government and leadership to play a more active role in brokering a peace accord between Israel and Palestine, a number of American clergy representing the Abrahamic faith religions worked together to urge our government to be more proactive. A *Washington Post* interview was arranged, and I was nominated to represent the Muslim position and join with three clergy: the Reverend Mark Hanson, presiding bishop of the Evangelical Lutheran Church in America, representing Protestant Christianity; Cardinal Theodore McCarrick of Washington, D.C., representing Catholic Christianity; and Rabbi Paul Menitoff, executive vice president of the Central Conference of American Rabbis, representing Judaism. To the surprise of all involved in the effort, the article that appeared under the heading "Clergy Urge More Active White House Effort for Mideast Peace"[54] quoted remarks from all the clergy except me. Is it any wonder, then, that the popular impression Muslims have is that the American media is not interested in recognizing Muslims as moderate? And is it any wonder that Muslims are constantly and angrily asked, "Where is the moderate Muslim voice?"

In his penetrating comments, the late Edward Said (who was an Episcopalian Christian Arab, not a Muslim) reminds us that studying human societies is not like studying inert objects.[55] People respond to how they are looked at and treated. And the West for a long time has looked down upon the Arab world (which is about 15 percent Christian) and the Muslim world. When we treat people honorably they will respond honorably; treat them dishonorably, and they will respond in kind.

America has been a superpower since World War II. Oil and other economic, political, and security interests defined by the cold war have shaped American involvement in the Muslim world. Since the Second World War, the United States has taken the position of dominance and hegemony in the Muslim world once held by France and Britain. The Arab and Muslim world is so dominated today by American power and influence, and yet Americans know so little of the passion and human detail of Muslims' lives. American news coverage of the Muslim world is usually limited to the points of intersection with powerful American interests. When the media looks at the Muslim world, it's like a young man looking at an attractive woman from whom he wants something.

Human study of any subject begins with the idea that all knowledge is interpretation and that interpretation must be conscious of itself, of its methods and its aims, if it is to be vigilant and to arrive at a correct understanding of the truth. But underlying every interpretation of other cultures—especially Islam—is the choice facing the individual scholar or intellectual: "whether to put intellect at the service of power or at the service of criticism, community, dialogue and moral sense."[56] In the language of our man-woman analogy, is the young man approaching the woman with the intention of a mutually respectful relationship, or does he want to use her for his own purposes? In Muslim eyes, Western scholars have only just begun to approach the Muslim world with the intention of equal and respectful dialogue rather than, as in the past, in the service of use and abuse, power and dominion.

Because the relationship between the West and the Muslim world was heavily influenced by the West's power and dominion over Muslims, any effort to bridge the chasm between America and the Muslim world must start with the right motivation. Our choice of dialogue and moral values must underpin our effort at interpretation. As Said presciently pointed out, the history of knowledge about Islam in the West has been too closely tied to conquest and domination, and "the time has come for these ties to be severed completely. . . . For otherwise we will not only face protracted tension and perhaps even war, but we will offer the Muslim world, its various societies and states, the prospect of many wars, unimaginable suffering, and disastrous upheavals, not the least of which would be the victory of an 'Islam' fully ready to play the role prepared for it by reaction, orthodoxy and desperation."[57]

America has had a peculiar insularity, probably a product of its geography and strong isolationist tendency. A distant cousin of mine from Egypt doing his doctoral studies back in the 1960s at Purdue University in Indiana once got on a bus in Lafayette and struck up a conversation with a friendly local American passenger. Noticing that my cousin spoke with a different accent, he probed, "Where are you from?" "The Mideast," my cousin answered. "The Mideast? Where's that?" he blurted, completely puzzled. "All I know is the Midwest!"

It is clear from this story that the American media plays a defining role in painting the picture that Americans carry in their heads about the Muslim world. And it has not been a pretty one. For the general public in America and Europe today, "Islam" is made to cover everything that one most disapproves of from the standpoint of civilized, and Western, rationality.[58] Describing an oil supplier as "holding America hostage" to oil is a strange way indeed of describing an appetite America has for a product belonging to someone else.[59] To Muslim ears, this sounds like accusing McDonald's of holding us hostage to our appetites for hamburgers.

The American news media cannot divorce itself from the viewpoint of American culture and American political needs. (This is true of any media in any country in the world.) The media decides *what* and *how* news is news, and it does so voluntarily, not by conspiracy but rather from culture: the media "are responsive to what we are and want."[60] If we accept this as true, this suggests the rather dramatic conclusion: *if and when Americans are motivated by a genuine desire for a positive relationship between America and the Muslim world*, the media coverage will adjust to this need.

Muslims find the American media particularly challenging because they watch their image being created by others who never consult them about how they see themselves. The "experts" on television who explain to the American public why Muslims do what they do often make Muslims feel like goldfish in a bowl, being studied from outside the glass wall of the bowl. Although they may make accurate and complete observations about Muslims on the inside of the fish-bowl, they rarely ask themselves, and never try to find out, how it feels to be a Muslim or how the observers' presence makes Muslims feel. And they rarely ask if Muslims are acting *as Muslims*, if a response is a peculiarly *Islamic* response, or whether the behavior is natural to being human, a response that any human in the same position would make. The same can be said for the Middle East Muslim media's portrayal of Americans, a portrayal that bears little resemblance to how Americans view themselves. It would be wrong, for example, if the Muslim world chose to regard all that happened in the United States as a reflection of Christian values.

Part of the problem lies in our human inability to see the other except through the lens of our own experience and our choice of language. When the issue is phrased as "the West against Islam," we pit a region of the world against a religion rather than one religion against another or one interpretation of religion against another. The result is that the Muslim world finds itself in the position of defending not only its political and economic aspirations, but also occasionally the role of religion in society and even differing interpretations and attitudes toward religion in society.

This observation leads to the insight that because the West regards much of its progress as the result of separating religion from affairs of state, it associates the continued backwardness of Muslims with religion, in this case Islam. All social or political problems in the Muslim world are seen not as political or social or economic but as *Islamic.* Thus we have the "Islamic crisis," the "Islamic resurgence," and "Muslim rage."

A Native American saying advises us not to criticize others until we have walked a mile in their moccasins. What Muslims want is for non-Muslims to walk this proverbial mile in Muslim moccasins. My attention was caught by a news item after September 11 that featured a number of American women who decided to wear the veil for a day and see how people reacted to them, as a way of empathizing with the Islamic experience. I understand that it was quite an eye opener for them. While some began to understand and empathize with Muslim women because people reacted to them with suspicion or fear, other women in this experiment loved how Muslim women's modest dress gave them freedom from the roving eyes of men. Another stereotype that non-Muslim women have come to understand from this type of exercise is that covering up—*if* it is purely voluntary—can actually empower women by allowing them to rise above fashion, appearance, and figure. Rather than being evaluated physically, they are taken at face value on their intelligence, personality, and performance.

What I appreciated most about this initiative was the attempt to understand Islam from the inside. An American media that continues to make Americans equate Muslims with anti-Americanism, terrorism, and a lifestyle that stands for the opposite of our deepest values does America a great disservice. So do American policies that feed a Muslim media misperception that American values are fundamentally anti-Islam.

What is needed is a new level of interfaith work between the media in both the Western and Muslim worlds that changes the discourse from one of "look at how bad you are" to "look at what we can do together," a tone that educates, enables, and ennobles the population, especially opinion leaders on each side, to fathom the other side's issues and to help in building harmony.

IS A "NATION" A PEOPLE OR A GEOGRAPHY?

People historically identified themselves as nations according to tribe, language, culture, tradition, and religion. Geography was part of the definition but rarely the primary or sole definition. This flows naturally and organically: an individual is part of a family, then of a clan and tribe, then of a nation.

At some point, certain groups of people began to think of nation as primarily centered in geography, and they projected their group identity onto the land. You could live in a certain geographical territory only if you belonged to a specific group of people who shared a common language, ethnic appearance, and tribe, who owned the land, defined as a nation-state or country. You can see how this idea would begin to seed conflict between people pushed out of ownership based on any one of the identity markers. The corollary is, you are included only if you give up a part of your inalienable rights to your own identity.

After World War I, Britain, Russia, and France divided up the Ottoman Empire and created new national identities based on geography. Territorial boundaries previously fuzzy were fixed, not always with regard for regional differences of culture and religion. New national identities were created along geographic lines. Some long-standing societies were split asunder, which started and then continued to fuel a pernicious resistance to pluralism in societies that up until then had lived together in the same geography.

For example, in the area where Iran borders Central Asia and India, Iranian Farsi-speaking people bordered on and mingled with Uzbeki- and Pashtu-speaking people. The territory called Afghanistan was drawn on the map, dividing the Uzbekis within the boundary from their compatriots outside it, in Uzbekistan; the Farsi-speaking Shiite Hazaras were separated from theirs in Iran; and the Pashtu-speaking Pashtuns were separated from Pashtuns in Pakistan, which was once a province of India. How does one convince the three groups to submerge their identities into this overarching identity based on geography? How are they expected to relate to their tradition of Uzbek, Pashtu, and Hazara, from which they were split?

Iraq was another "nation" created by drawing lines that split communities apart. This time the Kurds lost out. Instead of having a Kurdistan, they were split up between Iraq, Iran, and Turkey, although they had a strong sense of cultural and ethnic identity. Those responsible for this decision, the British, never considered how Kurds, split by an artificial boundary from their own people, were to define themselves into a new Turkish or Iraqi identity with others who spoke a different language or were Shiite while they were Sunni Muslims. These are among the challenges facing the United States today as it tries to forge a new Mideast and Muslim world order.

Imagine if at the end of World War I, the Versailles Treaty had erased the boundaries of Germany and Austria from the map and awarded the territory to neighboring countries. A segment of Germans now became part of Poland, another part of France, another part of Holland, and another part of Italy. Let's further assume that the division was made such that a sizable number of German Catholics were under Dutch Protestant rule and that the Vatican in Rome was deeply concerned about the status of Catholics suffering under "Protestant oppression." Would it be surprising if this "nation" of people with a strong Teutonic identity militantly agitated in France for a "Teuton-land"—a Deutschland in German—or that Italy would retain special bonds of relationships with German Catholics? That's similar to the Kurds split between Turkey and Iraq, and the Shiites between Iraq, Iran, and Afghanistan.

Breaking up people who are part of one nation, language, or cultural group and forcing them to be part of another identity, or creating alto-gether new identities and expecting them to take root based more on ge-ographic identity, has been a recipe for conflict in the Muslim world.[61]

The original Islamic idea of an *ummah,* a community or society, was always based on people, not on geography. When Palestine and Egypt were conquered during the second caliph Umar's rule, the Christians, Jews, and other religious groups not only were free to practice their re-ligious traditions, but Umar invited seventy Jewish families to take up residence in the city of Jerusalem, from which Jews had been banished in 70 CE. Evidently Umar did not think that geography required a uni-fied religious identity because he created a religiously pluralist one. Egypt did not become a majority Muslim society until more than half a millennium later.

As Muslims between the seventeenth and nineteenth centuries be-came influenced by European norms, the unnatural idea of an Islamic nation-state—a pure "Muslimland" based on geography—germinated in the Muslim consciousness. It finally came into being in August 1947 on the Indian subcontinent when India was split geographically along religious lines into India and Pakistan. A million lives were lost, and a conflict was born that rages to this day between two countries who are now nuclear powers.

For centuries Hindus and Muslims had lived in India, less divided by religion than they became after the creation of Pakistan. Until the mid-twentieth century the word *Hindu* was used to mean "from the land of India," so much so that in writings and speech on the subcon-tinent the term *Hindu-Muslim* was used to mean an Indian Muslim. Now the term is obsolete. But you find today Hindu and Muslim Gujaratis who speak the same language, Hindu and Muslim Kashmiris who speak the same language, and so on for many states and provinces of India and Pakistan. Are Muslims and Hindus on the subcontinent better off with the religious nation-state, or would they have been better off if they had managed to continue to live under one nation in a society that was more religiously pluralistic, as before? Which model is more consonant with the Abrahamic ethic, which underlies the Islamic ethic and the human ethic?

The creation of a religious nation-state that has contributed to a painful global conflict was the creation of the state of Israel in 1948. Up until then, Jews lived all over the Muslim world, from Morocco in the west to Afghanistan and Uzbekistan in the east, from Turkey and the Balkans to Yemen in the southwest corner of the Arabian peninsula. Major Jewish communities existed in Egypt, Syria, Iraq, Iran, and Turkey, the centers of Islamic culture during various parts of Islamic history. Having lived in these areas for many centuries, they looked, spoke, and ate—even sang—like the rest of the people around them, except that their liturgical rites were those of Judaism rather than Christianity or Islam. The creation of Israel, and the manner of its creation, began a most unfortunate schism between Jews and Muslims, who until then throughout most of their history had experienced a deeply intimate kinship with each other.

In non-European eyes, Israel was a European creation, a by-product of the nation-state idea. Because of the conflict, Sephardic Jews became unfortunately victimized in many Muslim societies, a sad situation not only for the Jewish communities but also for the Muslim communities, who by losing their Jewish citizens became less pluralistic. Imagine if the majority of American Jews had left the United States for Israel right after 1948. Would not America have suffered a terrible loss? Historically, the robust presence of American Jews has profoundly shaped American understanding of civil liberties and contributed to American culture, American education, and the American economy.

Until the mid-1960s, Egypt too was a highly pluralistic society, encompassing not only old-time communities of Copts and Jews, but also sizable communities of Greeks and Italians, who maintained their Greek and Italian cultural and language identities. Unfortunately, this diversity is a thing of the past. We can better understand how this happened if we again suppose that American Jews had left the country in 1948. Would America have remained pluralistic, or would it have become more sharply defined by a strongly partisan Christian ethic? Some argue that Jews and Muslims are better off living separately. I think the model of the United States shows without a doubt that societies are healthier when they evolve toward increasing pluralism, enhancing their economies by according equal participation to all peoples living together on the same land.

I shall never forget in 1973, when as a graduate student I accompanied the famous Egyptian businessman Ahmad Aboushaqra, founder of a chain of shish kebab stores—the "Colonel Sanders" of the Mideast—on a nationwide quest to find his childhood buddy, Albert Mizrahi. Aboushaqra is a deeply religious Muslim, Mizrah an Egyptian Jew. The two were finally reunited in Kansas City, and the love, affection, and tears of joy with which they greeted each other was as intense as that of two siblings discovering each other after a forced separation. Palestinian Muslims of my father's generation tell me that when they were children their parents would scold them if they did not, out of respect, kiss the hands of the rabbis as they did those of the priests and the imams. Many hope that with a genuine peace between Israel and Palestine, such mutual respect will sprout once again. Because many Muslims in the Muslim world no longer grow up with and know personally any Jews, is it any wonder that the tension between the faith communities has become increasingly virulent?

In addition, as discussed in the introduction to this book, European colonialism created what Harvard political scientist Samuel Huntington calls a "torn" society: a community whose leaders were ethnically traditional but whose mind-set belonged to the colonizing people. Two examples of this in the Muslim world were Kemal Atatürk in Turkey and the Shah of Iran. Atatürk was a Turkish general, a military hero. In 1924 he terminated the Ottoman Caliphate, which was based in Istanbul. The trauma of this event is still felt by many in the Muslim community. This was what Osama bin Laden meant in one of his tapes when he referred to an affront "eighty years ago," a reference that puzzled most Americans.

In Huntington's language, Atatürk and the Shah "tore" their societies. They were European in mind-set and sought to forcibly transform their societies according to a Western image. With the end of colonialism in the first half of the twentieth century and the rise of militantly secular regimes in what were then the major Islamic capitals of Turkey, Egypt, and Iran, Muslims found themselves ruled by unelected, secular leaders who forced their populations to imitate the West, sometimes in absurd ways. Turks were forced by Kemal Atatürk to change their clothing into Western clothing, wearing the hat instead of the fez. In the 1930s the Shah of Iran had his police use their bayonets to force women to remove their veils (*chadors*).

Americans may wonder why all this was so significant. Remember that we in the United States don't even force our children to wear school uniforms in our public schools, and we lovingly accommodate them when they insist on spending lots of money on brand-name sneakers with flashing lights. To fathom what Atatürk did in eliminating the caliphate, imagine if Mussolini had terminated the papacy and made the Vatican a museum. How would you feel if you were a Catholic? And as to what the Shah did, imagine if an American president who loved French culture ordered the National Guard to force American women on Florida beaches to remove their bikini tops in the name of "civilization": How would you feel if you were Baptist or Jewish? Wouldn't Southern Baptists regard that as a slide into immorality, as Iranian clerics deemed the Shah's actions?

Unlike Atatürk and the Shah, a notable example of someone who was brought up in the colonizer's tradition but who did not turn his back on his native tradition was Mahatma Gandhi. Returning to India, he did the exact opposite: he gave up Western dress, and he knew how to draw the line between the identity of the colonizer and the colonized and how to champion the dignity of the native, holding the native identity equal with that of the foreign in a way that was appreciated by people on both sides of the divide. He opposed the split of India into Pakistan, a position in line with the Abrahamic ethic. He was also against the social injustice of the Hindu caste system and treated Muslims as brothers and sisters, again in line with the Abrahamic ethic. Which of these examples has history demonstrated to be more truly resonant with native tradition and aspirations and at the end of the day more admired, even in the West?

• • •

Truth is not just about facts; it is as much about how we perceive the facts. What we see as truth is often our own interpretation of the facts, shaped by values so deeply embedded in our subconscious that we often don't notice them. Frequently we don't see the other side's truth until an analogy in our own context opens our eyes.

CHAPTER 5

We're All History

Our history shapes how we continue to act, and thus our future. It is important to be aware of events from the past, for they still determine people's attitudes and worldviews today. It is impossible, for instance, to understand Iranians' fear of the United States without factoring in the CIA's overthrow of popularly elected Prime Minister Mossadegh in 1953.[1] To ignore our history is to remain trapped in behaviors of the past.

And yet history is more than, as the great Muslim historian Ibn Khaldun (1332–1382 CE) points out, "information about political events, dynasties, and occurrences of the remote past, elegantly presented and spiced with proverbs." He says, "The inner meaning of history . . . involves speculation and an attempt to get at the truth, subtle explanation of the causes and origins of existing things, and deep knowledge of the how and why of events." According to Ibn Khaldun, history is more like philosophy and therefore "deserves to be accounted a branch of it."[2] Thus, in this chapter we take a look not only at our histories, but at the meaning of our histories—how the views of history in the Muslim world and in the West have led us to pursue different courses in our respective societies.

Take, for instance, the views of history of various major religions and philosophies. Here I would like to look briefly at the Hindu (as representative of the Far Eastern), atheist, and Abrahamic religions' views of history. Comparing these widely varying views of history will help shed light on both the differences *and the similarities* between Western and Eastern worldviews and may help people of goodwill in various traditions understand what makes the others tick. I am indebted, in this overview, to the late professor Wilfred Cantwell Smith, especially his book *Islam in Modern History*.[3]

According to Smith, the Hindu worldview is that the world and all its activity is *maya*, a meaningless illusory veil that can be pierced by proper religious insight. *Samsara*, the endless cycle of birth, death, and rebirth, is to be transcended. History is the sum of our individual actions working themselves out karmically in the accumulated effect on our lives. Salvation for Hindus lies in extrication from *samsara*, an extrication from history by creating the right kind of karma through improved behavior so that we don't have to continue to be reincarnated in this cycle of human suffering.[4]

The atheist worldview is the opposite of this. Atheism asserts that any ideas of God, of a life beyond this, are illusion, often articulated as a crutch for the weak and weak-minded. Atheism's exclusive concern is with this world. "There is no meaning, no value, and no reality to human life other than its meaning as an item in the on-going historical process."[5] A human being has significance merely as a means to an end within history. The atheist impulse is to shape history according to purely rational human self-interest without any reference to divinely inspired morality.

The Abrahamic faith traditions fall in between these two worldviews. For them, history is fundamental but not exclusively so. For the Christian, God's activity in history was crucial. The cross and crucifixion illuminate both the love of God and the evil wickedness of human beings. The duty of Christians is to try to save the world, even consecrating their lives to the process, while accepting with equanimity the possibility of failure. The world is filled with sin, so let's try to improve it; our goodness lies in loving our enemies and hopefully transforming them, and if they do not transform, we try to be forgiving; and so be it if we die failing. History is therefore the field of Christian endeavor based on love as the divine purpose. Morality flows out of salvation, not into it. For the Christian, the significance of the historical process is best defined not by some notion of social progress and how much we accomplish but by how devotedly and how well we love.

In the Semitic (Jewish and Islamic) worldview, the eternal Word of God is the imperative, not as *flesh* but as *law*.[6] The concern of Islamic law, or Shariah law, is to elaborate this imperative as it was embodied in the Quran and the exemplary actions and teachings of the Prophet. It means that the Muslims have to uphold the Law, to make the Law dwell among us. *Therefore the social order and its activities are as much the expression in a practical form of Muslims' personal faith as are liturgical rites that describe how people worship God.* Salvation for the Muslim is admittedly by faith, but faith alone without works is insufficient; faith (*iman*) must be consummated and expressed by righteous action (*'amal salih*). The Muslim ideal is to shape history according to God's dictate and deeming it a failure if we do not achieve it.

As followers of a religion of adversity, Christians generally do not regard a disintegration in temporal affairs as a *religious* failure; Muslims do. Jesus Christ left earth in an atmosphere of persecution, and Christians continued to be persecuted. By contrast, as the historian of Islam Bernard Lewis has said, the Prophet Muhammad left this earth as a political success story; thus for Muslims, whose earliest history was associated with political success, the ideal is not just to struggle *against* history but *for and with* it.

It is worth noting that the crossfire of an increasingly globalized world has produced combinations and permutations of the above worldviews. One may therefore meet a deeply moral atheist who believes in reincarnation, a ritually observant Muslim who feels free to use and discard others for personal self-interest, or a Christian who believes in retribution over forgiveness. The syncretism may be conscious or unwitting.

HISTORY IN QURANIC PERSPECTIVE

Muslims assert that history began with God and to Him it shall return, and the human endeavor is to redeem history, to integrate temporal righteousness in this world with a timeless and eternal salvation in the next. The Quranic view of history begins with Adam; it is of a Paradise lost: of the eviction of humankind from Paradise because of disobedience to God. The Quran's intention is to establish humanity on a path that leads back to it, to a Paradise regained in the Hereafter, and to live a life on earth that is reflective of a Paradise regained, a life surrendered to God and therefore reflective of how humans would behave toward each other in a paradisal state. Living a life that ignores God thus leads to destruction even in this world: "Those who believe [that is, have faith] and do good works, their Lord guides them because of their good works toward rivers flowing beneath them in Gardens of bliss . . . and surely We destroyed many generations before you when they did wrong; in spite of sending many messengers to them with clear arguments they still did not believe. Thus do We recompense the guilty people" (Quran 10:9, 13).

Human history in God's eyes, from the Quranic perspective, is about society failing to act in accord with the Abrahamic ethic, in spite of repeated admonitions to do so. The Quran urges its readers to "Consider the end of those who worked corruption in the land" (Quran 7:86). "Don't they see," it asks, "how many a generation We destroyed before them, whom We established on the earth even more than We established you, and sent the clouds pouring abundant rainwater, causing rivers to flow beneath them? Then We destroyed them because of their sins, and raised after them another generation" (Quran 6:6). Individuals who corrupt their societies bring about dire results not only upon themselves but also upon their communities. The Islamic objective, therefore, is to establish a society expressing the Abrahamic ethic of righteousness to God. A prosperous society not only is one that consists of believers who accept and worship God correctly; it is also one that establishes a just and equitable society, a society of moral integrity, a decent society that protects and furthers the "pursuit of happiness."

In the Muslim worldview, every mundane event has two references and is seen in two contexts. Every human action has an eternal and a temporal relevance, and each human individual will be held accountable on the Day of Judgment for his or her personal share. Deeds have consequences of one kind in this world and consequences of another in the eternal world to come. Therefore, each action must be assessed both in itself and in its relation to historical development.

Collectively and individually, Muslims have sought Paradise both beyond this world and within history, in a kind of society they believe is correct both for the individual in the next world and for the community in this. The Quranic supplication taught to Muslims, asking that God "grant us good in this world and good in the hereafter" (2:201), added to the Prophet's advice to "strive in your worldly affairs as if you will live forever, and strive in your affairs of the hereafter as if you will die tomorrow,"[7] prompted the earliest Muslims to take on the burden and opportunity of government and of cultural creation in the widest sense.

Muslims thus are deeply convinced that what happens here below is of inescapable and lasting significance (we are referring here to the history of the community and not to individual karmic actions). And therefore the building up of a proper community life on earth is a supreme and religious imperative.

Muslims have historically executed this assignment with remarkable distinction, creating beauty on earth as an expression of God and their understanding of Paradise. Muslims tried to recreate earthly representations of the many Quranic references to the paradisal "gardens of Eden beneath which rivers flow" (Quran 2:25). Muslim attempts to create a kingdom of God on earth were modeled on their understanding of the heavenly rewards granted to the righteous believers in Paradise. These were not just constructs of beauty for beauty's sake but acts of worship and glorification of God. In walking the gardens of the Alhambra in Granada, Spain, one is struck by an ambiance of peace and serenity, which belongs to proximity to God, in addition to the many direct reminders of God in the calligraphic inscriptions all over the palace walls. Such feelings of being close to God were recreated all over the Muslim world, from the gardens of Isfahan and Shiraz in Iran to the Mogul gardens of Kashmir to the ambiance of the Taj Mahal in India, and in all the great mosques from Cordoba to Cairo, from Marrakech to Samarqand, and from Istanbul to Jakarta.

With Christians, Muslims share the conviction that the transcendent reference is in the final analysis more important: the course of history is ultimately less significant than the quality of one's personal life. Yet Muslims are convinced that the course of history and the social shape it assumes are profoundly relevant to the quality of personal life within it. Muslims believe that there is inherent in the structure of the world and its development a proper course, a right social shape; that the meaning of history must lie in the degree to which these laws of nature and therefore of God become actualized; and, finally, that they who understand the essential laws, and who accept the responsibility thereof, are entrusted with stewardship of the task of executing that actualization, of guiding history to its inevitable and resplendent fulfillment.

Note how similar this viewpoint is to the American worldview, in which inalienable human rights (of life, liberty, and pursuit of happiness) are given to us by the Creator (who created "all men equal"). As long as the government secures God-given, inalienable rights, and as long as it governs in a manner that respects these rights, it is legitimate (that is, "Islamic"). When it desecrates these rights, it is not legitimate (that is, it is "un-Islamic"). The moral authority of any of its laws must be in keeping with this; otherwise the government is not constitutional, not an expression of what we in America call natural law.

I believe that the American Declaration of Independence and Constitution express the Islamic ideal, which is itself but an expression of the Abrahamic ethic, which according to Quranic history was attempted time and time again by each prophet. This observation is enormously relevant to non-American Muslims, and it is the duty of American Muslims and non-Muslims to convey this understanding to Muslims in the rest of the world. For if they recognize in the American form of governance a genuine substantive workable expression and model of their centuries-old longing for the kingdom of heaven on earth, they can formulate their understanding of an Islamic state along these lines.

SHAPING AN ISLAMIC HISTORY

To further a workable vision shared by America and the Muslim world, it will be helpful for each to have fuller understanding of the history of the other. Only by understanding the ideas that shaped the collective history of each can we hope to create channels of communication that can further our goals of increasing respect between these two great traditions.

Islamic history is essentially about, in biblical terms, establishing the kingdom of God on earth or, in Greek terms, forging the good society. For the purpose of this book we shall segment the fourteen centuries of Islamic history into five epochs that exhibited specific ideas worth highlighting. (Readers should note that Islamic history can be segmented differently.)

Abrahamic Ethic I: The Model Universal Islamic Community, 622–632 CE

The first thirteen years of the Prophet's mission, from 610 to 622 CE, were focused on teaching his contemporaries the notion of one God. The Meccans got tired of the Prophet's insistence on preaching his message and in 622 hatched a plot to assassinate him. He got wind of this, and since life in Mecca had become untenable and dangerous for him and his community, the small Muslim community of some seventy families quietly left Mecca in small groups for a town called Yathrib, which the Prophet had been invited to be the leader of. In time Yathrib was called "the Prophet's town," *medinat un-nabi,* or Medina, for short.

The ten years from 622 to 632 saw the Prophet and his nascent community plant in Medina the seeds of an Islamic good society. Defining Islam not in the Quranic universal sense but as "that which came through Muhammad," we might call this the first chapter in Islamic history.[8] During the time of Umar, when a decision was made to establish the Islamic lunar calendar, year 1 was set at 622 CE, that of the emigration (*hijra*) from Mecca to Medina, for that event birthed the Islamic community historically as a society. During the next ten-year period, a live connection, mediated by the Prophet, continued to exist between God and this budding human society seeking to establish a kingdom of God on earth. During this interval the community in Medina developed a sense of how the human-divine relationship might work on a societal basis.

For Muslims, this era of life in the company of the Prophet in Medina remains the finest example and model for the good society on earth. Every revival attempt throughout Islamic history has been an attempt to recreate this ideal. The ideal or perfect man was the Prophet, and Muslims value his precedent and practice, called his *sunnah,* and try hard to emulate it at a personal level. Therefore at the individual level, Muslims model themselves after the Prophet, and at the collective and social level, Muslims seek to model their societies and communities according to their understanding of the Prophet's community in Medina.

What makes this period unique in Islamic history is that here was where God worked with human material to develop a set of guidelines that could inform a universal or global Islamic community. Of course certain aspects of this society were part of its time and place, and the greatest juridical works of Muslim thought have been those that helped thinkers trace the boundaries separating that which is universal and global to Islam (the eternal, timeless aspects) from that which is local and specific to the Prophet's time and place. The Prophet revived an Abrahamic ethic, which had suffered a long absence in Arabia and which in the intervening centuries had been maintained by the Children of Israel, but in a way that could embrace all.

The community led by Muhammad until his death in 632 put into practice the commandments revealed to him in the Quran, as had been revealed to the prophets before him. Muhammad's establishment of the first Muslim community liberated the Arabs from their *jahiliyyah*, their unawareness of God and the concomitants of such a covenantal relationship with the Creator. A social model was created for future Muslims to strive toward. Membership in the Muslim community, the *ummah*, was open to anyone who surrendered to the One God, a concept that refreshingly transcended the social stratification of the old tribal ways.

Abrahamic Ethic II: The "Rightly Guided" Caliphs, 632–661 CE

The second period of Islamic history is that between 632 and 661 CE, called the era of the Rashidun, or "rightly guided" caliphs. With Medina still the political capital of the Muslim world, the community was led by close companions of the Prophet steeped in an understanding of the Quran and the Prophet's example and teachings.

After the Prophet's death, various Arab tribes tried to break away from the *ummah* and reassert their former independence. Their actions were driven not by religious dissatisfaction but by economics. Historian of religion Karen Armstrong points out that, for centuries, "the Arabs had eked out their inadequate resources by means of the *ghazu* [raids on other tribes]. But Islam had put a stop to this because the tribes of the *ummah* were no longer permitted to attack one another." The first caliph, Abu Bakr, forced the Arab tribes to adhere to the sociopolitical unity of an Islamic *ummah*. But "what would replace the *ghazu*," she asks, "which had enabled the Muslims to scratch out a meager livelihood?"[9] The obvious answer was a series of economically driven conquests in the neighboring countries.

Under the second caliph Umar's leadership, the Arabs overcame the Persians in 637, conquered Jerusalem in 638, and controlled the whole of Syria, Palestine, and Egypt by 641 CE. Many of the Christians, who had been persecuted by the Greek Orthodox, and the Jews preferred the Muslims and welcomed their rule over that of the Byzantines.

Armstrong invites her readers to "look what had happened once they [the Muslims] had surrendered to God's will! Where Christians discerned God's hand in apparent failure and defeat, when Jesus died on the cross, Muslims experienced political success as sacramental and as a revelation of the divine presence in their lives."[10] It's always satisfying for us to say that the past happened because God wanted it that way, no matter how much of it was our own doing. But it was much later that Muslims began to give these events a *religious* interpretation. Armstrong correctly points out that there was nothing religious about these campaigns; they were not about Muslims conquering the world or converting the non-Arabs to Islam. Because these early conquests were *economically* driven, the conquered people were not forced to convert, and until the middle of the eighth century conversion was not in fact encouraged.

Umar was a strict disciplinarian. The Muslim soldiers were not allowed to seize the conquered lands for themselves or to settle in the cities. The existing populations lived pretty much as they had except they paid a tax to the Muslim state, which was responsible for protecting them (a tax that was refunded when they could not be protected). New garrison towns were built for the Arab Muslims at strategic locations: Kufah and Basrah in Iraq, Qum in Iran, and Fustat by the Nile in Egypt.

This period of expanding Muslim rule over the neighboring ancient societies of Egypt, Byzantium, and Iran also brought a unique challenge, which was how the rulers in Medina were going to administer an empire containing members of other faiths. Two more of the Prophet's closest companions, the Rashidun—"rightly guided" caliphs—successively ruled the Muslim *ummah* until 661. Their rule was formative in that the *ummah* was defining itself and the forms it would take. Although the rule of the Rashidun was characterized by morality and compassion, the seeds of future political problems were planted then, especially during the rule of the third caliph, Uthman, problems the fourth caliph, Ali, tried to correct.[11] The subjects of the conquered lands were treated well; it was a matter of honor for their rulers, the Muslim Arabs, to help those in difficulty and avenge any wrong done to them. The subjects were also given the freedom to practice their own faiths in a pluralistic society, as stipulated in the Quran.

Most contemporary Muslims are unaware that Muslims did not become the majority religious group in Egypt until well into the second millennium some six centuries later. Neither do most of our Jewish friends know that it was the second caliph, Umar, who invited Jews back to Jerusalem after having been banished. Seventy Jewish families were invited to emigrate from Tiberias to Jerusalem to once again establish a Jewish presence in that city sacred to all the Abrahamic faiths. Islamic rule over these ancient societies established a norm of a religiously plural society in accord with the Abrahamic ethic. Although the success of the Islamic expansion was certainly thought to be testimony to the message of Muhammad, the goal of this expansion was economic. It is erroneous to think, as is done in the West, that it was about spreading Islam "by the sword."

Three of these four caliphs were assassinated: Umar, Uthman, and Ali. Ali had to wage a number of civil wars, which weakened him and resulted in the strengthening of Muawiyah, the politically savvy governor of Damascus, who was a scion of the Arab family of Banu Umayyah. Muawiyah succeeded in consolidating his power and establishing the beginnings of dynastic rule by appointing his son Yazid as the next caliph, thereby establishing what came to be known as the Umayyad Dynasty. This was highly unpopular with the Muslim masses, who sided with Ali and his descendants, but ever since then, and until the end of the Ottoman caliphate in 1924, Muslims have been ruled mostly by a series of dynastic rulers. This was not true in the early decades of Islam, when rulers were elected on the basis of merit rather than ruling by virtue of bloodline.

Intellectual Fermentation Period: Living Like a King, 661–1258 CE

The Intellectual Fermentation period was marked by much intellectual development, by translation into Arabic of Greek rationalist works on philosophy, and by incorporation of the arts and sciences from all parts of the then-known world. The major capitals during this period were Damascus, Baghdad (which included areas of Iran), Cordoba, and Cairo. This era saw the birth and development of the sciences of religious study, that is, Arabic grammar, Quranic exegesis, collecting the Prophet's hadith, the development and intellectual formulation of Islamic jurisprudence, and the intellectual and institutional development of spiritual Sufi orders.

From 661 CE on, the era of dynastic political rule began, starting with the Umayyads in Damascus, followed by the Abbasids in Baghdad and the leftover Umayyad Caliphate of the West in Cordoba. Included within this period are the several dynasties such as the Fatimids in Cairo (909–1171), the Almoravids (al-Murabitun), and the Almohades (al-Muwahhidun) in northwest Africa, and other regional dynasties that ruled over smaller geographic regions. The rulers were predominantly of Arab or Arabized stock.

The Umayyads. The Umayyads ruled from 661 to 750 CE from their capital of Damascus in Syria. Ever since the fall of Medina as the capital in 661 CE, the majority of the Muslim community has felt that the Muslim world never quite retained or established a form of governance that fully expressed the principles of a good society as was established by the Prophet and his close companions, the Rashidun. This sentiment has been the driving force behind every renewal attempt since 661.

Crucial questions were raised by this early history, which Karen Armstrong pointedly reiterates:

> How could a society that killed its devout leaders (*imams*) claim to be guided by God? What kind of man should lead the *ummah?* Should the caliph be the most pious Muslim (as the Kharijites believed), a direct descendant of the Prophet (as the Shiites believed), or should the faithful accept the Umayyads (or any other dynasty), with all their failings, in the interests of peace and unity?[12]

And how Islamic were the Umayyads (or any other dynasty)? Could rulers who lived in such luxury and condoned the poverty of the vast majority of the people be true Muslims? And what about the position of the non-Arab converts to Islam, who had to become "clients" (*mawali*) of one of the Arab tribes? Did this not suggest a pre-Islamic (*jahili*) chauvinism and inequity that was quite incompatible with the Abrahamic ethic of the Quran?

These political questions shaped the religion, piety, and political history of Islam for the following fourteen centuries, and they are the questions that still occupy Muslim thinkers today. Every attempt to revive the faith by a reformer (*mujaddid*) was an attempt to create a reality that matched the ideal established by the Prophet in Medina. In contemporary words, it is about how to answer the question "What would an authentic Islamic state look like today?"—a question that makes the American experiment in Iraq after Saddam Hussein extremely noteworthy.[13]

The Umayyads lasted barely ninety years, and the Abbasids took over, originally supported by the majority of Muslims, who believed that they would establish a rule that was more Islamic than that of the Umayyads, the majority of whom were highly unpopular. But the principle that "Power corrupts, and absolute power corrupts absolutely" was not then a common saying. Muslims thought that a pious man, especially a descendant of the Prophet, would rule wisely and justly. There was continued widespread support and sympathy for the family of the Prophet, whom many believed had the rightful ownership to the caliphate. Because they were oppressed in the Hijaz (the area of western Arabia that includes Mecca and Medina), many of the Prophet's descendants emigrated. The descendants of Ali's son Hasan emigrated primarily to North Africa, the area from Egypt to Morocco, which is why you see many kings of Morocco named Hasan (the last being Hasan V). The descendants of Ali's younger son, Hussein, emigrated primarily to the south of the Arabian peninsula and to the east toward Iraq and Iran, explaining the greater prevalence there of the name Hussein over Hasan.

The Abbasids. The Abbasids established their caliphate in 750 CE and ruled until 1258 CE in Baghdad. They were no less ruthless than the Umayyads in holding on to power and rule. The first Abbasid caliph, Abu'l Abbas as-Saffah (750–754), massacred all the Umayyads he could find. One escaped, Abd ar-Rahman I, who founded the successor Umayyad dynasty in Spain around 756. The second Abbasid caliph, al-Mansur (754–775), murdered the Shiite leaders (whom we'll discuss later), a situation not that different from the rule of Saddam Hussein. Muslims therefore felt cheated of a ruler who would rule like the "rightly guided" caliphs did. By the time of Harun ar-Rashid (the fifth Abbasid caliph, who ruled from 786–809), the transformation to an absolute monarchy was complete.

Ar-Rashid was a patron of the arts and scholarship, and under his son al-Ma'mun (who ruled from 813 to 833), cultural and academic renaissance reached its peak when al-Ma'mun established a House of Wisdom (*bayt al-hikmah*) in Baghdad. Its principal activity was the translation of philosophical and scientific works from Greek originals that the caliph had imported and that considerably influenced the development of Islamic thought and culture. The institution also housed astronomical observatories, where Muslim scholars devised new tables, correcting the ancient ones furnished by Ptolemy. Other parts of the Muslim world also established "houses of wisdom or knowledge" (*dar al-hikmah* or *dar al-'ilm*), such as an academy founded in Cairo in 1005 CE by the Fatimid caliph al-Hakim. They focused on classical, pre-Islamic sciences (*'ulum al-awa 'il*)—bodies of knowledge amassed by Greek, Roman, and Far Eastern scholarship—as well as traditional Islamic learning, including studies of the Quran and its exegesis, Hadith, and Arabic grammar. Containing a library and reading rooms, such academies served as meeting places for traditionists, jurists, grammarians, doctors, astronomers, logicians, and mathematicians.[14]

In spite of the absolute power these two dynasties wielded, the period of the Umayyads and Abbasids ushered in what many scholars have called the classical period of Islamic history. This was the time during which Muslims and others translated into Arabic all the works of knowledge they could get their hands on (Greek, Indian, and Chinese) and absorbed and advanced their ideas. The period from 800 to 1200 CE was the boom period of Islamic intellectual ascendancy, during which time Islamic jurisprudence was developed and rationalist ideas were adopted and applied in all areas of intellectual endeavor. From Cordoba in Spain to Central Asia, a *pax Islamica* ruled over the most civilized, most prosperous, highly educated, pluralist, and literate region of the world. Until 1258 the Muslim world was marked by a pronounced Arab culture and spirit, where an Arab spirit pervaded the Islamic civilization,

Historian and professor of Islamic studies Philip Hitti believes that the glory of al-Ma'mun's age was in the "impetus the caliph gave to learning and intellectual activity," developing it "into one of the most momentous in Islam if not in history of thought." The ninth-century Arabs were not only translators and transmitters, "their reservoir of knowledge had many outlets, as it had inlets, and much of what they passed on was enriched by their original contributions."[15]

Often a few small steps open up entirely new vistas. One example took place in mathematics: intellectuals of this time rendered Indian mathematics into Arabic. The Indians had invented the numerals 1 to 9. The Arabs added the idea of the zero (called *sifr,* from which the English word *cipher* comes) and thereby introduced to the world what became known as Arabic numerals and the rules of arithmetic. For the first time, schoolchildren could perform addition and even multiplication. Imagine adding 1304 + 2650, which any schoolchild today can do in a jiffy, if you had to do it the old-fashioned Roman way, by adding MCCCIV + MMDCL. The Arab way is easy, and this made the Arabs look real smart and increased their prestige throughout the known world.

Al-Khwarizmi, whose name gave us the terms *algorithm* and *logarithm,* was one of the greatest minds of the age. He composed the first book on algebra (from the Arabic *al-jabr*), called *Hisab al-Jabr wa'l-Muqabalah.* His works introduced Europe to the use of Arabic numerals, algebra, and logarithms. Together with other works that Arabs translated from the works of Indian astronomers, and added to, Muslims introduced to Europe the scientific knowledge extant at the time.

From the Indians and Persians the Arabs adopted delightful storytelling. The most famous collection of stories was "A Thousand and One Nights," known in the West as *The Arabian Nights* and translated by Sir Richard Burton into sixteen volumes occupying almost two feet of shelf space in my personal library. The fables of *Kalilah wa-Dimnah,* reminiscent of Aesop's fables, was a delightful collection of fables in which animals are personified and carry on dialogues discussing their experiences. The author of the fables was the Hindu philosopher Bidpai, who wrote the original *Panchatantra* in Sanskrit. Its Persian intermediary was lost, and the tales survived in Arabic.

Arab translators and researchers transmitted Greek philosophy as well to the West. The Spanish Muslim Ibn-Rushd, known in the West as Averroës (1126–1198 CE), was the last link in a chain of scholars that reintroduced Aristotle to the continent of his birth.[16] Further, the Greek originals of Aristotle and Plato survived in the Muslim world, which the West regained when Constantinople was recaptured in 1204.

Among the most influential people were the scholars, the people of religious knowledge, who were concerned about the correctness of actions from a religious viewpoint—whether actions were religiously legal or illegal. The Quranic injunction to let there be a people who deepen their understanding of religion so they can guide the community led naturally to the development of understanding (*fiqh*) of religion (Quran 9:122). From this, circles of scholars ('*ulama*') evolved, and by the mid-ninth century the most notable of them grew into schools of legal thought that developed what was called the Shariah. One of the most important jurists to develop this science of jurisprudence was Imam Al-Shafi'i (died in 820), founder of the Shafi'i school of jurisprudence. Shariah became the foundation for law in Muslim societies and the foundation for much legal reasoning in the Jewish tradition as well.

Because the population rarely regarded the caliphs as rulers equal to the Rashidun in character and sagacity but saw them instead as people leading dissolute lives, the scholars of law developed a legal perspective on the limits of the caliph's power. Armstrong points out,

> The Shariah totally rejected the aristocratic, sophisticated ethos of the court. It restricted the power of the caliph, stressed that he did not have the same role as the Prophet or the Rashidun, but that he was only permitted to administer the sacred law. Courtly culture was thus tacitly condemned as un-Islamic. The ethos of the Shariah, like that of the Quran, was egalitarian . . . an attempt to rebuild society on criteria that were entirely different from those of the court. It aimed

to build a counterculture and a protest movement that would, before long, bring it into conflict with the caliphate. . . . If Muslims lived according to the Shariah, they could create a counterculture that would transform the corrupt political order of their day and make it submit to God's will.[17]

Much of the impulse behind the desire in contemporary Muslim societies for the establishment of Shariah law is precisely that—seeking the rule of law against an existing power structure that does not have a formal opposition or any checks and balances to its power. The rulers, by contrast, sought to co-opt all the sources of power and influence.

The chief threat to the dynastic rulers was that power might be taken from them by the Prophet's descendants, popularly called *ahl al-bayt,* literally, "members of the [Prophet's] household." This was the preferred position of the majority of Muslims.

Al-Ma'mun was an intellectual himself, and he placed himself in the position of arguing with the scholars on their own turf. He took the radical step of raising rationalism to a state religion, adopting the views of a group of rationalists who were called Mu'tazilah. His mistake was in forcing it upon the populace. Whether the Quran was created or uncreated, for example, was one of these arguments—possibly a carryover from the Christian debates as to whether Jesus Christ (as the Word of God) was coeternal with God or created by God. Since Muslims believe that the Quran is the literal word of God (as Christians believe Jesus is), an argument developed on this point. Al-Ma'mun believed the Quran was created, and he transformed this small question into a major issue by forcing everyone who worked in his administration to be subjected to an inquisition-style interrogation and to admit, on pain of dismissal from office, that the Quran was created. After al-Ma'mun's death, the revenge of the *'ulama* took place, and the Mu'talizite doctrines were discredited.

Scholars were generally regarded by the governors and the caliphs as the opposition party, and not a single one of the major founders of Islamic schools of law (which they fully developed and systematized by the end of the ninth century) escaped punishment in some form or other: being jailed or whipped for taking a position antithetical to the political powers, which vastly contributed to their popularity with the masses.[18] The Umayyads and Abbasids sought to establish themselves above the law, a natural human trait. Scholars argued for a rule of law that applied to all, and they sought to establish, as we would say in modern terms, a judiciary independent of the political establishment.[19]

These ideological struggles resulted in what became known as the Sunni position, namely, that the community need not be headed by a descendant of the Prophet as long as it was governed by the rule of Law. The Shiites maintained the idea of rule by the Rightly Guided Imam, understood to be a descendant of the Prophet, until the Iranian[20] revolution in 1979 and Imam Khomeini's articulation of the idea of the *Vilayet-i-faqih* (rule by the jurisprudent), which regarded the jurist abiding by the Shariah as a stand-in for the Rightly Guided Imam.

Closing the Gates of the Muslim Mind. After September 11 the United States veered uncritically to the right, transformed overnight from a nation delighting in a pluralism of opinions, such as exercising one's constitutional right to burn the U.S. flag, to being politically incorrect if you did not sport a flag on your lapel. A similar defensive reaction took place in medieval times among Muslims who were attacked.

In 1258 the Mongols erupted out of central Asia, invading and destroying Baghdad and the eastern regions of the Muslim world. And from 1250 to 1500 CE in the West, the Muslims (together with the Jews) were ejected from the Iberian peninsula by the Spanish Inquisition.

The effect of these two destructions on Muslim history, coming right on the heels of the Christian Crusades in the area of Palestine, cannot be overstated. The Mongols under Genghis Khan developed themselves into a fighting machine of fearsome destructive power. They completely laid Baghdad to waste, killing millions in their rampaging path. The manuscripts of Baghdad's libraries were burned or thrown into the Euphrates, blackening its waters with their oozing ink. The Mongol army continued eastward until 1260, when it was defeated by the Mamluk sultan of Egypt, Baybars, in a place aptly called Ain Jalut (Goliath's Eye) in Palestine. The Mamluks were emancipated Turkish slaves who ruled Egypt from 1250 to 1517. It takes fire to fight fire as Americans say, and it took a warrior people, the Turks, to stem another warrior people, the Mongols.

This attack by non-Muslims on the Muslim world resulted in a circling-of-the-wagons mentality among Muslims. They were petrified.

With their libraries burned and invaluable manuscripts lost, they intellectually froze, and this freezing of Muslim thought was called by a special name: the "closing of the gates of *ijtihad*." Muslims veered sharply to the right and became defensive.

Muslim intellectual vibrancy has never quite been the same. Since then Islamic intellectual effort was focused on maintaining the survival of what was learned rather than on expanding knowledge further. This is not unlike what happened to Western civilization in the trauma caused by the fall of Rome. Both the economy and culture of the West declined during the Middle (or "Dark") Ages and would not recover for many centuries.

Non-Arab Muslim Rule, 1100s–1800s

The major developments within Islam in the period from roughly 1100 to 1924 were the institutionalization of Sufism and the forms of political governance. Political power shifted to the Seljuk Turks (1077–1307), followed by the Ottomans (1281–1924), whose capital was in Istanbul, Turkey. This period also includes the Safavids (1501–1732), whose capital was in Iran, and the Moguls (1526–1858), among whose capitals were Agra and Delhi in India. Arab dominance faded during this time, and the Muslim world was ruled by non-Arab Muslims. Dynastic rule remained the norm, however, under the model of empire. From the 1700s on, the Muslim world began to be colonized by European powers, but we leave the European paradigm for the following section.

In spite of the traumatic historical setbacks in Baghdad and Spain, three major Islamic dynasties came into being after 1258: that of the Ottomans in Istanbul, Turkey, from 1281 to 1924 CE, the Safavids in Iran from 1501 to 1732 CE, and the Moguls in India from 1526 to 1858 CE. The Moguls were descendants of the Mongols, who became Islamized, culturally and religiously. The historic expansion of Islam after 1258 is noteworthy for its being shaped by a *non-Arab spirit*, namely by Turks, Persians, and Indians. This second wave of Islamic resurgence expanded the geographic boundaries of the Muslim world: north into Asia Minor and the Balkans in Europe, deeper into Central Asia, south into Africa, and east into Indonesia and the Philippines. The Islamic faith and orthodoxy expanded into different and new cultures. The re-

sult was an Islam that, while clearly defined in its theological and juridical orthodoxy, was restated in a variety of cultures. This Islamic
character of this era was culturally different from the Arab Semitic and
African tone of Islam, which had clearly defined it up until the beginning of the first millennium.

These new Muslim societies did not continue to advance the
boundaries of knowledge as had their predecessors of the classical period. The rulers of the classical period fancied themselves equivalents
to our Rhodes Scholar presidents; the Mogul and Turkish rulers fancied themselves more Pentagon-style rulers. While holding on to the
knowledge of the past as best they could, they aimed to contribute
more in governmental framework and political theory, in economic
structure and social organization, and in cultural and aesthetic values,
architecture, art, and poetry—the vestiges of courtly power and prestige. During this era, Islamic artists and architects pushed the envelope.
The Ottoman architect Sinan, whom the *Encyclopedia of Islam* regards as
"an Islamic equivalent to Sir Christopher Wren," transformed architectural understanding. His Suleymaniye Mosque in Istanbul (1556),
with its signature domes and pencil-thin soaring minarets, is considered the masterpiece of the age, and his 334 architectural works, mostly
mosques, not only defined Ottoman architecture but also influenced
architecture all over the Muslim world up to today. The architectural
features of the Islamic Center in New York City, built in 1980 on
Ninety-sixth Street and Third Avenue, bears the stamp of Sinan's influence. The beautifully detailed floral designs of Iranian mosques,
palaces, and gardens evoked the peaceful paradisal quality of the Alhambra in Granada, Spain. And the Taj Mahal in Agra (1650) and the
Red Fort in Delhi, India, defined the apex of Mogul architecture. During this period too, the art of Islamic calligraphy reached its greatest
heights, especially in Turkey and Iran.

By the eighteenth century this second efflorescence of Muslim society was in serious decline, coinciding with the robust expansion of
Europe and rise of European colonialism. In the Muslim world, military and political power disintegrated, and the commercial and other
economic life became feeble. The sense of being under attack, this time
from a powerful European colonialism, continued the stagnation of Islamic intellectual effort.

Spiritual and Political Expansion. Up until the time of Ghazali, the great scholar and mystic of the eleventh century, Shiite tendencies, fueled by love of the Prophet and his family, remained strong. The Seljuk Turks were Sunnis, and they effectively suppressed Shiite rule, which had attained political power in the dynasties of the Fatimids in North Africa and Egypt and the Buwayhids (or Buyids) of Persia. The Turks established themselves by reorganizing Islamic education. Previously study was undertaken by independent students gathering under independent masters. The Seljuks, politically savvy, understood that scholars can create a counterculture, so they reorganized the *madrasas* (schools); instead of being private independent schools, madrasas became official institutions run by the Seljuks. They ensured loyalty by appointing teachers sympathetic to their religious and other policies. In these new madrasas, stress was placed on the religious sciences, while the profane sciences, which had flourished equally under the early Abbasid and Shiite dynasties, were discouraged or banned. Once education is run by government authorities, it becomes less education for education's sake than for ensuring the right political environment, the "right kind of citizen."[21] The new form of madrasa soon spread from Iraq into Egypt and Syria and, in the thirteenth and fourteenth centuries, into Morocco.

From the eleventh century, Sufi cloisters and lodges (*zawiyahs, ribats, khanaqahs,* and *dergahs*), which provided temporary resting places for traveling Sufis, played a decisive role in introducing Islam to the borderland and non-Arab regions in central Asia and North Africa. Sufi migrations became a rural and urban movement of the spirit.

The two-century period from the Mongol invasion in 1258 to the founding of the Safavid dynasty in Iran was a time of ferment. The role of Sufism in educating the population on Islam was significant not only as a spiritual way for Muslims wanting to deepen their faith, but also in introducing Islam to non-Muslims. Two of the first Mongol princes to adopt Islam sought out a Sufi teacher, before whom they made their public declaration of faith. Berke, khan of the Golden Horde and a grandson of Genghis Khan, went specially to Bukhara to acknowledge Islam at the hands of the Kubrawi Sufi master Saif uddin al-Bakharzi, while Ghazan Khan of Tabriz sent for the Shii Sufi Sadr ud-din Ibrahim from Khorasan to act as officiant at his ceremony in 1295. Sufism received official favor from the Seljuks and their rulers and from Saladin and his successors. The Persian poet Rumi was highly honored by the court of Konya, and there are many references to official patronage at other courts.[22]

By the 1700s, many orders declined. Without the sustaining power of continuing live masters, some orders stressed the peripheral instead of the essential and thereby degenerated, which compromised the pure nature of Sufism. This led to a flurry of revival attempts.

The Western and European Paradigm, 1700s–1900s

From the late 1700s and especially throughout the twentieth century, European ascendant power dominated and colonized the Muslim peoples. Western norms, ideas, and culture infiltrated the Muslim world. During this period of Muslim history, initiatives were shaped by the Muslim world's interaction with the West: Islamic nationalism, apologetics, and the quality of Islamic activism were primarily reactive rather than proactive.

Among the ways of thinking the colonizers introduced to the Muslim world was that of the nation-state based on geographic boundaries. Some Muslims adopted that idea, like Turkey under Atatürk. Others found themselves in new nation-states with identities imposed by the colonizers. The Kurds after World War I found themselves grouped with either Turkish or Iraqi nationals. The end of this period saw the gradual but fitful political independence of the majority of Muslim peoples. Nostalgia for the national identity prior to the imposition of geographic boundaries has given rise to more than fifty Islamic nation-states belonging to the Organization of Islamic Conference.

Most of the revivalist movements in the Muslim world, and political dynamics of our times, have their genesis in this period: from the Wahhabis (in the late 1700s) in what is today Saudi Arabia to the Indian revivalist movements beginning with Shah Waliyullah (in the mid-1700s). Late-nineteenth-century thinkers such as al-Afghani and Muhammad 'Abduh sought to revive Islam's past glory and were as concerned about independence from the West as about learning from it, taking what was beneficial and discarding what they regarded toxic.

Two Approaches to Reform. When people seek reform or wish to correct the mistakes of the past, they do it in one of two ways. Either they work constructively, incorporating learning from the past, or they work critically, seeking to start over by discarding learning from the past. The advantage of the first approach is that it focuses people on what needs to be done by educating and developing them. It is also the more permanent and lasting approach because people are taught how to think through new situations and come up with a right answer—and to recognize when there is, and can be, more than one right answer. The advantage of the second approach is that it is much simpler to teach and inculcate. Crimes are easier to identify, cheaper to punish, and they invoke more passion than does education. And people are driven by passion. Moreover, it is much easier to find teachers to teach the second, critical, approach than the first, constructive, approach. However, the second approach creates heresies out of any idea that differs from its own and finds it difficult to coexist with other approaches. Its life is also naturally short, since it is defined by what it stands against and therefore does not outlast its opponent.

Aberrant Islamic practices (called *bid'a*) naturally led to these two responses in Islamic history. Both regarded themselves as efforts leading to a pure Islam—that of "our original pious predecessors," *as-salaf as-salih*—and thus in the nineteenth and twentieth centuries they became known as the *salafi* movements. The first category of responses included attempts to revive an authentic Islamic impulse free of the excesses that had accrued over the centuries; the second category was reactionary responses to excesses that arguably threw the baby out with the bathwater. Of the latter, the most influential over the past half century has been the Wahhabi movement.

Wahhabi Islam: The "Let's Start All Over Again" Approach. By the 1700s the Ottoman, Safavid, and Mogul dynasties had all passed their prime. Muslims felt the need for reform to counter the lethargy that had overtaken their communities. The Arab world chafed under Turkish Ottoman rule and yearned for a return to the simplicity of an idealistic and in some ways idealized, unadulterated, and pure Islam.

Reform movements tried to revive themselves by self-correcting rather than starting over—except most notably one, that of Muhammad ibn Abd al-Wahhab (1703–1787), from Najd, the northeast area of the

Arabian peninsula. Abd al-Wahhab's revivalist movement rejected most of the Islamic heritage of the past eleven hundred years and tried to imagine an Islamic society that began all over again as in the time of the Prophet, based solely on the Quran and the Prophet's *sunnah.* Ignoring the rich contributions of non-Arab cultures to Islamic history, he initiated the most drastic instance of starting all over again ever attempted in Islamic history.

He could realistically think of doing this for several reasons. For one thing, he was about as pure an Arab as could be, unlike most of the other reformers, who from his point of view were foreign. Also, eighteenth-century Najd, located in Arabia, was culturally more similar to Mecca and Medina of the Prophet's time than to Damascus or Baghdad or Istanbul, seat of the Umayyad and Abbasid and Ottoman caliphates, which by then had ruled the Muslim peoples for over a thousand years. Had he originated in India, he could not have ignored Indian pluralism or, if in Egypt, Egyptian society's diverse cultural and religious history. But from Abd al-Wahhab's point of view, most of the Muslim intellectuals—like Ibn Rushd (Averroës), who was a "Westerner" from al-Andalus (Spain)—were foreign, not only geographically but also intellectually and psychologically. Abd al-Wahhab wanted to adhere to the tradition of *his* pious predecessors, not to traditions of "foreigners" beyond the Arabian peninsula. We might colloquially say that Abd al-Wahhab yearned for an *Arab* Islam, not a Turkish, Persian, or Indian Islam, for wasn't the Quran after all an *Arabic* Quran?[23] Too, Abd al-Wahhab's geographical remoteness made it possible to entertain such a vision of a purified Islam. Because Abd al-Wahhab lived in the relative isolation of central Arabia, in a society that was culturally and religiously homogeneous relative to the neighboring countries, his project was theoretically doable.

Abd al-Wahhab established his movement in his home territory in the Najd province. His message was straightforward: a return to a classical Islam that was pure, puritanical, simple, and therefore vigorous. He rejected philosophy, and he publicly burned a number of philosophical books, including some of Ghazali's works. Anything that he deemed a source of dissension, including the Shiah, was equally rejected. In addition to preaching, he formed an alliance with a local ruling prince, Ibn Saud, so that his vision could be implemented in society. Ibn Saud's power was helpful in quelling the resistance to his vision that inevitably arose. Without Ibn Saud's political support, Wahhabism would not have gained the influence it did in the Arabian peninsula.

What was compelling about Wahhabism was the attempt to implement a historical ideal: the Quran and *sunnah* as practiced by the Prophet in Medina in seventh-century Arabia—an attractive idea to the lay Muslim. Taken to its theoretical limit, this is impossible, for much that is necessary to Islamic life was developed in the first few centuries after the Prophet, such as the rules of *ijtihad*, that is, the effort expended by Muslim jurists to arrive at a correct legal opinion or judgment; the formulation of the rules of Arabic grammar, which was necessary to jurisprudence; and the development of Arabic dictionaries. Even the recording of the hadiths of the Prophet and the compilation of a written Quran were begun after the death of the Prophet. (The Prophet dictated the Quran, as it was revealed over twenty-three years, to different scribes, but the entire text was not collected, compiled, and collated into one manuscript until after his death.) The principle of multiplicity of legal interpretation that the jurists recognized as essential to truth and a harmonious Muslim society arose only by the third century after the Prophet. Wahhabism resulted in a selective interpretation of Islam that tried to filter out most of what it viewed as introduced by foreign elements, especially philosophical rationalism, spirituality, and foreign cultural elements.

The understanding of Islam that Wahhabis were fighting against, and that by then had become universal, was that Islam is God's purpose for humankind as expressed in the Quran and *sunnah, and as it is worked out in the ongoing community's understanding of these two.* Abd al-Wahhab's interpretation attempted to stop at the *sunnah.*

We pointed out that Muhammad's message included three segments: (1) *islam,* freely choosing to obey God (will); (2) *iman,* seeking God's Truth with your mind (intellect); and (3) *ihsan,* loving God above all else (heart) and opening oneself to union with God (soul). The Wahhabis focused most of their efforts on the first segment: "doing the right thing," believing that if we truly did that, most everything else would fall into place. Only the strictest interpretation of the Law, stripped of the various opinions and interpretations of the intervening centuries and schools of thought, was deemed valid. This, they preached, was pristine Islam; all else was superfluous and wrong.

Essential to al-Wahhab's success was the alliance that he effected with Ibn Saud and the ensuing success of the family of Saud in consolidating its power over the other tribes of the Arabian peninsula and forging them into the nation that is today Saudi Arabia. And now, for a moment, we turn our attention to the twentieth century. With Saudi takeover in 1924 of the Hijaz (the western part of the Arabian peninsula where Mecca and Medina are) from Sharif Hussein (grandfather of the late King Hussein of Jordan and father of King Faisal, who was depicted in David Lean's film *Lawrence of Arabia*), Mecca was no longer the center of Sufism, no longer the venue where ideas percolating in the Muslim world were subjected to the rigor of cross-examination by the leading thinkers of the Islamic world. It gradually became the most efficient and most influential point of dissemination of Wahhabi thought.

The Wahhabi influence on the Muslim world was not that pronounced until the second half of the twentieth century, partly because central Arabia, where Wahhabis established themselves, was geographically remote and not regarded as a place of importance. Arabia then had no important centers of learning and no economy to speak of. But after World War I, with religion increasingly on the defensive in the historical centers of Islam (the capital cities of Turkey, Egypt, and Iran), Saudi Arabia became the haven to which Muslim activists, particularly those from Egypt, who were denied participation in developing the religious voice in Egypt after the Abdel Nasser takeover, fled.[24]

However, in the mid-twentieth century oil was discovered, and by the 1960s the Saudis had the largest proven oil reserves of any country. When the price of oil multiplied in 1973, the Saudis went on a massive development campaign and needed to hire tens of thousands of employees, which they did especially from the large-population countries of Egypt, Pakistan, Bangladesh, and Indonesia. As these employees returned home from their expatriate work stints, they, in combination with the increasing numbers of pilgrims amounting to more than two million annually, began to influence the Muslim world with what they believed to be the Islam as practiced in the land of the Prophet at the *time* of the Prophet.

Wahhabism's excesses were most cogently expressed by the recent incident at a girls' school in Saudi Arabia, where a fire broke out and the *ikhwan* (religious police) refused to let the girls climb out unless they had their veils on. The result was that many girls were killed in the fire, an incident that provoked an uproar in Saudi Arabia and has led to soul searching among the Saudis. (As we saw in the previous chapter, this is in fact contrary to Islamic law, which stipulates that if application of a law results in the endangerment of life, the law is to be suspended.)

Sufi Revivals: The Constructivist Approach. The mystical way of Sufism has often been the channel through which Islam has spread to the hearts and minds of most peoples. The first documented evidence of Sufi penetration into the Malay archipelago (which includes Indonesia) was that of the Sufi Hamza Fansuri in Sumatra (who died around 1610), although Sufi influence was already indicated since the 1200s.[25] The Islamization of Java is associated with a legendary story of nine Sufi saints (*wali songo*).

The locus for this spread of Islam had traditionally been Mecca. The city operates psychologically as the religious capital of the Muslim world, and it exerts a profound influence upon the pilgrims who come annually for the hajj from all over the world. It has the ring of the Vatican to a Catholic, combined with the emotion of the Holy Land. Many a Muslim's ambition is to die and be buried in Mecca or in Medina, close to the tomb of the Prophet.

What is little known today was that Mecca in the nineteenth century had become the most important Sufi center in the Muslim world. Almost every order of Sufis was represented there. The Wahhabis had abolished the Sufi orders in those parts of Arabia that they controlled, primarily in the Najd, but they had not yet taken over Mecca and Medina. Mecca at this time served as a center for diffusing Sufi traditions, for Sufis initiated pilgrims into their orders, and these pilgrims returned home and often wielded an influence in their homelands far outweighing that of the official representatives of Islam. For example, the first Minangkabau sheikh of the Naqshbandi order received his initiation in Mecca around 1840 and introduced his order to Indonesia.

When it came to revival movements, Sufism's approach was to recognize and save what is spiritually beautiful and valuable. Some focused more on the contemplative life and avoiding involvement in politics and worldly affairs; others were fully engaged in worldly life.

An example of focusing on the contemplative life was the Darqawi order, founded by Abu Hamid ad-Darqawi (1760–1823), based in Morocco, whose followers spread through North Africa. Although he tried to avoid political involvement, he got caught up in it anyway. Another group in the Maghrib (northwest Africa) that did not avoid worldly affairs was the Tijaniyya order, founded by Ahmad at-Tijani, who was born in South Algeria in 1737 and died in Fez, Morocco, in 1815. His order is today widespread in north and west Africa, from Algeria and Morocco to Senegal, all the way into the Sudan in northeast Africa.

Another important revivalist initiative was founded by Ahmad ibn Idris, born in Fez, Morocco, in 1760. He not only taught the litanies (*wirds*) and ethics of Islamic contemplative life, he also spoke for the unity of the Islamic endeavor united in the bond of Islam. Ibn Idris's influence was felt more through the work of his followers, for he inspired the reawakening of Sufi orders during the beginning of the nineteenth century. One of his students was Muhammad as-Sanusi (1787–1859), founder of the Sanusi movement, whose presence was most felt in the central Sahara region of Libya. As-Sanusi established a *zawiyah,* a cloister, in 1838 on a hill in Mecca called Abu Qubais facing the Ka'bah. The order gained the allegiance of some of the Bedouins, and *zawiyahs* were founded in other parts of the Hijaz. He left Mecca in 1840 and established a *zawiyah* in the hills of the northeast part of Libya.

As-Sanusi's successor, Ahmad ash-Sharif (1873–1933), was involved in fighting the Italians during their colonization of Libya. This story of Libyan political independence continues with his cousin's representative, Omar al-Mukhtar, who fought the Italians until he was caught and publicly hanged on September 16, 1931. His story was depicted in the movie *Lion of the Desert* starring the late Anthony Quinn as al-Mukhtar. After the Second World War, Libya attained independence in 1951 through the efforts of the United Nations and was ruled by a Sanusi king until deposed by Muammar Qadhdhafi in September 1969.

Another of Ibn Idris's students founded the Mirghani (also known as the Khatmiyya) order, most prominent in the Sudan and continuing to be active in Sudanese politics well into the twentieth century.[26]

The Sufi intellectual gnostic tradition in the Arab world represented by Ibn al-'Arabi (1165–1240) had waned by the nineteenth century. His ideas were difficult to comprehend, which led some people to the easier reaction, namely, to reject them as unorthodox. Ibn al-'Arabi's teachings did not develop into a school, although there were individuals who felt drawn to be part of this intellectual Sufi tradition. Perhaps the most notable of this period is the Amir Abd al-Qadir of Algeria (1808–1883), who fought the French occupation until they captured him and eventually sent him to Damascus, where he lived the rest of his life and died there, interred in the same city as his intellectual forebear Ibn al-'Arabi. (At the request of the Algerian government, Abd al-Qadir remains have recently been moved to Algeria.)

In Iran, however, an intellectual Sufi tradition flourished with Mulla Sadra (1571–1640), who wrote on Ibn al-'Arabi's ideas on the unity of being (*wahdat al-wujud*). His influence was limited in the immediate generations succeeding him, but it increased markedly in the 1800s when his ideas helped inspire a renewal within Twelver Shiism (the Shiism associated with Iran) and were revived by the efforts of Mulla Hadi Sabzawari (1798–1878).

Political power usually plays an important role in furthering the destiny of revival movements and even of approach in Islamic thought. We have noted, for example, Ibn Saud's partnership with the Wahhabi movement, without which it could not have attained the ascendancy it did in the Muslim world, in conjunction with Saudi Arabia's growing fortunes.

In India a Naqshbandi known as Shah Wali Allah of Delhi (1703–1762) sought to reconstruct Islamic thought in a most comprehensive way. He wanted to reconcile the dichotomy that people thought existed between Shariah (law) and Sufism, to blend together a pure understanding of each that would more completely reflect the Prophet's range of imperatives. Growing up and watching the Mogul empire crumbling, he held the vision of a purified Islam that retained a strong devotion to Sufism. His movement laudably sought to retain the widest range of all that was valuable in the history of Islamic thought. But at the same time, India was coming under the rule of the British, and therefore the struggle for him and his successors was as much against external threat and domination by the colonialists as for Islamic regeneration.

European Hostile Takeover: 1700s–1900s. In 1798 Napoleon conquered Egypt, and by the beginning of the 1800s most of the Muslim world had fallen under the dominion of European colonial power. The Portuguese were the first to penetrate India and the Far East but were later displaced by the Dutch and then the British, although the Dutch retained what is today Indonesia. By the mid-1700s, India had become dominated by the British through its East India Company.

Modern Americans forget that they too were victims of British colonialism, and the thirteen American colonies, after various periods of colonization by the British, waged the American War of Independence from 1775 to 1783 to gain independence from the British. What the English king did to the American colonies, the colonial powers did to the Muslim world. The British, the French, the Russians, and to a lesser extent the Dutch and Italians, divided up the Muslim world into their colonies. From the very beginning of the period the Muslim nations fought for their political independence, but it was not until the twentieth century that they gradually gained it.

Blending Best of East and West. European power excited the admiration of many Muslim thinkers. Many of them recognized in European civilization much of what once had made Muslim society great and what Muslims had lost. One of the most important leaders who galvanized Muslim societies along these lines at the end of the nineteenth century was Jamal ad-Din al-Afghani (1839–1897), whose career encompassed the Arab world, Turkey, Iran, India, and the European West. He united with traditional Islamic scholarship a familiarity with European and modern thought. He inspired a whole generation of political revolutionaries and venerable scholars, giving many a sermon based on the Quranic verse "Indeed God does not change the condition of a people until they change that which is in their selves" (Quran 13:11). He appreciated the vigor of Western science and scientific techniques and spoke of adopting and adapting the discoveries of the West into the Islamic context. This approach of not rejecting Western learning and accomplishments but of adopting them became the hallmark of much of early-twentieth-century Islamic thought and activism.

Al-Afghani devoted himself to Muslim revival and anticolonialism. As a philosopher, writer, orator, and journalist, he catalyzed the incipient national liberation movements in the Muslim world. He

criticized the lethargy of the Muslim countries and the increasing control of their economic and political life by European powers. His dream
was to see the Muslim states unite and recreate the glory of Islam's
past.

Among those influenced by al-Afghani's ideas was the Egyptian
reformist thinker Muhammad 'Abduh (1849–1905), grand mufti of
Egypt in 1889 and, finally, a member of the supreme council of Cairo's
Al-Azhar University. His reform movement, known as the Salafiyya,
from the phrase *salaf as-salihin* ("the pious ancestors"), gained momentum in Egypt.

Like his mentor, al-Afghani, Muhammad 'Abduh was enamored
by much of Western civilization and sought to retain the best of Islamic
thought and blend it with the positive things learned from the West.
Although he provoked hostility in some conservative circles, his ideas
met with remarkable support among serious-minded Muslims, and
they still resonate with many today. His program was threefold: re-
forming people's understanding of Islam by bringing it back to its
original condition; recognizing the rights of people in relation to government; and emphasizing a greater understanding of the Arabic language, the language of Muslim scripture. The challenge that Muslim
thinkers faced at the time was that while they favored assimilation of
some aspects of Western civilization without losing their cultural and
religious heritage, they were simultaneously struggling for independence from political and economic control from the West.

Like many of the revivalist thinkers, 'Abduh wished to see Muslim
societies rid themselves of the abuses that falsified Islamic practice and
kept it out of step with the times. He wanted to adapt Islam to modern
exigencies by going back to its true and fundamental principles or, in
other words, to reform along orthodox lines, a path laid out by the
school of Ibn Taymiyya and Ibn al-Qayyim al-Jawziyyah and leavened
with al-Ghazali's ethical concepts of religion. 'Abduh sought to revivify Muslims' understanding of *ijtihad* and to make it applicable to the
times. This is important because Islam, as we have seen, is a religion of
law. Unless Muslims have a common understanding of the basis of
how their laws are derived, and how laws are to be determined as
shar'i, which is the equivalent of "constitutional" in the mind of a Muslim, conflict is bound to occur. He believed that there was no conflict

between religion (properly understood) and knowledge, and thus there was no conflict between reason and revelation.

In 'Abduh's theology, the religious content consists of humility before God, reverence for the Prophet, enthusiasm for the Quran, and the observance of an ethical system favorable to progress. He criticized the closing of the Muslim mind, the ossification of Muslim scholarship, and the adherence to uncritical imitation, called *taqlid*. Realizing that knowledge and Europe's wealth, progress, and power all resulted from investing in education and the sciences, he sought to revamp Islamic education in Egypt, especially at Al-Azhar University, which at the time relied on rote memorization without the kind of dispute and debate that leads to intellectual development.[27]

Muhammad 'Abduh sought to revivify Islamic intellectual thought, and his effect upon Islamic education in Egypt and the Muslim world was profound. Within a generation, Al-Azhar graduates were sent to study in the West, to explore what Western hermeneutics and methodologies would add to classical Islamic hermeneutics and methodologies.

Salafiyyah was centered in Egypt, where 'Abduh held the post of grand mufti, but it had profound influence on other Arab countries, and similar movements sprang up in other parts of the Islamic world, such as the Aligarh in India and the Muhammadiyah in Indonesia. The Salafiyyah movement aimed to restore the original Islam in the modern context, which as we know is the eternal challenge all religions face. Salafiyyah emulated the endeavors of Christian missionaries and sponsored propagandists to spread the message of Islam and counter their efforts at converting Muslims. The movement called for humanism and progress, declaring that there was no conflict between orthodox Islam and modern needs. In embracing the theory of evolution, the movement took modern science as an authority whose knowledge adds to revealed knowledge of the Quran, and the first feminist movements found support in the Salafiyyah.

Today, the movement is no longer in operation. Its ideas have unfortunately been overshadowed by fundamentalist reactions, and the term *salafiyyah* is applied inaccurately (in terms of its original intent) to groups who believe in applying Islamic law rigidly rather than in adapting it to modern times.

The attempt to blend the best of East and West during this turn-of-the-century era found its subcontinental voice in Sir Muhammad Iqbal (1873–1938), a Muslim thinker whose exposure to the West yielded an inquiry into Islamic thought. Iqbal was an Indian philosopher, poet, politician, and president of the Muslim League who studied at Cambridge University and the University of Munich. His written works focused on religious reform and self-advancement, combining the ideas of Western philosophers with the Quran.[28] True to his poet nature, he saw beauty in many things. Although he shared with other thinkers the desire to blend the best of Western civilization with Islamic civilization, he did not establish a movement that sought to further his ideas.

Blending Gone Sour: Coups by Western-Influenced Strongmen and Subsequent Fundamentalist Reactions. After a time, the blend of East and West went sour. Complicating the picture were aggressive attempts by the Soviets to export communism, viewed by Muslims as an insidious Western -ism. Thinkers such as al-Afghani, 'Abduh, and Iqbal had recognized what was positive in both the West and the Islamic traditions of their time. They had sought to blend what they recognized as the best of Western ideals with a revival of Islamic civilization and to discard the worst of each—not to throw out the proverbial baby with the bathwater.

Political events intruded. Atatürk ended the Ottoman Caliphate in Turkey in 1924. The regimes that took over in Turkey under Atatürk, in Egypt under Abdel Nasser, and in Iran under Reza Shah Pahlavi (who ruled from 1925 to 1941) and his son Muhammad Reza Shah (1941 to 1979), influenced by Western secularism, suppressed and marginalized the religious element. By the 1970s, important Islamic institutions such as Al-Azhar in Egypt no longer produced the kinds of intellectual thinkers who could continue the heritage of Muhammad 'Abduh, resulting in a reversal and a massive reclosing of the Muslim mind. Religion was under attack all over the world, and Islam was under attack even in its capitals. In the meantime Wahhabism, being the strongest element on the Islamic scene, found itself in the role of primary defender of the faith.

By this time the cold war between the United States and the Soviet Union shaped world politics. Both sides preferred to have in office one strongman whom they could control; the tragedy was that the United States did not during this period (1952 to the end of the century) support the democratization process in the Muslim world. To those in the Muslim world, oppression came in the form of Western-influenced dictators who suppressed traditional Islamic culture and religion; thus political freedom has appeared to consist of opposing Western influence and reclaiming Islamic tradition, often in the most fundamentalist form possible. Had the United States opposed such dictatorial regimes over the past half century, the link for Muslims between the West and their lack of freedom might have been broken—and the power of fundamentalist tendencies weakened.

Sayyid Qutb (1906–1966), an Egyptian writer of Indian origin, is considered the main ideologue of modern Muslim fundamentalism. He became an opponent of the West after traveling through Europe and North America in the early 1950s, repelled by what he saw as superficial religion. For him, rulers like Abdel Nasser were guilty of working with the West to enhance the influence of secularism on religion. Qutb felt the need to respond to this from a Muslim perspective. Qutb was a member of the Muslim Brotherhood, an activist group started by Hasan al-Banna, who sought to establish an Islamic regime in Egypt. In 1954 he was accused of being involved in an attempt to assassinate Egyptian president Gamal Abdel Nasser and was sentenced to fifteen years in prison. He believed in an Islamic democracy based on the Quranic idea of *shura* (consultation). While he was in prison, his opinions hardened against the Nasser regime and its violent oppression of those it did not agree with. Angered and hurt by this violence, he developed in prison an absolutist view of Islam. Released in 1964 with help from the then-president of Iraq, he was arrested a year later and accused of treason, planning a coup d'état, and attempting to assassinate Nasser. He was executed in August 1966 in spite of entreaties from many, including the then-president of Pakistan, Ayyub Khan, to stay his execution.

In November 1964 Qutb published his book *Landmarks*, in which he accused Muslim societies of being *jahili* (an anti-Abrahamic ethic). This book contains the seeds of modern Islamic fundamentalism and has had vast ideological influence in Egypt and other Muslim countries, including revolutionary Iran. Qutb's anger against the West was directed at what he saw as Christianity's modern legacy, which was the idea that religion should be confined to a small corner of life. Qutb also blamed Zionism for what he saw as an eternal campaign by Jews to destroy Islam. He also attacked one other group, the Muslims who had gone along with Christianity's errors—"the treacherous Muslims who had inflicted Christianity's 'schizophrenia' on the world of Islam."[29] He thus found an enemy in each segment of the Abrahamic faith traditions.

America on the Horizon of the Muslim World. Until the turn of the twentieth century, America was relatively isolated from European affairs, its involvement in world affairs being largely confined to North and South America. But by the time of the First World War (1914–1918), America was actively induced by the European powers to be drawn into European politics. To tell this part of the story—our joint history—requires more insight into America's past, and so we turn now to the history of the United States.

In discussing American history, I will emphasize those points of intersection with Muslim history—the issues and developments that have had the greatest impact on America's relationship with the Muslim world. Overall, we might conceptualize this story as the growth of the Abrahamic ethic in the West, in the form of freedoms extended to greater numbers of people in this country and increasing opportunities for "life, liberty, and the pursuit of happiness."

AMERICAN HISTORY: FROM THE PURITAN ETHIC TO LIBERAL DEMOCRACY

As we have seen, America was founded upon religious values, as expressed in its Declaration of Independence and Constitution. In all societies, however, the ideals expressed by the founders often encounter challenges when they are implemented in real life. This is true in American history as well. The on-the-ground reality of life in America often has not matched the Abrahamic ethic of respect for all expressed in its founding documents. In particular, the realities of slavery, lack of rights for women, and prejudice toward newly arriving immigrants of different races and religions have been areas of life in which American society has had to evolve toward a fuller expression of its own Abrahamic ideals. We will take a look at each of these topics below and note that the battle between the Abrahamic ethic and the Protestant ethic resulted in the latter's giving way to the Judeo-Christian ethic and then into increasingly purer expressions of the Abrahamic ethic. But first we delve a bit more deeply into the theology that shaped America: the Puritanism of its early New England settlers and the Protestant ethic that grew from it.

Puritanism was a version of Calvinism, founded by John Calvin (1509–1564), whose writings profoundly influenced the course of the Protestant Reformation. Calvin asserted that hard work, thrift, and the accumulation of wealth were not only consistent with a fervent belief in God but also a "calling." He pointed out that the profession of being a businessperson can be as much a sacred act as that of being a priest.

Calvin also declared the revolutionary notion that interest on monetary loans was not usurious, an idea whose impact on the futures of Europe and America cannot be overemphasized and to which we will return in a moment.

Calvin's ideas provided a much sharper definition to the Protestant Reformation initiated by Martin Luther (1483–1546). Luther and Calvin introduced into Christianity a different way of thinking about and practicing Christianity. For example, Luther's slogan *sola scriptura* ("by Scripture alone") and the evangelical Protestantism that grew out of it are close to Islam, where the Quran is primary. Calvin's emphasis on predestination—that God has chosen some for salvation—is similar to what became the majority opinion in Islamic Sunni (Ash'arite) theology, that God had decreed those souls destined for Heaven and those destined for Hell.

Another similarity Protestantism shares with Islam is its iconoclasm. Calvin strongly opposed the use of graven images, feeling that such use encouraged the unlettered in superstition and the temptations of idolatry. Oliver Cromwell's army in England desecrated statues in English cathedrals and parish churches, an act that must have aroused in Catholics of the time feelings that many had when the "puritanical" Taliban regime in Afghanistan destroyed statues of the Buddha.

The Protestant ethic shared with Islam other defining ideals, such as that religion and knowledge are compatible[30] and that religion and wealth are compatible,[31] ideals that in Islam had fueled the rise of a vast intellectual heritage and the active Muslim role in world trade. These values, which Muslims shared with Puritans, strongly influenced the culture of the American colonies and later of the United States. The Puritans (who were the "English Calvinists," so to speak) spoke English, practiced a Protestant faith, valued hard work and commercial success, and believed in the importance of education. Over time, many people came to equate these characteristics with Americans in general. Because America was founded by the English Puritans as well as other European Protestant immigrant groups, all of whom were influenced by Luther and Calvin and who became anglicized upon emigrating to America, we may equate the Puritan ethic with the Protestant ethic in America.

Where the Spirit of Capitalism Is Found

In his classic and most famous work, *The Protestant Ethic and the Spirit of Capitalism,* sociologist of religion Max Weber traces the ethos or spirit (*geist*) of capitalism to this Protestant ethic, in particular the Puritan ethic. By *capitalism* he meant not the pursuit of gain as such, for that pursuit has existed in humans from time immemorial, but rather a disciplined labor force and the accumulation of wealth for its own sake rather than for the material rewards it can bring. Weber was trying to answer the question, What made people work so hard—in fact, endlessly, in an "iron cage"? What led them to desire and work for profit for its own sake rather than as an aid in improving life? Weber pointed to the Protestant ethic; he believed that Calvinism "supplied the moral energy and drive of the capitalist entrepreneur."[32]

In my view it was not the Protestant ethic as such but rather the corporate ethic that locked people in an iron cage, seeking to maximize profit for the corporation's own sake. To understand this better, let's spend a few moments looking at the corporation.

Since the times of Phoenicians and Assyrians, the idea had existed of an organization doing business.[33] However, the corporation as it came into being through Western capitalism was defined by three new ideas:

1. The corporation was a separate independent person, with the same ability to do business as a real person.

2. By selling tradable shares, the corporation could be owned by an unlimited number of investors.

3. The investors, who are the corporation's owners (shareholders), were free from responsibility for any liability incurred by the company, especially unpaid debt.

It must be noted that unpaid debt was deemed abhorrent under all laws of the time and is still so under Muslim law. Debt had historically been looked upon as a weakness, a liability not only in the financial sense but also in the moral or religious sense. To take advantage of someone who needed a loan by charging that person interest was morally repugnant; it was usury, which, in all religions of the time, was sinful. Today when you go to buy a new car, the salesperson runs a credit check on you, and the larger the number, the better off you are considered both financially and morally. Your ability to assume large debt is considered a sign of your financial strength and economic astuteness. But prior to the Protestant way of thinking, the Catholic Church, like most Muslim scholars then and now, maintained that any return on a loan was usurious.

With the coming into being of the corporation, the company could take on debt, lose it, *and claim bankruptcy without bankrupting its owners.* The creditors had no recourse against the corporation's owners, who were limited to losing only the funds they had invested. This was new—and profoundly revolutionary.

The firewall between the shareholders and the company's liabilities gave the owners the ability to own all of a corporation's assets but none of its liability. *Unlimited* liability would have restricted a company's ability to raise capital. *Limited* liability, by contrast, unleashed the possibility for entrepreneurs to raise previously unheard-of sums of money, safe in the knowledge that investors could lose only what they had put in. Limited liability made possible the accumulation of capital.

And the corporation, as a fictional person, was theoretically immortal; it could go on accumulating capital and doing business forever.

Unlike a human person, it did not have to plan for the end of its life, and therefore its ability to grow was also unlimited. "Companies . . . possess most of the legal rights of a human being, without the attendant disadvantages of biology: they are not condemned to die of old age and they can create progeny pretty much at will."[34] These elements—unlimited life, potentially unlimited assets from investors, *but* limited liability on the part of those investors—allowed the corporation to grow beyond all previously known bounds. The corporation has an insatiable and endless appetite for its objective, whether that objective is money, as in the for-profit company, or social values, as in the nonprofit corporation. It is the corporation, or corporate ethic, not the Protestant ethic, that created the conditions under which people now work endlessly to accumulate wealth.

And it is also the corporation that enabled the West to wrest supremacy from the Muslim world, and from the rest of the world as well. The corporation, which combined the Puritan ethic with easy access to capital, provided America with powerful tools to develop its capitalist base, upon which to build the world's largest economy. The limited liability corporation provided northern Europe and the modern West its great competitive advantages over the southern European, the Islamic, and the Far Eastern way of doing business, for whom the notion of not paying your debt was not only sinful and immoral but also unthinkable. (Until the Muslim world finds a way to openly embrace these concepts and ideas in a manner consistent with Islamic law, it will continue to lag economically.)

The corporation made possible the creation of other entities that theoretically could live forever. Any idea or activity could be institutionalized, thus making it permanent and able as the need arose to evolve. One of the earliest and most important of such incorporations was the university, which "incorporated," that is, provided a *body* to the *spirit* of the empirical method, a key tool in the advancement of science, thus institutionalizing the empirical method and enabling it to last.

The early American states used chartered corporations endowed with special monopoly rights to build some of the vital infrastructures of the new country—universities (like America's oldest corporation, Harvard University, chartered in 1636), banks, churches, canals, municipalities, and roads.[35]

The Company Helps Build Democracy

The corporation led to the creation of the private sector as a growing force and power center of its own. As an economic entity, the corporation crystallized and formalized the gradual separation of the powers of the economy from that of the state. As business strategist Peter Drucker put it, "This new 'corporation' . . . was the first autonomous institution . . . to create a power center that was within society yet independent of the central government of the national state."[36] The Virginia Company helped introduce the revolutionary concept of democracy to the American colonies, to the fury of James I, who called it "a seminary for a seditious parliament."[37]

This is because if we imagine the corporation as a republic, and its shareholders as its citizens, the directors, whom the shareholders elect, are its representative government, whose role is to represent and protect the interests of the shareholders. The corporation's officers and employees who manage the company's day-to-day affairs are equivalent to the civil servants who run government. By creating a power center separate from the state, the corporation certainly accelerated, if not introduced into politics, the notion and model of modern representational democracy. Some companies became so strong that they were able to defy government control, which led to the United States breaking up monopolies in the twentieth century.

And since the objective of the corporation was to earn results for its shareholders, defined primarily as financial profit, we observe a parallel between the establishment of the United States of America and a corporate structure. And just as a corporation's shareholders are those who have purchased stock in the company (those who hadn't purchased stock couldn't vote for the corporate officers), America's first citizens with voting rights were originally those who owned land.

America's Too Good Not to Be Better: Civil Rights and Black Muslims

The story of America's intersection with Islam cannot be told without the history of black people in America. The first Muslims in America were brought over from Africa as slaves to work on the cotton plantations of the south. Approximately 10 percent of slaves were Muslim Africans,[38] and many of them were highly literate. As slave owners tried to wipe out their charges' identities, many of the names and stories of these first American Muslims have been lost. But a few remain. Umar Ibn Said (ca. 1770–1864), a Muslim scholar and trader who hailed from present-day Senegal, was enslaved and arrived in Charleston, South Carolina, in about 1807.[39] It is known that he was literate because in 1819 Francis Scott Key, the composer of "The Star Spangled Banner," received a letter from a white Protestant North Carolinian asking for an Arabic translation of the Bible for Umar. The Arabic Bible, restored and housed in the Davidson College library of North Carolina, contains Umar's notations of praise to Allah.

Unfortunately for themselves and for the relationship between the Abrahamic faith traditions in America, the first Muslims were brought in as slaves. Historically in most of the world, slavery was more of an economic than a racial structure. It had the quality of bonded labor, in which you purchased the individual's future labor instead of hiring it, somewhat like purchasing a house or a car instead of renting or hiring it weekly or monthly. Premodern societies therefore had slaves of various races and ethnicities, and slaves could and did have families who could not be broken apart, and they could and did purchase their own freedom and live as free men and women. But the evil of American slavery was that it was compounded by a noxious racism that disregarded slaves' rights.

America's Constitution did not originally fully express the values of the Abrahamic ethic toward nonwhite races. As we noted, Native Americans were completely excluded from the family of human rights, and the Africans who were brought to America as slaves were for representational purposes deemed three-fifths of a person (in article 1, section 2).

After a bloody Civil War that almost tore America apart, slavery was abolished by the Thirteenth Amendment to the Constitution in December 1865, and African American men were constitutionally granted the right to vote by the Fifteenth Amendment in March 1870. A century after the Emancipation Proclamation of 1863, America still struggled to repair the moral ravages of slavery. African American rights were still denied by many whites who could not bring themselves to accept racial equality—and who rejected the amendments to the Constitution that brought its ideals closer to a fuller expression of the Abrahamic ethic of human equality and liberty. It took another century and the civil rights movement, which galvanized individuals and civil rights organizations, to bring about substantive change. Starting in 1955, groups organized protest marches, demonstrations, boycotts, and sit-ins at whites-only restaurants and diners and in the fronts of buses, where blacks were denied seating. Such refusal to abide by segregation laws challenged segregation and discrimination.

After the Civil Rights Act of 1964, affirmative action policies were used in the United States to increase opportunities for blacks (and other minorities) by favoring them in hiring and promotion, college admissions, and the awarding of government contracts. Depending upon the situation, the term *minorities* might include any underrepresented group, especially one defined by race, ethnicity, or gender.

The term *affirmative action* was first used by President Lyndon B. Johnson in a 1965 executive order that declared that federal contractors should "take affirmative action" to ensure that job applicants and employees "are treated without regard to their race, color, religion, sex, or national origin." While the original goal of the civil rights movement had been so-called color-blind laws, simply ending a long-standing policy of discrimination did not go far enough for many people. As President Johnson explained in a 1965 speech, "You do not take a person who for years has been hobbled by chains and . . . bring him up to the starting line of a race and then say, 'you are free to compete with all the others' and still justly believe that you have been completely fair."[40]

The civil rights movement cannot be given its full due without factoring the role of Black Muslims, a term coined by C. Eric Lincoln in 1956 for followers of the Nation of Islam movement. The Nation of Islam was founded in the 1930s and was led by the Honorable Elijah Muhammad from 1934 until his death (1897–1975). Lincoln was teaching a course in religion and philosophy at Clark College in Atlanta, Georgia, in the fall of 1956 when a student's term paper on Christianity shot at him the following words:

The Christian religion is incompatible with the Negro's aspirations for dignity and equality in America. It has hindered where it might have helped; it has been evasive when it was morally bound to be forthright; separated believers on the basis of color although it has declared its mission to be a universal brotherhood under Jesus Christ. Christian love is the white man's love for himself and for his race. For the man who is not white, Islam is the hope for justice and equality in the world we must build tomorrow.[41]

Challenged to study this alternative, Lincoln produced his important study, *The Black Muslims in America*, suggesting that this "hate that hate produced" phenomenon was "about the voiceless people who want to be heard in the councils of the world,"[42] an insight worth remembering as we explore what fueled the fundamentalist and militant religious movements of the past century.

Unlike Martin Luther King Jr., Elijah Muhammad did not advocate a rapprochement with white people. Not only did he teach American blacks to be proud of their race and color, Elijah Muhammad advocated an autonomous state for Black Muslims. His most well known and articulate speaker was Malcolm X, who on first hearing Muhammad speak "lost his shame on being colored."[43] The Black Muslims focused on the rehabilitation of American blacks, achieving such success in prisons that parole officers and police admitted that the Black Muslims were the best rehabilitation agency at work. Their method was to convince the convict that he fell into crime because he was so ashamed of being black, that the white man had so conditioned him psychologically that he was unable to respect himself. Then they convinced the prisoner that being black was a blessing, not a curse, and that in keeping with that blessing he had to clean himself up and live the life of decency and respect. "As a result," philosopher Louis Lomax points out,

> You never see a Muslim [follower of Elijah Muhammad] without a
>   clean shirt and tie and coat.
> You never see a Muslim drink.
> You never see a Muslim smoke.
> You never see a Muslim dance.
> You never see a Muslim use dope.

You never see a Muslim woman with a non-Muslim man.

You never see a Muslim man with a woman other than his wife.

You never see a Muslim without some means of income.

You never see a Muslim who will not stop and come to the aid of any black woman he sees in trouble.

You seldom see a Muslim lapse back into crime.[44]

Promoting self-reliance of black people, strong family values, no drugs, and no smoking or drinking, Elijah Muhammad's movement spread quickly and prospered, especially in the 1960s. He differed with traditional Muslims in his belief in the superiority of the black race over the white race and in proclaiming himself the last Prophet (traditional Muslims believe that the last Prophet was *the* Prophet Muhammad, who taught that no one is better than another except by the ethics of their deeds). But these theological differences could not override the social appeal of his message of black pride and self-discipline.

Interest in Islam was partly furthered in the black community because of a growing recognition that Islam for many of them was the faith of their ancestors. In his best-selling book *Roots: The Saga of an American Family* (1976), Alex Haley traced his ancestral history and lineage to a Muslim family in Mali, West Africa. Many African Americans became interested in their genealogy, and in exploring their own roots, they traced their religious ancestry to Islam.

Elijah Muhammad and Martin Luther King Jr. at first were bitter ideological opponents; King would accept neither black supremacy notions nor a blanket indictment of white people, a position that is true to the Abrahamic ethic. Malcolm X later recognized this position as being the orthodox Muslim belief after his hajj to Mecca in 1964 and meeting Muslims of all colors from other regions of the world.

Malcolm X broke off from the Nation of Islam in 1963 and was assassinated in February 1965, and his position as head of Elijah Muhammad's New York City mosque was assumed by Louis Farrakhan, who for a long time maintained the principles of black separatism. After Elijah Muhammad's death in 1975, his fifth son, Wallace (who took the name Warithuddin Muhammad), took over leadership of the Nation of Islam and brought it in line with orthodox Islamic theology and practices. Warithuddin downplayed black nationalism and admitted nonblack

IMAM FEISAL ABDUL RAUF

members. He changed the group's name to the World Community of Islam in the West and, later, to the American Muslim Mission.

Not Fair to Women!

The Abrahamic ethic is about the equality of all human beings before their creator, regardless of race or gender. But even after black men gained the right to vote in 1870, American women were still constitutionally prohibited from voting until August 1920, when Congress ratified the Nineteenth Amendment. Enfranchisement of women never attained the status of a major political issue until after suffrage had been won by formerly disfranchised groups of the male population. This was what happened in America and western Europe, and it is what we see in some countries like Kuwait, where women have nearly but not quite joined men in winning the right to vote, which their sisters in Bahrain recently won.

American democracy is representational, which means that the population at large elects the least number of people who can represent them efficiently. As I have explained above, electing government representatives is analogous to the stockholders electing the directors of a corporation. In America, being a stockholder meant being a landowner, in addition to being white and male. The requirement of being a landowner was dropped by the early 1800s, and voting rights were extended to all adult males. The abolishment of slavery and granting the American black male the right to vote in 1870 extended democracy to a broader base of men. By definition, laws that changed the rule that required you to be a landowner to vote resulted in women being denied suffrage solely on the basis of their gender. Whereas women property holders in Massachusetts had voting privileges from 1691 to 1780, American women after 1870 found out that where once they had two-thirds of the legal qualifications for voting (compared to white male landowners), the elimination of property ownership as a requirement for voting deprived women of the only legal claim for a right to vote that they previously had.

After a lot of agitation, Congress ratified the Nineteenth Amendment in August 1920: "The right of citizens of the United States to vote shall not be denied or abridged by the United States or by any State on account of sex." Another barrier preventing a fuller expression of the Abrahamic ethic fell away.

Muslim countries too face challenges in fully expressing the Abrahamic ethic with regard to the roles of women and men in society. Americans often ask me about the status of women in Islam, believing that Muslim women are oppressed and have no rights compared to Western women—and, further, that gender inequality is sanctioned by Muslim law. But something is amiss in the perceptions here. Four of the most populous Muslim nations have, or have had, women heads of state: Indonesia, Bangladesh, Pakistan, and Turkey. Could one argue, then, that the United States lags behind the Muslim world in granting equal rights to women—and that the reason America has never had a female president is because of its Judeo-Christian ethic?

The problem lies in confusing cultural norms with religious belief or law. Unless we separate the theological from the sociocultural dimensions of the issue, we are likely to misread the situation. What complicates the understanding of the gender issue, even by Muslims, is that Muslim jurists regarded the custom (*adah, 'urf*), or common law of a society, as a source of law when the Quran or the *sunnah* was silent on an issue. Thus, what was custom in a particular time or place found its way into Islamic law.

Today, the Muslim world is a vast and varied cultural landscape; the realities of women in Malaysia, for example, are not the same as the realities of women in Saudi Arabia, Bosnia, or Senegal. So to investigate the status of women in Islam, one must start with a look at the realities of Muslim women from a *theological* perspective.

Gender equality is an intrinsic part of Islamic belief. The Quran says God has "prepared a forgiveness and a great reward" for "the submitting men and women, the believing men and women, the pious men and women, the truthful men and women, the patient men and women, the humble men and women, the charitable men and women, the fasting men and women, the men and women who guard their chastity, the men and women who remember God frequently" (Quran 33:35).

The Quran places equal responsibility on men and women for all religious obligations. Women are equally obliged to pray, to fast, to give charity out of their wealth, to perform the pilgrimage, and so forth.

Islamic theology emphasizes social justice, and this includes justice in domestic affairs. The Quran gave women marriage, divorce, and inheritance rights centuries before women in the West were granted such rights.[45] The Quran says, "Men shall have a share in what parents and kinsfolk leave behind, and women shall have a share in what parents and kinsfolk leave behind, whether it be little or much—a share ordained by God" (Quran 4:7). Although females inherit half of what males do, they are not required to pay out of their wealth for the support of their dependents; males are. The Quran enjoins men to be caring and kind with women, and one chapter even begins by saying, "God has indeed heard the words of her who pleads with thee concerning her husband and complains unto God" (58:1). This verse illustrates that justice between men and women—especially in the domestic context—is a matter of importance to God.

Other rights given to women included abolishing the pre-Islamic habit of female infanticide and emphasizing the respect due to the mother and, by association, to all women. A man once came to the Prophet Muhammad and said, "Messenger of God, I desire to go on a military expedition and I have come to consult you." The Prophet asked the man if he had a mother, and when he replied that he did, the Prophet said, "Stay with her, then, for Paradise is at her feet [meaning, is found in serving her]."[46]

The Prophet Muhammad implemented the rights of women, as laid out in the Quran, and worked to level the imbalance between men and women in his society by providing a living, working example: he himself and his own household. Karen Armstrong notes how companionable Muhammad was with his wives, how they stood up to him and answered him back. "Muhammad scrupulously helped with the chores, mended his own clothes and sought out the companionship of his wives."[47] He would consult with them, seek their advice on matters pertaining to the community, and take their words seriously.[48] In his last sermon, Muhammad highlighted the mutual rights due to each between men and women: "O men, it is true that you have certain rights with regard to your women, but they also have rights over you. If they abide by your right then to them belongs the right to be fed and clothed in kindness. Do treat your women well and be kind to them for they are your partners and committed helpers."[49]

As one wades through the Quran and *sunnah*, it becomes clear that there are certain inalienable rights due to women in Islam, and certain women have drawn from these rights to become exemplars and role models for others. Of the host of female saints and scholars, mothers and warriors, businesswomen and performers who parade through Islamic history, the women who stand out in striking detail are the wives of the Prophet. As Muhammad is the exemplar for all Muslims, his wives are also role models for Muslim women.

Khadijah, Muhammad's first wife, was a wealthy, successful, single businesswoman when she commissioned Muhammad to oversee a caravan of goods to Syria in about 605 CE. Upon his return, she offered him her hand in marriage. She was forty and he twenty-five. Muhammad's marriage to Khadijah is considered a turning point in his life, and her support was crucial to the early days of his prophethood. "As is explicitly stated, she supported and encouraged him, fostering his confidence in himself and his mission."[50] They were happily married for twenty-five years before Khadijah's death. Muhammad was devastated, but his life was soon to be filled with other influential women.

Aisha was his youngest wife, known to have been strong-willed and feisty as well as observant and intelligent. Because of her quick mind, her years of intimacy with the Prophet, and the fact that she lived for several decades after his death, many of the hadith are attributed to her. When the Prophet knew that his life was coming to an end, it was to Aisha's room that he retreated. There she nursed him for the few days of his illness, and his grave was made in the floor of her chamber. After the Prophet's death, Aisha was active in the political life of the time. She was once among about a thousand men on a mission against the assassination of the third caliph, Uthman, and later one of the three leaders in opposition to Ali. Later in her life, she was noted for her piety as well as for her knowledge of poetry, Arab history and other subjects, and her eloquence.[51]

In surveying the women who have been prominent in the history of the Islamic world, it becomes increasingly clear that there is a strong prototype for Muslim women and that women's rights are alive in the very theology of Islam. But, as in most countries the world over, the reality for women does not match the ideals we all know are right and just. As American women are fighting for equal pay for equal work, for reproductive rights and affordable childcare, Muslim women are fighting for compulsory education (in Afghanistan), the right to drive (in Saudi Arabia), and the right to cover their hair (in France and in Turkey). As American women are knocking through glass ceilings to acquire the rights due to them in the Constitution, Muslim women are doing the same to gain full access to their rights as laid out in the Quran and *sunnah*.

Many of the limits placed on women in Muslim (and non-Muslim) societies are the result of custom, and these limits continue because people have a hard time changing their customs. In terms of realizing social rights, the Muslim world is following a similar trajectory as in the West, and changing a society's notions of what is acceptable in gender roles takes generational change. Just as in America roles have changed dramatically, especially in the last hundred years as America has implemented the Abrahamic ethic to a greater degree, it is reasonable to expect that Muslim societies implementing the justice called for in Islamic theology will undergo parallel transformations.

This is why granting political rights is the most effective way to redress legitimate women's grievances. For as a nation becomes increasingly democratized, the ballot box becomes the means by which each constituent group in society attains its objectives.

From Protestant Ethic to Judeo-Christian Ethic

American Muslims today face similar hurdles to full acceptance as American Catholics and Jews faced in earlier years. By studying the evolution of American faith traditions, and especially that of American Catholics and American Jews, we gain a knowledge of the patterns of immigrant American religious social development that is useful in understanding what is happening and is likely to happen to American Muslim society.

Most Muslims are unaware that what they are going through is a *sociological* phenomenon, not a *religious* one, that is remarkably paralleling the historical experience of immigrant Catholics and Jews. Although the experience of African American Muslims is rooted in the historical experience of slavery and therefore is sociologically different, African American Muslims share with immigrant Muslims the sense that their faith is still generally regarded by American non-Muslims with suspicion and hostility.[52] Catholics and Jews felt this way a century ago. If the experience of Muslims follows that of Catholics and Jews, it will take another generation or two before American Muslims reach that point achieved by their Catholic and Jewish predecessors in the mid-twentieth century, when American Catholics and American Jews could establish their Catholic-ness and Jewishness not apart from or in spite of their Americanness, but precisely in and through it.

The crucial need of our day is to find ways to accelerate the process whereby American Muslims will be able to establish their Islamic identity not apart from or in spite of their American identity, but precisely in and through it.

It therefore behooves American Muslims and non-Muslims interested in Muslim issues, domestically and internationally, to study this history and experience, for this knowledge can help chart the course of American Islam, its potential role both as a mediator between America and the Muslim world and its role in shaping the Muslim world globally.

Although not all of the earliest immigrants from Europe were Puritans, they were overwhelmingly Protestants, and in spite of the ideals of the Declaration of Independence and Constitution, they brought with them their prejudices against non-Protestants and nonwhites.

Although Catholicism was present on American shores from the start, its story is more that of a foreign church that struggled to find its place in a growing American culture. The earliest Catholic settlement in Maryland in the seventeenth century, the New Orleans center of Catholicism acquired in the Louisiana Purchase of 1803, and the Southwest center of Catholicism, acquired from Mexico in 1848, played lesser roles in what became American Catholicism than did the Irish form, product of the great Irish immigration of the nineteenth century.

Catholics had a difficult time in colonial America, their churches proscribed in most of the colonies and actively persecuted in some. Some states continued discriminatory laws until well into the nineteenth century. In a country where Protestantism was generally identified with the new American character, becoming an American meant getting rid of one's foreignness. Catholicism, especially its theological and social opposition to Protestantism and Puritan ideals, was therefore difficult to maintain. Some Catholic immigrants actually became Protestants; many more simply lapsed and remained unchurched.

Immigration from Europe in the 1800s brought large numbers of Irish Catholics to America. The anti-Catholic movement in America was directed primarily at the Irish "foreigners," who were felt to be imperiling the livelihood of "native" Americans, as well as their culture, their religion, and their American way of life. Confronted with notices such as "Men Wanted—No Irish Need Apply," Irish Catholics even had their churches burned to the ground.[53] In time, however, the Irish defined the Catholic Church in the United States and performed an indispensable task in mediating between the Catholic Church as a strange and alien body and the emerging American culture.[54] "Not the least of the contributions of the Irish," a Catholic historian suggests, "was their work in Americanizing Catholics of other nationalities."[55]

The Americanization of the Catholic Church, and its secure establishment in American society, was considerably accelerated by the fairly rapid advancement in social and cultural status of the Irish, German, Italian, and other Catholic ethnic groups. In a process characteristic of the American pattern of life, the church played a crucial role as a vehicle for the social, economic, and political ambitions of immigrant groups bent on building themselves from poor foreigners to middle-class Americans.[56] Especially through its widespread network of institutions and activities,[57] and in particular through its Catholic schools and colleges, the church accelerated the emergence of a Catholic middle class, enabling the Catholic community to become more American—America being preeminently a middle-class country. And with the advancement of large segments of the Catholic community, the church too advanced. It thus became possible to be an American not only without falling away from the church, but precisely in and through being a Catholic. In this critical development, the long-range policy of the Irish-dominated church fell in with the underlying trends of contemporary American society, each reinforcing the other.[58]

Muslim immigrants today in America number roughly 60 percent of an estimated Muslim population of seven million, and the immigrants see themselves as reliving much of the Catholic experience. Most mosques and Islamic centers reflect the sociology and shifting demographics of their constituents. In New York City, for instance, mosques tend to project a strong ethnic identity, with African American, Latino-American, or immigrant flavors, the latter spanning the range from Arab, Bengali, Pakistani, Turkish, and Albanian cultures to Indonesian and even West African, French-speaking culture. The new generation of American-born Muslims is just coming of age, and as they and the next generation mature they will need to shape their Islamic identity in a culturally American context. Among the key fronts where this challenge is taking place is in the private Islamic schools, as was true for Catholics.

Another aspect of the Americanization of American Catholicism was the radical revision of Catholic thinking on the issue of church and state so as to bring it in line with American experience and tradition. The conventional position of the church was to affirm the union of church and state on the model of the Catholic monarchies up until the seventeenth and eighteenth centuries. However, in the early twentieth century, American prelates and theologians began to take a new line. In 1916 Cardinal Gibbons declared without hesitation:

> Sixteen millions of Catholics prefer the American form of government before any other. They admire its institutions and its laws. They accept the Constitution without reserve, with no desire as Catholics to see it changed in any feature. The separation of church and state in this country seems to them the natural, inevitable, and best conceivable plan, the one that would work best among us, both for the good of religion and of the state. Any change in their relations they would contemplate with dread. They are well aware, indeed, that the church here enjoys a larger liberty, and a more secure position, than in any country today where church and state are united. No establishment of religion is being dreamed of here, of course, by anyone; but were it to be attempted, it would meet with united opposition from the Catholic people, priests and prelates.[59]

Some thirty-two years later, in 1948, Archbishop John T. McNicholas, speaking for the entire American hierarchy, declared, "We deny absolutely and without qualification that the Catholic Bishops of the United States are seeking a union of church and state by any endeavors whatsoever, either proximate or remote. If tomorrow Catholics constituted a majority in our country, they would not seek a union of church and state. . . ."[60] By the mid-twentieth century Catholic opinion was substantially in line with the American tradition embodied in the First Amendment.

More important, perhaps, was the reorientation of Catholic thinking on this matter at the theological level. John Courtney Murray, S.J., one of American Catholicism's outstanding theologians, undertook a systematic reexamination of Catholic teaching on church and state and developed a viewpoint and approach capable of relating basic Catholic doctrine to American democracy in a way that did violence to neither. The brilliance and cogency of his writings made a deep impression beyond the boundaries of the American Catholic Church. And while Murray's thinking met with sharp opposition from some more conventionally minded European and some American theologians, these new currents of thought made themselves felt in the Vatican and contributed substantially to Vatican II.

The most striking evidence of the Americanization of the Catholic Church in America probably came around the middle of the twentieth century, when American Catholics and non-Catholics alike began to regard Catholicism as one of the three great American religions.

> By the second quarter of the present [twentieth] century the American Catholic, like every other American, was thinking of his church as one of the three "religions of democracy," side by side with the other two; he could hardly imagine an America without Protestants and Jews—even though he might be deeply suspicious of Protestants and not altogether free of anti-Semitism. . . . Under the pressure of the American environment in which they so successfully adapted themselves, American Catholics—like American Jews and in part even American Protestants—learned to operate with a double vision: in terms of a self-enclosed microcosmic community within their own church and its complex of Catholic institutions, and in terms of a tripartite macrocosm in which Catholics, Protestants and Jews were conceived as living in harmonious coexistence, if not cooperation, under the benevolent aegis of American democracy.[61]

American Muslims today, especially in immigrant mosque centers, operate with a similar double vision: in terms of their own small community with their own ethnic institutions often tied to a "back home" worldview, and in terms of a much larger pluralistic and democratic society.

Writing in the mid-twentieth century, historian Will Herberg incisively points out, "It is because it has become one of the three great 'religions of democracy,' and not because of its claim to speak as the Universal Church, that American Catholicism is today listened to with such respect and attention by the American people."[62]

Having bought in to the American way of life, American Catholics adopted key aspects of the Puritan and Abrahamic ethic. The Abrahamic ethic became, in fact, the umbrella religion of religions, that all may freely come together in it. But since American Catholics practiced their own rituals and liturgy, the *Protestant* ethic needed to be broadened. Catholics couldn't say that they were part of the "Protestant" ethic, but they *could* be part of a "Christian" one.

As we shall see next, American Jews followed a similar path in becoming part of American society. Thus the Protestant ethic broadened to those outside Christian circles, and the Judeo-Christian ethic became the hallmark of twentieth-century American religion.

Although the first Jews to come to America landed in 1654, American Jewry is predominantly the product of the great wave of immigration from Germany and Eastern Europe in the 1800s. Their high degree of dispersal and the relative prosperity they achieved made their accommodation into American life remarkably easy. By the mid-nineteenth century they were already busily erecting a network of community institutions (synagogues, hospitals, schools, and community centers) that reflected conditions of settlement and not simply traditions carried over from the past or abroad.[63]

Sporadic attempts had been made to unite the Jewish community in an overall organization and to establish a central authority for American Jews, but they failed: American Jews remained loosely and autonomously organized, reluctant to follow the British Jews in establishing an authoritative Board of Deputies. In this respect, they were American, following closely the Protestant American pattern of decentralization and voluntarism.[64]

Around the turn of the twentieth century, 1.7 million Eastern European Jews arrived in America. Because religion and immigrant culture were so thoroughly fused as to seem almost indistinguishable—as it is today for many immigrant Muslims—the East European immigrants came up against a shattering crisis in their interaction with their American-born sons and daughters—again, as is happening to many Muslim parents today. Desperately anxious to become unequivocally American, the second generation born and raised in the New World rejected the foreignness of their parents, which sometimes also meant rejecting Jewishness and Judaism. The new Conservative movement, more traditional than the Reform but equally American, felt this to be their opportunity. Solomon Schechter, head of the Jewish Theological Seminary, saw the lines of development that American Jewry would take; he predicted the ultimate dissolution of the transplanted Yiddish culture and urged American Jews to make themselves at home in America, master English, and learn Hebrew.[65] An American Orthodoxy also emerged in the 1920s when its seminary, the Yeshiva University in New York, was established, along with its rabbinical council and its synagogal federation, Union of Orthodox Jewish Congregations.

An earnest effort to win the American second generation was made by Reconstructionism, created by Mordecai M. Kaplan, which strove to combine a liberal theology with a conception of Judaism that saw the Jews in America as living in two civilizations, one American and the other Jewish. Note here the similarity with the American Catholic experience, which separated the theological or "vertical' dimension of faith from the sociological or "horizontal" dimension of faith, seeking to incorporate the American way of life as part of its sociological belief structure.

By the mid-twentieth century the shape and form of American Jewish religion was characterized by a far-reaching accommodation to the American pattern of religious life. The institutional system was virtually the same as in the major Protestant churches—the same corporate structure, the same proliferation of men's clubs, sisterhoods, junior congregations, youth groups, discussion circles, adult education projects, and so forth. With minor variations, "the arrangement of the synagogue, the traditional appurtenances of worship, and the religious ceremonies showed the effects of change wrought by the American environment."[66] Even the central place of the sermon, congregational singing, mixed choirs, organs, responsive readings, abbreviated services, the concluding benediction, and many other commonly accepted features obviously reflected the influence of familiar Protestant practice.[67]

Most American Jews came to America from Eastern Europe at a time when the walls of the ghetto were crumbling and the East European Jewish community was beginning to feel the effects of the social and intellectual forces of the Enlightenment. Within one or two generations the great mass of East European Jews were compelled to pass directly from the Middle Ages into the nineteenth or twentieth century. The confusion and disorientation were further accentuated by the abrupt break with the past that took place with their being uprooted and resettled in the New World. As Herberg points out, "For various reasons, the Orthodox Jewish rabbi, the only kind of rabbi known to most East European immigrants, seemed neither willing nor able to serve as a link between his ethnic-immigrant group and the larger American community in the way in which the Catholic priest or Lutheran pastor so frequently served his group. On the contrary, the Orthodox rabbi tended rather to shut himself off from the new world which he found alien and unacceptable."[68] This changed as orthodoxy began to adapt to its American environment.

Many contemporary immigrant American imams are in the same position. Hailing from West Africa and the Middle East, from Pakistan and Bangladesh and Indonesia, they are often unequipped to serve as effective links between their communities and the larger American community. Even for those African American imams who were brought up in the civil rights era, alienated from the white majority population by their early experience of racist segregation, the task of being effective links to the larger American community entails unique challenges. This is changing, though, with bicultural younger imams coming on the scene increasingly anchored in the issues and concerns of the younger generation.

By the mid-twentieth century the American Jewish community had become integrally part of American society. American Jews, like American Catholics, were now in the position to establish their Jewishness not apart from or in spite of their Americanness, but precisely in and through it. Judaism had achieved its status in the American way of life as one of the three religions of democracy.[69]

The struggle that Catholics and Jews went through with regard to the Protestant community paradoxically *secularized* the American religious landscape. Protestant fears of Catholicism were not primarily religious or theological, as they had been in previous centuries in Europe, but were characteristically *secular*. Catholicism, Protestants feared, was "un-American, undemocratic, alien to American ways, and prone to place loyalty to church above loyalty to state and nation."[70] Compared to the Protestant churches, the Catholic Church had a global organization. American Protestants who advocated separation of church and state with regard to Catholics were trying to ensure that what appeared to them as the Catholic organizational steamroller would not take over America, resulting in a union of *Catholic* church and state in America.

American Protestants' complaints about the lack of separation of church and state in Catholic societies in the mid-twentieth century are echoed now in complaints about American Muslims and their views of church and state. American Muslims feel they are regarded by many contemporary non-Muslim Americans as un-American, as not believing in democracy, as alien to American ways, and as rejecting the separation of church and state even in America.

We have pointed out that when Christianity and Judaism arrived in America, each over time developed its own uniquely American character and identity—and each eventually had a substantial modernizing effect on its parent religion worldwide: Vatican II and modern American Judaism are cases in point. This process deserves review, because it too has implications for Islam in America.

The Second Vatican Council, which profoundly opened the church to relations with other religions, would not have unfolded as it did without the role of American Catholics. It signaled the moment when the Catholic Church accepted the modern world and, in the words of one commentator, moved philosophically from an old atmosphere of "severity and condemnation" to a new one of "mercy and understanding"—a shift that many Americans would like to see in Islam. The church began to encourage interfaith dialogue and to suggest that other faiths were to be not merely tolerated but respected. Redressing centuries of anti-Jewish teachings, the Vatican II Declaration on the Relation of the Church to Non-Christian Religions stated, "In her rejection of every persecution against any man, the Church, mindful of the patrimony she shares with the Jews and moved not by political reasons but by the Gospel's spiritual love, decries hatred, persecutions, displays of anti-Semitism, directed against Jews at any time and by anyone."

Expanding on this sentiment of inclusiveness, the proclamation adds, "We cannot truly call on God, the Father of all, if we refuse to treat in a brotherly way any man, created as he is in the image of God. Man's relation to God the Father and his relation to men his brothers are so linked together that Scripture says: 'He who does not love does not know God' (1 John 4:8)." The Vatican II Declaration on Religious Freedom, *Dignitatis Humanae,* adds an endorsement of every individual's freedom of conscience: "Every man has the duty, and therefore the right, to seek the truth in matters religious in order that he may with prudence form for himself right and true judgments of conscience, under use of all suitable means."

In the view of many observers inside the Catholic Church, American priests, bishops, and cardinals provided the critical support for these Vatican II steps toward spiritual renewal, pluralism, and inclusiveness.

In a similar way, Jewish observers recognize the influence that America's society, politics, and climate of religious freedom have had on Judaism. Both Reform and Conservative Judaism flowered in the relatively open society of the United States. Jewish historians have noted that America was the first country in which Jews lived in unsegregated communities. Through coexistence with other religions in the free atmosphere of American society, Judaism experienced a separation between the spiritual and purely cultural expressions of its faith, whereas before, cultural and religious traditions had been deeply interwoven and no such separation existed. The eventual result was the adoption by Jews of mainstream American culture and a distinct evolution of a Judaism that reflects the values of a pluralistic, free society.

Ultimately, growing as they did in the unique soil of America, Christianity and Judaism both evolved in ways distinct from the religions in their European countries of origin. In turn, these new American progeny bridged the gap between American religion and the practices overseas.

From this bit of Jewish and Catholic history, we can see that in time an American Islam is bound to evolve that will also have a profound impact on Islam in the Muslim world. There is a long-standing belief among Muslims that a renaissance of Islam will rise in the West. With help from our Jewish and Christian predecessors on American soil, we can accelerate this process for the betterment of all of humanity.

Based on the Jewish example, for instance, American Muslims may find ways to practice their traditions and have them recognized by the wider American society. Earlier, in chapter 3, I offered suggestions for implementing Muslim law in ways that are recognized by American courts. The Muslim community might follow the example of the Jewish community in establishing the equivalent of their Beth Din, a legal system for Orthodox Jews in which rabbinic judges adjudicate a case, and the decisions are legally binding in American courts because the cases "are conducted in a manner consistent with the requirements of secular arbitration law."[71] Jewish and Catholic experiences in America have paved the way for Muslims to have their religious needs recognized in American society and law and therefore help to influence the development of Islamic tradition outside the United States.

With this fuller understanding of American history as the working out of an Abrahamic ethic in a liberal democracy, let us return now to considering America's interaction with the Muslim world from the early twentieth century onward.

WHITE KNIGHT OR HOSTILE TAKEOVER? AMERICA ON THE HORIZON OF THE MUSLIM WORLD, 1900–PRESENT

As mentioned above, until the early twentieth century America did not involve itself in European affairs. But by the time of World War I, America began to be drawn into European politics.

From 1913 to 1921, America was governed by the administration of Woodrow Wilson (1856–1924), grandson of a pastor and son of a Presbyterian minister. Wilson was a visionary, a progressive reformer who believed in the principles of the Abrahamic ethic and sought to implement its ideas in governance (the most notable exception being his poor record on the rights of black Americans). He believed, and said, that the president should be a national voice in the affairs of the people, not forcing views upon them but interpreting their wants, and that the moral judgment of the people needed channels for self-expression. The role of the president, therefore, was to initiate and guide national legislation in accord with the chief executive's interpretation of the will of the people in this regard.

Wilson's social, economic, and political policies, known all together as New Freedom (from the title of a book published by him in 1913), were instrumental in paving the way for America's growing prosperity and international leadership in the twentieth century. His institutional reforms furthered and refined the meaning of life in a free and democratic society, thus amplifying the Abrahamic ethic and taking it to new levels.

Examples of this on the domestic front were his legislation for the following:

- Elected by sidestepping the political machinery of the parties, he advocated the Seventeenth Amendment to the Constitution, ratified in 1913, which required U.S. senators to be elected by the popular vote rather than by state legislatures. This gave more power directly to the people than to the political machinery governed by large interests.

- He oversaw the creation of the Federal Reserve System in 1914, which has had a profound stabilizing effect on the American economy through monetary polices, such as expanding or contracting the money supply to suit the national need, and through supervision of the banking industry. Up until then banks were totally dependent on their own currency resources. They could thus be jeopardized by rumors or special financial crises, despite their good financial condition, and bank failures were a not-uncommon occurrence.

- Credit and loans were made available to farmers through the Federal Farm Loan Act of 1916, which established twelve federal land banks to make money available for long-term farm mortgages at reasonable rates.

- In the same year, Wilson established the Federal Trade Commission to prevent business monopolies (one company or group of companies gaining control of an entire industry and jacking up the prices artificially). At the same time, he passed legislation that affirmed the right of unions to strike, boycott, and picket.

- He introduced the eight-hour workday for railroad workers on interstate lines.

- He lowered taxes on imported goods by eliminating tariffs.

- He pushed through a bill prohibiting child labor in 1916 (which, interestingly, was then declared unconstitutional by the Supreme Court in 1918).

- Wilson also achieved a victory when the Nineteenth Amendment to the U.S. Constitution, legalizing women's voting rights, was passed in 1919 and ratified in 1920.

The above are among the institutional aspects of American democracy (and American *democratic capitalism*) that many Americans take for granted as naturally flowing from democratic rule. However, it took the United States well over a century after the Constitution was drafted to think of and implement them. Without these and other corrections done over the past two centuries, American democracy would not be the liberal democracy it is. These are some of the very corrections that democratic regimes in other parts of the world need to implement, without which they are illiberal democracies, unable to provide for their people the quality of life Americans enjoy.

It is to the credit of the American leadership that they democratized their capitalism by introducing legislation, borrowed from socialist movements, that helped the less fortunate members of society participate in the general well-being. During the Great Depression years, the jury was out on whether Communism and socialist policies were better than capitalism. Franklin Delano Roosevelt's New Deal policies from 1933 to 1945 continued the legacy of Wilson in furthering

institutions that would protect the American economy and its democratic principles. These were important for the survival of the American
democratic regime, for they attenuated a pure capitalism by ensuring
the security of its people. Historically, FDR's New Deal was prompted
by the need to recover from the economic depression that followed the
financial crash of 1929 and to stabilize the national economy to prevent
severe economic crises in the future.

The earliest sufferers from the crash of 1929 were investors in securities and depositors in banks. The Federal Securities Act (1933),
through federal supervision of new issues of securities and other
means, protected investors against fraudulent practices. This protection was then broadened by an act (1934) that provided for a Securities
and Exchange Commission to regulate stock exchanges. To protect
bank depositors, Congress in 1933 passed the Emergency Banking Act,
which gave the president the power to reorganize insolvent banks, and
the Banking Act of 1933, which insured bank deposits by the Federal
Deposit Insurance Corporation.

One of the most important locomotives of the American economy is the housing industry. Housing legislation introduced by FDR
included the institution of the Home Owners' Loan Corporation, the
Federal Housing Administration, and the U.S. Housing Authority.
By passing the Social Security Act in 1935, the United States took a
great step toward providing economic security for its population;
this act provides retirement benefits, unemployment compensation,
and welfare services for mothers, children, elders, and people with
disabilities.

Many in the Muslim world, especially in high-population countries such as Indonesia, Pakistan, Egypt, and Turkey, still do not enjoy
these benefits, which Americans have come to regard as their rights
and *implicitly as part of their democracy.* What Muslims need in their societies, more urgently than the ballot-box definition of democracy, are
local versions of these reforms, which were part of Wilson's New Freedom and Roosevelt's New Deal, so that they can attain what President
Teddy Roosevelt intended by his "Square Deal."

By modifying the American free-enterprise system, the New Deal
saved the country from adopting, possibly by revolutionary means, either a socialist or fascist system. It was severely condemned by others,

however, who saw in Roosevelt's policies only a dangerous curtail-
ment of the rights assured by the free-enterprise system.

As the United States is now involved in nation building in Iraq,
and to some extent in Afghanistan, it is important to bear in mind that
what Muslims are looking for is a Square Deal.

GLOBALIZING THE AMERICAN
DECLARATION OF INDEPENDENCE

On the overseas front, Wilson's presidency overlapped with the First
World War. America was then much more a nation of immigrants, and
different immigrant groups attached themselves emotionally to different
sides of the war, complicating the decision-making process of the U.S.
leaders and suggesting a neutral stance as more domestically desirable.

Wilson, however, was under pressure to participate in the war, and
he was aware that the Allied governments (the British, French, and
Russians) had formed secret agreements with one another to expand
their empires through their involvement in the war. The secret Sykes-
Picot Agreement (1916), for example, provided for Britain and France
to divide up the Middle East, most of which was then part of the Ottoman Empire. Other agreements provided for Russia and Italy to
annex portions of what is now Turkey. Wilson's political confidant
Edward Mandell House remarked, on seeing the secret agreements,
"They are making it a breeding ground for future war."[72]

Much of the conflict of the past century between the Muslim world
and the West has its roots in this Western-initiated breakup of the Ottoman Empire, which carries strong religious overtones. The reader
should be reminded that Osama bin Laden mentioned this when he referred to "what happened eighty years ago" in one of his broadcast
announcements on American television. Most Muslims regard the
breakup of the Ottoman Empire and especially the militant seculariza-
tion that ensued in Turkey and other parts of the Middle East a deliberate attempt by Europe and the West to destroy Islam. Imagine if
Mussolini had destroyed the Vatican and imposed a Middle Eastern
dress code on the Italians: wouldn't the Christian world have regarded
that as an anti-Christianity posture supported by the Muslim world?

Upset at the intentions of the Allies to colonize more people,

Wilson outlined to a joint session of Congress on January 8, 1918, the conditions and goals under which he would participate in the war. His Fourteen Points expressed his ethics, among which were:

- No more secret agreements between countries

- Diplomacy and negotiation always to take place in the public view

- Freedom of the seas

- Freedom of trade

- An end to tariff and other economic barriers

- General disarmament and the establishment of an association of nations to guarantee the independence and territorial integrity of all nations

Indicating that the Allies had colonial ambitions in the Middle East, much of which was then ruled by the Ottoman Empire, point 12 stated, "The Turkish portions of the present Ottoman empire should be assured a secure sovereignty, but the other nationalities which are now under Turkish rule should be assured an undoubted security of life and an absolutely unmolested opportunity of autonomous development." This point meant that the Middle East should not be divided among the belligerent powers; that people hitherto ruled by the Turks should become autonomous.[73]

On February 11, 1918, Wilson spoke to Congress and defined the four principles upon which the peace settlement should be made. The second and third were:

- That peoples and provinces are not to be bartered about from sovereignty to sovereignty as if they were chattels or pawns in a game, even the great game, now forever discredited, of the balance of power; but

- That every territorial settlement involved in this war *must be made in the interest and for the benefit of the populations concerned,* and not as a part of any mere adjustment or compromise of claims amongst rival states. . . .[74] (italics mine)

Wilson's peace proposals were received with ardent enthusiasm by Congress but not by the Allied governments because he revealed their intentions. At the time the United States had no significant political or economic interests in the Mideast. In off-the-record comments made aboard ship en route to the peace conference in 1919, Wilson told his associates, "I am convinced that if this peace is not made on the highest principles of justice, it will be swept away by the peoples of the world in less than a generation. If it is any other sort of peace then I shall want to run away and hide . . . for there will follow not mere conflict but cataclysm."[75]

The hoped-for white knight did not completely come through for the Muslim world. Wilson did not succeed in having the Allies grant the people of the Middle East their independence, although his efforts did have an attenuating impact on the ideas current during that time. The Great Game, as it was called, resulted in the area from North Africa to Afghanistan being divided up among Britain, France, and Russia. However, Russia continued to give Britain problems by seeding dissension, especially in Afghanistan, Iran, and Iraq.

More far-reaching was Wilson's active push for an association of nations, which became known as the League of Nations. It lasted from 1920 until 1946. Just as the American federal government was a national government established by the American states, one can see in Wilson's attempts an effort to project the notion of the American Declaration of Independence and its inalienable rights internationally and to establish the seeds of some form of international governance, especially in resolving matters of conflict that in the past had led to war. The League of Nations was unable to prevent the outbreak of the Second World War. But World War II resulted in such a loss of life and wealth and bred so much destruction that the nations that engaged in it came out of the war either destroyed or much weakened, except for Russia and the United States. By war's end, most of them were ready to accept the notion of no more war among themselves, and the League of Nations evolved into the United Nations.

The Allies' demand for reparations from Germany after World War I had created such hostility and hardship among Germans that it sowed the conditions for the rise of Hitler and another world war even more destructive than the first. Contrast this with what the United States did after World War II in Germany and Japan. By generously helping these nations rebuild their economies and introduce democracy, America helped create an environment in which war today with these nations is unthinkable, no matter what differences of opinion may arise.

Today's picture with regard to the Muslim world is no different. In its own interest, the United States, together with its allies, should focus intently on developing Muslim economies and speeding the adoption of these democratic-capitalistic reforms, without which nation building will not go far. As we have mentioned several times, the frustration expressed by today's Muslim world is due in part to the widely shared perception that the United States has done the precise opposite in the past by supporting regimes that in turn siphoned off their own nations' resources rather than distributing them equitably and thus raising their citizens' level of prosperity.

Franklin Delano Roosevelt, clearly inspired by the ideas and idealism of Wilson's New Freedom and Teddy Roosevelt's Square Deal, said in his annual message to Congress on January 6, 1941, "Just as our national policy in internal affairs has been based upon a decent respect for the rights and dignity of all our fellowmen within our gates, so our national policy in foreign affairs has been based on a decent respect for the rights and dignity of all nations, large and small."[76] The speech is known as his "Four Freedoms Address" to Congress, for in it he identified the four basic freedoms as follows:

1. Freedom of speech and expression—everywhere in the world.

2. Freedom of every person to worship God in his own way—everywhere in the world.

3. Freedom from want, which, translated into world terms, means economic understandings that will secure to every nation a healthy peacetime life for its inhabitants—everywhere in the world.

4. Freedom from fear, which, translated into world terms, means a worldwide reduction of armaments to such a point and in such a thorough fashion that no nation will be in a position to

commit an act of physical aggression against any neighbor—
everywhere in the world.

When Roosevelt invited comments from his staff members in the
Oval Office, Harry Hopkins, one his principal advisors, questioned the
phrase "everywhere in the world." "That covers an awful lot of territory, Mr. President," he said, adding, "I don't know how interested
Americans are going to be in the people of Java." Roosevelt's reply was
prescient: "I'm afraid they'll have to be someday, Harry. The world is
getting so small that even the people in Java are getting to be our
neighbors now."[77]

Forrest Church, writer and senior minister at the All Souls Unitar-
ian Church in New York City, suggests that "the Four Freedoms address finds its moral grounding in both Christian ethics and the
founders' vision."[78] I have already pointed out that this Christian ethic
seen in the founders' vision is just as strongly Islamic, and it forms the
common ground of all religious belief that accepts the Abrahamic
ethic, for it is that nature of self-evident good that any and all people
can endorse.

The Universal Declaration of Human Rights was prepared by the
Commission on Human Rights of the Economic and Social Council
(ECOSOC) of the United Nations. Eleanor Roosevelt, social activist,
niece of Theodore Roosevelt, and widow of Franklin D. Roosevelt,
chaired the commission. It was adopted by the United Nations in 1948.

These principles, enunciated by Wilson and Franklin D. Roosevelt,
excited the admiration of the Muslim world toward the United States.
Muslims were increasingly familiar with American democracy and its
influence upon developments in Europe, which fed their desires to establish independent democratic regimes of their own.

The rights described in the thirty articles of the Universal Declaration of Human Rights are an extension of and, in effect, an attempt to
globalize the American Declaration of Independence and Bill of Rights.
The thirty articles include the right to life, liberty, and security of person; to freedom of conscience, religion, opinion, expression, association, and assembly; to freedom from arbitrary arrest; to a fair and
impartial trial; to freedom from interference in privacy, home, or cor-
respondence; to a nationality; to a secure society and an adequate stan-

dard of living; to education; and to rest and leisure. The declaration also affirms the rights of every person to own property; to be presumed innocent until proven guilty; to travel from a home country at will and return at will; to work under favorable conditions, receive equal pay for equal work, and join labor unions at will; to marry and raise a family; and to participate in government and in the social life of the community.

All these rights are in fact amplifications of the Abrahamic ethic. They thus constitute the social basis of all the Abrahamic religions: Judaism, Christianity, and Islam. They are therefore *Islamic rights* as much as they are *universal* rights, for they emanate from a natural religious instinct, what we have defined earlier as the *din al-fitrah*, the natural human religion, insofar as it pertains to the relationship between human societies. To the extent that Muslims have been denied these rights, their societies can be called neither truly Islamic nor truly human nor free.

AMERICAN CALLS TO HELP DESTROY COMMUNISM, 1953–1989

Until 1952, the Muslim world was much enamored of the United States. By and large, Muslims wanted to develop their societies and to improve standards of living for their communities along Western lines. Unfortunately, after the Second World War, two superpowers emerged simultaneously with the birth of the atomic age. The Soviet Union and the United States could not fight each other directly, but they fought each other by proxy, setting up spheres of influence in much of the globe. It was the era of the cold war. Much of what happened in the Muslim world and in other parts of the world (such as Cuba and other Central American nations, for example) was determined by cold war calculus.

Muslims lived both within and outside the boundaries of Soviet and American spheres of influence. The central Asian republics of Turkmenistan, Tajikistan, Uzbekistan, Kazakhstan, and Kyrgyzstan were part of the Soviet Republics. Nations such as Turkey and Pakistan were quickly allied with the West, Turkey being made part of NATO. Saudi Arabia and the Gulf countries also allied with the West, especially because, being religious, they were clearly and strongly anti-Communist. Moreover, they became important because of the oil reserves that lay under their feet. Iran, Afghanistan, Egypt, and Indonesia were major population centers where cold war proxy fights ensued.

Budding democratic movements were destabilized by one superpower or the other when it felt that things were not going its way. Each side found it more reassuring to have in place authoritarian regimes who could ensure a policy that was either anti-Communist or anti-West. In 1953 the CIA overthrew popularly elected Prime Minister Mossadegh of Iran, thereby earning the hostility and distrust of the Iranian people for decades.[79] When after a quarter century of authoritarian rule the Iranians wanted a change of regime, the United States refused to support the principle of consent of the governed, this being one example of the United States fighting against its constitutional principles in the Muslim world. In 1965 it is estimated that between three hundred thousand and one million Indonesians were massacred, said to be Communists or Communist sympathizers. Suharto emerged as president of Indonesia with support from the United States. In a nutshell, between 1953 and 1989, when the Soviet Union imploded and the cold war officially came to an end, the Muslim world was a key part of the global chessboard on which the cold war was played. And a militant Islam was used by the United States in cooperation with the Saudis and the Pakistanis to make Afghanistan the Soviet Union's Vietnam.

WAHHABI CONTRIBUTION IN HELPING END THE COLD WAR

Earlier we reviewed the genesis of the Wahhabi movement and its solidification of power through alliance with the Saudi family. In the 1970s, I mentioned, the Wahhabis came to ideological prominence through the economic spotlight shined on Saudi Arabia and its oil reserves. A major twist in using religion—in this case, Wahhabism—to further political objectives took place in the events that led to the Soviet invasion of Afghanistan in December 1979. Afghanistan was ruled by a monarchy until 1973, when military officers led by Muhammad Daud overthrew the king and proclaimed Afghanistan a republic. In 1978

Afghanistan came under Communist rule when the military overthrew Daud and installed Noor Muhammad Taraki, who was overthrown and killed in September 1979 by Hafizullah Amin and his supporters. In December 1979 the Soviet Union mounted a full-scale invasion of the country, killed President Amin, and installed Babrak Karmal as the president.

It was evident to any observer of geopolitics that the three regime changes in less than two years, back and forth from Communist to non-Communist rule, revealed that Afghanistan had become one of the playgrounds for the cold war between the United States and the Soviet Union. The Soviets were concerned at the time because the five southern states (Turkmenistan, Tajikistan, Uzbekistan, Kazakhstan, and Kyrgyzstan) were populated by historically Muslim peoples, and the Khomeini revolution in neighboring Iran could potentially foment anti-Soviet sentiment within them. During the same time, Khomeini was criticizing the pro-American Shah, who finally fled Iran in January 1979. Not trusting that any religious regime would be anti-Communist, the Americans felt they could no longer rely on Iran as they had in the past to hedge the Soviets on the western flank of Afghanistan, so they had to count on Pakistan, which neighbored Afghanistan on the eastern side, and on the Saudis, who were just across the Persian Gulf west of Iran. If the Soviets took over Iran, Saudi Arabia would be threatened. The historically close relationship between the Saudi government and the U.S. government prompted America to play the Islamic (in this case Wahhabi) religious card in combating the Soviets, in partnership with the Saudis and Pakistanis. The still-recent (at the time) American involvement in Vietnam made Americans extremely reticent to place American troops in Afghanistan, and America preferred to fight this war by proxy. The Saudis were a natural partner because the Saudis were always anti-Communist, for the simple reason that Communism was de facto antireligion, and Pakistan was an Islamic state. Both the Saudis and the Pakistanis were Sunni, and the Wahhabis had historically been strongly anti-Shiite (which the Iranians were).

A jihad was called against the Soviets, and the Afghans developed their mujahideen fighters, with many joining from foreign countries. Thus the conflict broadened, with Muslims drawn in and strengthening the Wahhabi influence. President Reagan hosted some mujahideens in the White House, honoring them for their role in containing what he once called the Evil Empire of the Soviet Union. Receiving American military training and support, these Afghan fighters were also sustained by weapons and money from Saudi Arabia, Iran, and China. By the mid-1980s the United States was spending hundreds of millions of dollars each year to aid Afghan mujahideen based in Pakistan.[80] In 1986 the United States began supplying the mujahideen with Stinger missiles able to shoot down Soviet armored helicopters. In May 1988 Afghanistan, Pakistan, the Soviet Union, and the United States signed agreements providing for an end to foreign intervention in Afghanistan, and after heavy losses the Soviet Union began withdrawing its forces. The Soviet withdrawal was completed in February 1989.

The outcome of American participation in training a militant group of Muslim mujahideen fighters, including Osama bin Laden, over the decade of the 1980s has had profound implications, not only on the domestic politics of Muslim societies, but also on the relationship between them and non-Muslim societies.

The mujahideen fighters returned to societies that did not have job opportunities for them and did not value them highly, and this fueled an intense frustration. Disillusionment over Muslims' inability to create the good society in practical ways has been directed at the West, at local non-Muslims, at Muslims who disagree with them, and toward all outsiders. Witnessing less-than-ideal expressions of Islamic rule in their own countries, including Saudi Arabia, the mujahideen have taken on the role of self-proclaimed Robin Hoods. Returning from their holy wars (jihads) against the infidels (the Communists), they see their local equivalents of the evil Prince John and Sheriff of Nottingham committing injustices, and they decide that doing something, anything, about it is better than doing nothing. And so we have Muslim zealots.

As individuals, we are today what we are because of our history, our life events, where we lived, and the sum total of our experiences. The same is true of a society. I have provided some historical reviews because history is important in helping us understand why we are as we are and in understanding why people feel the way they do about others, especially why many Muslims and Americans feel the way they do about each other. Understanding each other's points of view—our fears, aspirations, and longings—is essential if we are to be successful in bridging the gaps that exist between us.

year of publication

OUR HISTORY BEYOND 2004: THE GLOBAL VILLAGE

The world has become a global village, and no one, America included, can be isolationist or ignore global opinion without paying a price.

The global village today is shaped in large part by the United States and the principles embodied in the American Declaration of Independence and the United Nations Declaration of Human Rights. Increasingly, peoples around the world are rejecting dynastic rule, and monarchies are surviving mainly where they permit themselves to be figureheads, as in Britain, Norway, and Malaysia. The nation-state concept is being eroded by the forces of technology and globalization. Populations around the world are increasingly insisting on rule by consent of the governed and on greater participation in governance—a gradually increasing trend to rule in accord with the principles of the Abrahamic ethic.

Over the past century, the Muslim world has entered a new era. The end of the First World War was followed by the establishment of the League of Nations and America's attempts to establish a new world order based on Wilson's principles, which later became part of the United Nation's Declaration of Human Rights. In the intervening eighty-plus years many notable dates in Islamic history have occurred. Among them are:

- 1924, a date Osama bin Laden referred to, when the Ottoman Caliphate ended and the British, French, and Russians divided up the empire into separate countries

- 1947, when India was split into Pakistan and India, a deliberate attempt to create a homogeneous Islamic nation-state defined by geography

- 1948, when Israel was created as a homogeneous Jewish nation-state within the geographical envelope of the Muslim world

- 1979 and the Khomeini Revolution in Iran

- 1989, when the Berlin Wall fell and the cold war ended, altering the political calculus regarding Afghanistan and most of the Muslim world

- September 11, 2001, when the most dramatic suicide bombing attacks in history took place on the American mainland

- 2003, when for the first time, the United States militarily occupied Iraq, at the heart of the Muslim world, with several hundred thousand troops trying to shape a new Iraq (and possibly a new Afghanistan)

The above dates constitute rare moments in a region's destiny, moments when the die is cast that affects the indefinite future and the lives of many. We stand today at such a time, a time when the possible implications of American action are likely to have the broadest repercussions in the Mideast and the Muslim world.

With a wise and proactive America, the next few years could shape the "last" period of Islamic history, a period in which the constructs of Muslim society could be established in a way that meets the aspirations that Muslims have held since the time of the Prophet, a history that is true to itself and harmonious with the rest of the world. This must be the goal that we set for ourselves. Anything less just will not do.

The Challenges of Globalization

Globalization means simply the human activity of moving our goods, our services, our ideas, and our selves around the world with national borders becoming increasingly porous.[81] *Globalization* is a new entry in our vocabulary, a technical term used often in conferences and contemporary intellectual discourses, but the process has been taking place since the dawn of human history, albeit rather slowly. What makes it look new is merely the speed with which such change is occurring, as a result of technology.

For example, the "typical" Italian meal of spaghetti with marinara sauce followed by a cup of espresso coffee is the result of cross-cultural fertilization—what we now call globalization—that took place over centuries. Rome did not know pasta until Marco Polo returned from China in the 1300s and introduced noodles to Italy. The Italians did not invent marinara sauce until Columbus and other voyagers to the Americas brought the tomato from the New World to the Old. And before the rise of the Ottoman Empire, Europeans did not know coffee, which they at first regarded as an "infidel" beverage (Turkish coffee) originating in southern Arabia around the town of Mukha', known in English as "Mocha." After six centuries of slow-moving globalization, we can now dine on an "authentic" Italian meal.

The reason globalization causes angst is because it is forcing societies to change—economically, politically, socially, and religiously. In the United States, for example, the major fear of globalization is economic: the erosion of American industrial prowess because of foreign competition, NAFTA, and the exporting of jobs to places such as Mexico and India. In Europe, a major anxiety about globalization is that it brings an increase in immigration of non-European nationals, especially from Muslim lands. England has a growing Indo-Pakistani population, Germany a growing Turkish population, and France a growing North African (Algerian and Moroccan) population, which leads to a concern about the growing penetration of Islamic values into the capitals of Western civilization.

In the Muslim world a major concern is the erosion of social, family, and moral values because of the encroachment of what is seen as immoral values by way of satellite TV and the entertainment media. Ancient and dearly held customs are in danger of disappearing, and people fear being caught up in a vortex of materialism and overtaken by a worldview devoid of their cherished values. A general concern in the developing world is the power of foreign—mostly American—capital to dominate and upset national economic infrastructures, such as when Southeast Asian currencies were shorted in 1997, to the impoverishment of millions in the region.

The rapid process of globalization is forcing us to evolve toward commonly shared norms and thus to become more alike. This naturally leads to tension between those struggling to hold on to those values that are challenged and in danger of disappearing, and those struggling to forge ahead and replace old values with the new.

The challenge globalization poses to humanity is: Can we develop a worldview that is based on certain values held to be universal while still maintaining our unique and diverse cultural identities?

THE END OF HISTORY: LIFE IN THE GLOBAL GOOD SOCIETY

Social theorist Francis Fukuyama in the early nineties wrote about "the end of history" as the time "when [hu]mankind had achieved a form of society that satisfied its deepest and most fundamental longings." Muslims have always yearned to establish the Islamic good society, defined as that society that is able to reestablish the values exhibited by the Prophet and his four immediate successors, the "rightly guided" caliphs, in Medina. This was the ambition of all the revivalist movements throughout Islamic history. In such a society, Fukuyama observes, "there would be no further progress in the development of underlying principles and institutions, because all of the really big questions had been settled."[82]

Writing in the *New York Times* a few years later, at the end of the nineties, commentator Michael Novak observed that in the twentieth century the world answered two out of three of the "really big questions." The first question was political: whether democracy or dictatorial rule (fascist or communist) provided the better blueprint for society. In the twentieth century democracy clearly proved itself to be the superior form of government. Colonialism and the era of empire building came to a permanent end, and a notion of a United Nations was born.

The second really big question was economic: free or state-controlled economies? Since the fall of the Soviet Union, the remaining socialist countries have rushed to adopt capitalist insights, practices, and reforms precisely to improve the economic conditions of their poverty-stricken populations. In addition, attempts have been made to strengthen economic infrastructures such as banking and stock and capital markets—structures associated with open-market economies—in nations such as China, India, and Indonesia, where, previously, powerful attempts had been made to establish socialist economies. The resolution of the above two questions gave birth to democratic capitalism, whose defining feature was the attenuating of raw capitalism.

The third really big question has now become paramount: How then shall we live? How *must* we live, to preserve free societies and to be worthy of the blood and the pain humanity has endured? This is "the unfinished business of the twentieth century," Novak suggests, adding that serious American thinkers have begun to take it up.

He diagnoses "the present American crisis" as religious,

> or at least as moral and religious, rather than simply as moral alone. For the underlying question is deeper than moral. Why are our sentiments about justice so strong? Why do we long for universal amity? Why should we trust reason? Why should we be moral, especially when no one is looking and no one is harmed and no one will ever know?[83]

The unfinished business of the United States is religious; it is the question of how to express a religious impulse more fully *while doing it within the guidelines set forth in the Constitution*. The answers of secular humanism no longer seem adequate even to the many who tried hard to be faithful to them. Today the religious question has arisen most insistently among some of the most successful and the most powerful, and not at their moments of weakness but during their hours of greatest triumph. Just when they have achieved everything they once thought would make them happy, they bump into their own finitude—and their infinite hunger. "There must be more to it than this!" is the essential cry of the human heart. Though we are rich and powerful, we still need our existential questions answered—and Novak predicts confidently that "the twenty-first century will be the most religious in 500 years."

Acknowledging God provides a norm of ethics that relieves us of our existential stress. Today it is often the brightest and the most able and the most fortunate who are becoming aware of their true nature—"a nature that sings to them of God."[84] America, or precisely the American way of life, has disproven the Marxist axiom that religion is the opiate of the downtrodden, the weak, and the impoverished. It has proven that the strong and the wealthy are just as much in need of religion, and it has prompted leading American voices of our age to call for greater attention to religion—and in the forum of public life, not only in our private enclaves. The question remains how to do this and be faithful at the same time to the principles set forth in the Constitution, especially the separation of church and state.

The unfinished business of the Muslim world is just the flip side of this. It is how to introduce democratic capitalism, *while doing it "constitutionally," that is, within the guidelines set forth in Muslim law.* Muslim societies, as we have seen, get the "religion" right; they follow the first commandment well, acknowledging God and making the worship of God the highest priority of daily life. Their cutting edge is the second commandment: how to implement the values of love of neighbor and institutionalize freedom and economic well-being for all. The dialogue between the Muslim world and the West is therefore a fruitful one; each has something the other needs. By combining our accumulated wisdom, we could transform life in the global village.

A globalized religiosity will be one that is based on principles and values that satisfy our universal human spiritual needs. In this worldview people recognize that humans experience anomie at the individual level and conflict at the interpersonal and collective levels if they are disconnected from God or, as some would say, from the higher creative power in the universe, the Absolute.

Finding the place where conflict between the material and the spiritual ceases can happen only when the human individual learns to know itself, recognizing itself as the threshold between two worlds, each with its realities: the reality of material existence, where the ego dwells, and the reality of spiritual Being, where the soul or essential self is held and nurtured in the embrace of the All-Compassionate.

Our spiritual masters have been educating our souls for many centuries. Their teachings and methods are based not on dogma and conjecture but upon a divine and objective foundation, which is the primordial, natural religion of humanity (the *din al-fitrah*). Their teachings offer a path to complete humaness, a state in which the spiritual and the human are unified, in which the world of spiritual qualities and material existence are seen as one.

The path of human happiness lies in recognizing that humans are created in the image of God and that, by extension, the best society is one that builds a fully mature understanding of what it means to be a nation under God. Herein lies the wisdom of America's founders, for even if they were not aware of it, they expressed the truth that a nation "under God" extended best the view of the human made in the image of God into the social intercourse of humanity. To Muslims, this is what is meant by building the kingdom of heaven on earth, and this is their aspiration for, and what they love about, America.

CHAPTER 6

A New Vision for Muslims and the West

In January 2002 I was invited to lecture at Greenwich Presbyterian Church in Connecticut. After an hour and a half of questions and answers, a wonderful woman stood up and asked, "What can a Christian woman like me do to help?" American Jewish audiences too are dissatisfied with the state of the relationship between the Muslim and Jewish faith communities, and they probe me insistently on what they can do to help change it. The most common and most challenging question people have asked me since September 11—in churches and synagogues as well as business corporations—is "What can we do to solve the problem between the Muslim world and the West?" Indeed, what can ease the underlying tensions between Muslim, Christian, Jewish, and other faith communities? How can we turn the tide of these relationships immediately, and proceed to heal them within a matter of years, not decades?

THE VISION "NEEDED YESTERDAY": HOW TO CHANGE MINDS AND WIN PEACE

The urgency of this question is underscored by a 2003 report titled "Changing Minds, Winning Peace," issued by the United States Advisory Group on Public Diplomacy for the Arab and Muslim World. This panel, formed by the U.S. State Department and chaired by Ambassador Edward P. Djerejian to study the dismal state of public relations worldwide between the Muslim world and the West, reported that "Hostility toward America has reached shocking levels." The Djerejian report adds, "What is required is not merely tactical adaptation [of American communications efforts] but strategic, and radical, transformation." I can think of no clearer words to describe this critical need.

Healing the relationship between the Muslim world and the West in an urgent time frame requires implementing a quick-acting, multi-track process to address a broad spectrum of issues that have fueled the conflict. We require a vision that defines the objectives of our effort, creates targeted strategies to attain these objectives, and convenes the essential players capable of implementing them.

The vision is this: America must do all it can to help champion the emergence of a strong, self-confident Islamic world that fulfills the principles of an Islamic good society as understood by the Prophet and his "rightly guided" successors—what we called in the previous chapter the unfinished business of the Muslim world—and ushers in its last stage or "end" of history. With the help of American Muslims, the United States should actively support the development of an Islamic democratic capitalism that addresses the Muslim world's three most profound issues of conflict: religion, control of power, and distribution of economic assets.

To that end, I offer ideas for what ordinary citizens—businesspeople, educators, Christians, and Muslims—can do as well as what the American government can do to heal the relationship between the Muslim world and the West. We already have the skills needed to implement all of these strategies, and some projects are already taking place. Everything here is doable, and yet, to succeed quickly, the strategies outlined here will be most effective if implemented as a network with cooperation from all sectors of society. Our efforts now must really be joint efforts.

Dialogue is the first step. Dialogue is absolutely essential, for without it no further changes will take place. Many of the ideas I offer below build on a foundation of dialogue, for only after we have replaced our fear and misunderstandings with friendship and empathy are we in a position to see what further steps are needed or even possible. Dialogue creates a changed climate in which deeper issues become easier to address. Refusing to dialogue continues conflict.

WHAT THE UNITED STATES GOVERNMENT CAN DO: DESIGN A WEAPON OF MASS PEACE

If America seriously wants to bridge the chasm between the Muslim world and the West, it must publicly declare that its foreign policy is returning to its original democratic values. It should articulate a vision of an Islamic democratic capitalism to ordinary Muslims in countries around the world. This effort would be best initiated by the president of the United States directly and dramatically addressing the Muslim world at large. The president's message should incorporate the ethical convictions of FDR's "Four Freedoms" address to Congress and the emotional tone of John F. Kennedy's *"Ich bin ein Berliner"* speech, to demonstrate emphatically that America's best interests coincide with the Muslim world's best interests. President Bush's speech at the twentieth anniversary of the National Endowment for Democracy was the closest that any U.S. president since Roosevelt came to speaking directly to the needs of the Muslim world along these lines.[1] However, this speech was made in Washington, D.C., to an American audience. His surprise visit to Baghdad for Thanksgiving Day 2003 was one of several missed opportunities for him to have directly addressed the Iraqis and others in the Arab and Muslim world via TV and radio, but no doubt other occasions will arise for the leader of the free world to wholeheartedly and publicly commit the United States to pursuing a new foreign policy toward the Muslim world.

Such a foreign policy would assist Muslim nations in attaining these major objectives:

1. Economic freedom (that is, freedom from poverty) for Muslims worldwide. This means offering help in establishing the basic economic infrastructures and controls necessary for Muslim countries to develop prosperous societies that will increase the quality of life for all citizens. The creation or reform of banking systems, capital and stock markets, and sound monetary policies are essential. Most Muslims live in economies whose currencies inflate rapidly, eroding individual savings and making life increasingly difficult for the average person. Muslim societies desperately need stable currencies and low inflation.

2. The rule of law for Muslims worldwide, which includes justice, security, and freedom from fear. Islamic law does not condone any group of individuals in society living above the law nor does it hold Muslims and non-Muslims to different standards of justice. Muslim societies need an independent judiciary, not

a judiciary whose decisions can be determined by individuals in political office. The combination of economic structures and the rule of law also implies essential economic legislation. Examples include antitrust legislation to eliminate monopolies and create greater equality of opportunity (the kind of legislation the United States had to implement to protect its democracy),[2] and the safeguards implemented during the Wilson and FDR administrations, such as providing deposit insurance, credit availability, and economic safety nets for various economic sectors and the population at large. While some form of direct financial aid might be needed from the United States and G-7 nations, the greater need of Muslim societies is for "structural" aid, that is, help in developing the right economic and economic-legal infrastructures. Fair trade policies constitute another item that would go a long way toward forging Muslim goodwill toward the United States.

3. Broader public participation in decision making and governance in Muslim countries, along with the protection of human rights. This does not mean a violent overnight conversion of all Muslim governments to full democracy—an impossible and as we have shown not altogether meaningful task—but it does mean building support for democratic principles within existing governments and allowing diverse population groups to participate more meaningfully in their own governance. Also a gradual evolution to some measure of term limits for the most powerful offices in the land. Term limits are highly preferable to the militant alternatives.[3]

4. An Islamically articulated separation-of-powers doctrine, which means:

   • A judiciary independent of the executive and legislative branches

   • An economy free from state control, combined with a non-monopolistic private economic sector with safeguards against corruption

- A military that does not interfere in the affairs of governance

- A free press with greater access to government actions, to help educate the populace and aid it in holding its rulers accountable

- Freedom of religious expression and conscience and protection of all religious institutions and houses of worship

Simultaneously and in addition to the above four nation-building objectives, the United States should commit itself to fully resolving three long-standing conflicts:

1. The Arab-Israeli conflict in the Mideast, which will eliminate Muslim-Jewish religious tensions

2. The Kashmir conflict between India and Pakistan, which will eliminate Muslim-Hindu religious tension

3. The Chechnya conflict with Russia

As it works to help Muslim nations attain the above goals, the U.S. government should actively seek the participation of the United Nations and the many nongovernmental organizations seeking the same ends. Only when such efforts are woven together can rapid transformation be achieved. A noteworthy example of the weaving together of strategic initiatives may be found in the Man-on-the-Moon Project. Countless scientists and engineers worked on separate components of the project, but all focused on the overall objective: landing a man on the moon. Without the organizational support provided by the National Aeronautics and Space Administration (NASA), which pieced together the people with the expertise to develop the technology and know-how, it is certain that John Kennedy's promise to land a man on the moon by the end of the 1960s would not have been fulfilled by that date, and perhaps not at all. In the same way, I am convinced that if the U.S. government committed itself to a Winning-the-Peace initiative between America and the Muslim world, a project of the magnitude of the Man-on-the-Moon project, it would lead to positive, rapid results.

Some of the players required for such a peace team would be the following:

- Islamic scholars, especially of law and jurisprudence
- Western scholars of constitutional law and other legal experts
- Religious scholars from faith traditions that intersect the Muslim world, and especially from Judaism, Christianity, Hinduism, and Buddhism
- Economists and banking experts
- Conflict resolution experts
- Education experts
- Communications and media experts
- Psychologists and social scientists

These people and skills are widely available in universities and academic institutions, nongovernmental organizations (NGOs), think tanks, the business world, and government. But I cannot emphasize enough that unless they are deployed as a team, the time span to achieve the objective will be decades instead of years, during which time increasing damage may occur.

For example, we have discussed some aspects of the vexing question of church-state separation as seen from both Muslim and American perspectives. This issue intersects Islamic law, American constitutional law, and government, and it is a subject of keen interest to scholars and thinkers of other religions as well. It is especially relevant to countries such as Israel, Pakistan, and Iran. Most people, even those in religion, are not adequately equipped to think through these issues in ways that can clarify it. Yet it is important that this issue is clarified and explained in a manner that is understandable even to the layperson.

The same applies to economic issues. Most people are unable to fathom the importance of antitrust laws, the role of monetary policies, and the financial architecture of an economy in ensuring a healthy and stable currency, and yet these are among the issues that fuel a lot of confusion in the Muslim world. For example, Abdul Hadi Awang, leader of a Malaysian opposition party in the state of Terengganu in Malaysia, has banned interest on state-granted housing and car loans to civil servants and eliminated what he calls "un-Islamic" local taxes and tolls.[4] While eliminating interest on housing and car loans is made possible by raising the price of homes and cars to reflect the cost of capital, it is not clear how it is possible to control monetary policies without interest-based securities.

As mentioned earlier, home construction and the automobile industry are the two largest components of the U.S. economy. Eliminate home mortgages and car loans, and the U.S. economy would suffer the equivalent of a major heart attack. How do we expect the economy of Muslim nations to take off without the powerful uplifting economic effect of home mortgages, which would also enable millions of Muslims to achieve home ownership? The Muslim world currently is forced to use interest-based instruments to fulfill its need for capital formation, financial liquidity, and monetary policy, but until Muslim governments find a way to inform their publics of how they address the usury problem, this remains a point of contention.

Broadly speaking, this Winning-the-Peace initiative is interdisciplinary work at a level never before undertaken: bringing disparate skills not just from different fields but also from different histories and different faiths and weaving them together in a focused way. Essential to the process are American Muslims, who truly understand both perspectives and who can act as critically needed translators in the cultural bridging work.

WHAT AMERICAN MUSLIMS CAN DO: EVOLVE FROM "MUSLIMS IN AMERICA" TO "AMERICAN MUSLIMS"

American Muslims, positioned as they are with a foot in both East and West, have a vital contribution to make. They are in a position to say not only that that no contradiction exists between Islam's theology and the longing of many Muslims for democratic values and equality of opportunity, but also that Islam's theology and jurisprudence demand it. Because they understand the aspirations of each side and have reconciled their American and Islamic identities, they have a central mediating role to play in building trust and brokering interreligious and intercultural communication between America and the Muslim world.

By forging alliances and coalitions with other American religious groups, particularly major Jewish and Christian institutions, American Muslims can assist in crafting the best language, innovative approaches, and, perhaps most important, the right working perspectives with which our nation could help the Muslim world solve its problems. In so doing, American Muslims meet their obligation to play a critically important role as mediators between the 1.2 billion Muslims worldwide and their great nation.

The ability of politically moderate, mainstream American Muslims to play a leading role in healing relations between the Muslim world and the United States has been challenged by a complex of issues. Sixty percent of American Muslims are transitioning from a first, immigrant, generation into a second generation of emerging American Muslims. African American Muslims, who constitute the other forty percent, are American nonimmigrant Muslims evolving from a first generation of predominantly Black Muslims, who accepted Islam during the Civil Rights era of the 1960s and were shaped by its dynamic, into a second generation whose Islam is shaped more by religious and spiritual considerations and the sociological challenge of how to integrate with their immigrant colleagues.

One of the challenges facing any immigrant community is how to move from being an immigrant to developing a local mind-set and way of living. When Islam spread from the Arabian Peninsula to the rest of what is known today as the Muslim world, it had to restate its religious principles in the cultural contexts of ancient pre-Islamic societies: Egypt, Mesopotamia, Turkey, Iran, Africa, India, and so forth. And we can witness shades of difference between Egyptian Islam and Indian Islam, between Turkish Islam and Senegalese Islam—not in the theology but in the sociology and laws that flowed from the different preexisting customs of each society.

A significant challenge today in the United States is the development of an American Islamic identity that can meaningfully encompass all the sundry immigrant Muslim identities as well as the local African American identity. The history between the Muslim world and the West (including America) has unfortunately led many Americans to equate being Muslim with being anti-American and anti-Western—an unfair blanket categorization.

The work involved in developing an American Islamic identity has to involve, by definition, a high appreciation both for what it means to be American and what it means to be Muslim. It cannot be just the accidental experience of being a foreign Muslim living in America, each part at odds with the other. Nor can it be an American becoming Muslim in order to reject America. It requires unpacking the psychological layers of past individual and collective experience, separating history from essential humanity, shedding what is irrelevant, and building an identity based on what is eternal to the human condition in a new America and a globalized world.[5]

One way to accomplish this goal is to engage with our predecessors in the immigration experience, Christians and Jews who had to develop an American Christian and American Jewish identity, learning from their experience as they evolved from being imported expressions of mainly European churches and synagogues into American expressions of Judaism and Christianity. While each experience is unique, many aspects of the process are common and can afford meaningful and fruitful opportunities for interfaith dialogue. As we saw in chapter 5, each community had to contend with the humiliation factor at the hands of mainline American Protestants. But as a saying goes, it's better to learn from the mistakes of others, for life is too short to commit them all. This means that the fast track for American Muslims seeking to find their American identity lies through learning from the immigrant experience of American Catholics and Jews. Blended with lessons gleaned from Islamic history, when the earliest Muslims spread beyond the Arabian peninsula to the ancient cultures from West Africa to Southeast Asia, this knowledge can help American Muslims more rapidly shape a new definition of what it means to be an American Muslim in a globalized world—as much for the sake of their children and grandchildren as for their 1.2 billion coreligionists around the globe.

Muslims face a unique challenge in this regard, for when Christianity and Judaism took root in Europe, they developed an Occidental character different from their Semitic roots. Islam has yet to develop an Occidental character; its history has been primarily Oriental and Semitic.

Out of such engagements and initiatives American Muslims should develop an informal network of Muslim and non-Muslim intellectuals, scholars, and religious leaders who share a mutual commitment to democratic values, pluralism, and a free society stated in Islamically orthodox vocabulary and theological constructs.

The long-term goal of the new network would be to accelerate the development of a healthy American Muslim identity that is fully Islamic, fully American, and fully committed to the values of the Abrahamic ethic. It could sponsor scholarly seminars aimed at clarifying the confusion between what is truly Islamic in a theological or jurisprudential sense and what is merely a holdover from the cultural and social traditions that Muslim immigrants bring to America from their native countries. In the international arena, by viewing the world with fresh eyes unclouded by cultural history, Muslim Americans could play a key role in leading the Islamic world toward the economic freedoms for which its citizens most deeply long and that Muslims in the West routinely enjoy.

WHAT EDUCATORS CAN DO: FORGE THE NEXT
GENERATION OF MUSLIM CITIZENS

As University of Chicago professor Allan Bloom pointed out in his *Closing of the American Mind*, every political regime shapes its citizens according to what it most needs. In some nations the goal is the pious person, in others the warlike, in others the industrious. Since the United States during the cold war helped to forge an Islamic warlike citizen—by supporting madrasas in Pakistan that taught radical ideology as preparation for fighting the Soviet Union—it now has an obligation to support reform efforts that seek to educate Islamic citizens who are both pious and pluralistic. President Pervez Musharraf of Pakistan, at the World Economic Forum in Davos, 2004, expressed his readiness to immediately establish five hundred madrasas to teach a different syllabus and counter the radical message, "but," he asked, "where is the money to pay for them going to come from?" The United States has a self-interest in paying for them, as education is one of the most effective ways to wage war against terrorism.

The informal network of Muslim and non-Muslim intellectuals, scholars, and religious leaders mentioned in the previous section could participate in and accelerate efforts already under way to design educational curricula for schools that will further this goal. Such a network could also support educational programs in existing academic institutions and organize symposia in which American Muslims could work on harmonizing the values that attracted so many to the United States in the first place with the religious traditions that they cherish. Such educational programs would help assimilate new Muslim immigrants into American society and would help young, American-born, second-generation Muslims articulate the American Muslim dream to their own nation and to the world. A central aspect of this network's educational mission would be to build informal communication links between existing American Muslim opinion leaders at home and abroad while encouraging young, emerging leaders to find their own voices. The network would provide intellectual mentoring for the next generation of democratic-Islamic citizens.

WHAT AMERICAN JEWS CAN DO: REDOUBLE EFFORTS FOR PEACE IN THE HOLY LAND

Because it remains the single biggest obstacle to healing the relationship between the United States and the Muslim world, the Israeli-Palestinian problem is one that our nation must face head-on in our traditional role as leader of the free world.

Achieving peace between Israel and Palestine is essential to building peace between the Islamic world and the United States. Additionally, such a peace would help eliminate Muslim-Jewish religious antipathy and stem the rise of anti-Semitism in the world. The Clinton administration tried to broker peace in 2000 but for whatever reason was not able to forge a lasting agreement. We came close to achieving peace at that time, and because we came close, we must attempt it again, redoubling our efforts to heal this gaping wound.

If the United States were to press for Middle East peace, even placing its troops between the Israelis and the Palestinians if necessary to keep the peace, as it has done elsewhere, it would be interpreted as an expression of its genuine desire to foster better relations with the Muslim world. By contrast, American willingness to allow the Palestinian problem to fester indefinitely is interpreted by Muslims as a dismissive attitude that ignores the concerns of the global Muslim community. Once the Palestinians accept a plan that allows them to start focusing on living their lives, the rest of the Muslim world will eventually go along with what the Palestinians accept, for they are the principal party involved.

Such a peace plan, however incomplete at its inception, must focus on alleviating the suffering of the Palestinian people and allowing them to live in dignity, freedom, and increasing prosperity. No plan could offer these benefits to the Palestinians unless it also offered Israelis the safety and security that they need to live their lives in peace. By also focusing on increasing job opportunities and the prosperity of the individual family, such a plan could plant the seeds of a lasting peace.

To extend a football analogy, what is needed is a series of quick, highly advertised first downs to rapidly excite ordinary Muslims and convince them that America is serious about pursuing a mutually respectful relationship. The world's sole military and economic superpower remains the key player in any effort to build peace. The United States possesses the most effective global bully pulpit to convene the United Nations or any particular subgroup of nations—such as the Arab states or the G-7 nations—to generate the necessary momentum and to focus the expertise required to achieve concrete results.

The quickest route through a mountain is often around it. If the road to peace between India and Pakistan is through China, the road to peace in the Middle East between Israel and Palestine is more likely to go through the United States. The United States remains the one nation of the world that, by exerting the full moral force of its leadership, could bring the warring parties together. America would reap an enormous outpouring of goodwill from the rest of the world if it exerted half the effort in building peace in Palestine that it used to topple Saddam Hussein. And imagine how much more secure the entire world will be, including the United States, once this conflict is put to rest.

The American Jewish community is the most important player on this field. It knows best how to quarterback the plays necessary to make Mideast peace the number one priority for leaders in the U.S. government and Congress.

To this end, I propose (and describe below) a series of Jerusalem Dialogues to explore what a secure home for each side would look like—and the American Jews, Christians, and Muslims engaged in this exploration would be ideally positioned to communicate their insights to American policymakers.

One hundred years of suicide bombings will not drive Israel into the sea. Nor will one hundred years of targeted assassinations and home demolitions by Israel dry up the reservoir of young Palestinian recruits eager to join organizations such as Hamas. Each act of violence against Israel has severely weakened Israel's peace parties and driven its public into the arms of extremist hawks. Likewise, the callous policies of those hawks toward the Palestinians have further deepened the frustrations and sense of hopelessness that feed international terrorism, anti-Semitism in Europe and the Muslim world, and the growing Muslim perception of Jewish terrorism, which in turn has fueled an even greater rise in terrorism committed in the name of Islam. And so the deadly cycle continues, with the death toll mounting on both sides.

Statements by some Israelis that they will never negotiate with terrorist organizations and statements by some Palestinians that they will never negotiate with an outlaw Israeli state simply ensure that the conflict continues to claim its tragic toll of innocent lives on both sides. The bloodshed will not end until both sides grow weary of the killing and are finally ready to talk. Not stage talk designed for the ears of the United States or the United Nations, but real talk. I am heartened by the Geneva Accord worked out between Yasser Abed Rabbo and Yossi Beilin (Palestinian minister of culture and information and Israeli opposition leader, respectively), for it expresses the sentiment of growing numbers of people on both sides.

Marc Gopin, a Tufts professor and conflict resolution specialist with the Harvard Program on Negotiation, suggests that what Palestinians need and demand of Israelis is dignity, while Israelis crave and need a long-term safe haven. Both sides are bitter about being deprived of the same need: a secure home. The Palestinians' overriding need is for what they have missed the most, the dignity of home and the actual ownership of ancestral lands, while the Jews crave what they have most missed, multigenerational safety from annihilation.[6]

Senior American Muslim and Jewish leaders rarely have the opportunity for a meaningful dialogue that transcends superficialities. Both of their communities would benefit greatly from increased communication and understanding—and both are vitally interested in finding a just and secure resolution to the Israeli-Palestinian conflict, which has provided the underlying fuel for so much religious fanaticism and terrorism worldwide. At the same time, increasing numbers of Jews and Muslims in the United States have become frustrated over the lack of resolution of this conflict and would like to see America playing a more decisive role in resolving it. American Jewish and Muslim leaders, if they could agree on certain key issues and speak together with a unified voice, could have a powerful effect on steering American foreign policy toward a role of more engaged and credible peace building.

As an example, senior Jewish and Muslim leaders might gather for a series of roundtable Jerusalem Dialogues, to which both secular and religious leaders would be invited. Muslim participants might include senior academic, business, and community leaders as well as imams representing some of the most important Muslim communities in the United States. Jewish participants might include the leaders of major Jewish organizations along with a variety of respected business and community leaders. In addition, prominent Christian leaders and certain nongovernmental organizations with experience in Middle East peace efforts would be invited, including both Palestinians and Israelis. Finally, nationally renowned conflict resolution specialists could be asked to moderate the group.

These dialogues would be aimed at building trust between American Muslims and Jews, exploring what a secure home for each side would look like, and entertaining possibilities for just and secure solutions to the Israeli-Palestinian conflict. The Muslim and Jewish leaders meeting in the United States would review many of the same issues being discussed by Israeli and Palestinian negotiators in the Middle East, but they would do so from a fresh and perhaps less politically constrained perspective, one that might be helpful in filling in many of the still unmapped quadrants of any future road map to peace.

Along the way, the American Muslim and Jewish leaders participating in this effort would likely create their own informal network, which would enable the group to confer quickly in times of national urgency when a coordinated Muslim-Jewish response might help defuse tensions within their communities and the nation. The American Muslim, Jewish, and Christian leaders engaged in this exploration would be ideally positioned to communicate their insights to American policymakers and together to lobby the U.S. administration and Congress for the implementation of a politically workable framework for peace acceptable to each side.[7]

WHAT AMERICAN CHRISTIANS CAN DO: VIGOROUSLY PURSUE INTERFAITH DIALOGUE

Wonderful work has already been done in this country by Christians engaged in interfaith dialogue. Wherever I speak here in America, especially since September 11, I find goodwill from Christians as well as an openness among many Christians to engage in dialogue regarding our common American identity. Many Christians are eager, both as individuals and as representatives of institutions, to cooperate in developing initiatives that will open doors of understanding between our two faith communities. Our country needs this continued spirit of openness, and I commend American Christians for the important steps they have already taken in interfaith dialogue.

American Christians have an important role to play also in the dialogue between Muslims and Jews. The structure of dialogue already set up between Christians and Jews can serve as a model for dialogue with Muslims as well, especially on the Israeli-Palestinian issue. American Christians would do well to include Arab Christians in dialogue. Muslims see among both Jews and Christians some reluctance to acknowledge those communities of their own faith who live in Muslim parts of the world. Arab Christians, for example, would like to participate as equal partners in dialogue on Mideast issues, for they feel linked to Christians in the West through religion as well as to the Muslim world through culture. Sephardic Jews, who represent a minority among Ashkenazi Jews of European descent, are also needed—and are eager to participate—in this dialogue. Arab Christians and Sephardic Jews understand elements of both the Muslim world and the West and thus have a vital role to play in bridging the chasm between them.

For all the wonderful work in interfaith dialogue already done by American Christians, more yet remains. The Reverend Franklin Graham, head of Samaritan's Purse and son of the Reverend Billy Graham, has called Islam "a very evil and wicked religion." The Reverend Jerry

Vines, past president of the Southern Baptist Convention, has referred to Muhammad as "a demon-possessed pedophile."[8] To an American who loves Islam deeply, I find these words unbearably painful to hear—and they are words that cause unspeakable anger in other parts of the world. Such words also represent false and un-Christian theology, for Christians are taught to "hate the sin but love the sinner," a teaching that is perfectly consistent with Islamic teachings and the practice of the Prophet Muhammad. Sadly, with similar emotion but expressed in reverse, some Muslim clerics in the Middle East refer to America as "the great Satan" and call for violent jihad against Christians and Jews. As one working with all his heart for peace, I feel great anguish at these words too, for they are theologically false and not based on the values of Islamic law and jurisprudence.

If American Christians could refrain from making incendiary remarks about Islam, this would help create a climate in which "fundamentalist" leaders on both sides might begin a process of trying to understand each other instead of hurling insults across the cultural chasm. In addition to exercising such restraint, Christian leaders who don't understand or who even fear Islam would do well to engage local Muslim leaders in their hometowns in an open and good-spirited dialogue aimed at building trust and tolerance on both sides.

I dream of the day when a prominent American Christian leader such as the Reverend Graham visits the home of an Iranian ayatollah and stays with his family for three days—and the ayatollah reciprocates by visiting the American's home, thus affording each a rich opportunity to learn about the other's tenets and the moral high ground of their respective faiths. If we are truly to learn to love our neighbors, we might start by simply trying to understand them.

WHAT THE AMERICAN MEDIA CAN DO: COVER ISLAM, DON'T VEIL IT

The American proverb "Smile at the world, and it will smile back at you" applies to the Muslim world as well. Smile at Muslims, and they will smile back at you. For too long America has growled at the Muslim world, and now it wonders why it's growling back. A drastic overhaul is needed—nothing less will do—of the American media's efforts in its attitude toward the Muslim world, for the West and the Muslim world cannot continue to regard each other as existential enemies.

The American media and movie industries would do well to stop depicting Muslims as bad guys, which feeds both an American antipathy toward Muslims and Muslim rage toward America. It is decades since Hollywood has depicted certain ethnic groups negatively because of the adverse publicity the studios would get, but somehow Muslims and Arabs have remained a free hit. The Westerns I used to watch in my youth invariably depicted Native Americans as barbarian savages, as did the Tarzan movies in their depiction of Africans. Today we look at these old movies and find the subliminal racist messages they convey offensive. Films, books, and newspaper articles that depict Muslims negatively add to the tension between the Muslim world and the West. The boys and girls of my childhood modeled themselves on the iconic figures found in movies and the media: Tarzan and Jane, John Wayne and Zorro. With millions of Muslim children throughout the world being influenced by American movies, what iconic figures has Hollywood offered growing generations of young Muslim boys to compete with the image of Osama bin Laden?

Muslims were therefore delighted when movies that depicted them and their culture in a positive light began to emerge. Examples were *Robin Hood: Prince of Thieves,* in which Morgan Freeman played the role of a highly educated Muslim aiding Kevin Costner's Robin Hood in gaining justice for the poor. Another was *The 13th Warrior,* in which Antonio Banderas played the hero, a Muslim noble who joins up with some Vikings to protect their villages. American Muslims have felt unfairly maligned for so long that movies depicting them positively are cherished and welcomed as a breath of fresh air. Honoring the culture of others results in mutual honoring; dishonoring a culture results in mutual dishonoring. What a world of difference they see when ethnic Chinese and Buddhists compare old films, which treated Chinese as abject cooks or untrustworthy people, with new ones such as *Crouching Tiger, Hidden Dragon* and others, which depict Asian people and Buddhist fighting monks in an admirable light.

The American print and broadcast media in particular need to do more to fulfill their civic objective, specifically in highlighting the efforts and, more important, the positions and arguments of important, well-informed, and educated Muslims involved in ongoing debates in the Muslim community here and overseas. Growing generations of Muslims, American and foreign, need hope, and they need to learn how they can be fully modern, fully pluralistic, and fully Muslim.

WHAT THE BUSINESS COMMUNITY CAN DO: REPLACE "DYING TO KILL" WITH "DYING TO MAKE A KILLING"

The journey toward achieving peace requires that we imagine what peace will look like between warring parties, that we know what we want to achieve and by when. Then we have to plan it and deploy enough force, energy, and skill to obtain it.

For example, I strongly believe that once a peace is established between the Israelis and Palestinians, no matter how imperfect it might look at the beginning, the growing economic bonds between Israel and its neighbors will create powerful bonding forces. The observations of Ashutosh Varshney, whom we met in chapter 4, indicate that by forming associational relationships—bonds created by business, trade, political, and professional ties—we can expect violence to subside. In the event of peace in the Middle East, among Israel's most important trading partners are likely to be its neighbors: Palestine, Lebanon, Jordan, Egypt, and Syria. I've often asserted that the three countries of Lebanon, Israel, and Palestine are likely to be among the economic locomotives of the Middle East because the Lebanese, Israelis, and Palestinians have global relationships in the fields of commerce, banking, and trade. The same is likely to be true for Palestine and Jordan: Israel will likely be among their most important trading partners. Strong regional economic ties will likely create pressures within a couple of decades for a common currency and a momentum toward an economic union not unlike that of the European Union. At that point in time, issues that are current stumbling blocks on the road to peace will be looked at from a wholly different perspective.

The same applies to the other major conflict areas in the Muslim world: Kashmir and Chechnya. India and Pakistan are likely to be among each other's most important trading partners in the aftermath of any peace plan that sticks, and within a generation or less the region that was split apart in 1947 will become another economic union, together with Kashmir and Bangladesh.

What makes me say this? Look at the effect of the rapidly growing economic relationship between India and China. In four years, the bilateral trade between China and India has mushroomed from less than $2 billion per year in the fiscal year ending March 31, 2000, to $7 billion in the fiscal year ending March 31, 2004, and it is projected to hit $10 billion the following year. Indian prime minister Atal Bihari Vajpayee admitted that "there was a period in the India-China relationship when our preoccupation with our differences prevented a pragmatic understanding of the mutual benefits from cooperation."[9]

This statement says it all: "preoccupation with differences" prevents people from understanding how much they will benefit by co-operating with each other. This is no more than applying the Sufi story (or Buddhist story, for these anecdotes travel the globe) about people who cannot bend their elbows finding themselves in heaven or in hell. Hell is where, seated in front of a feast, they are unable to eat because they cannot bend their elbows, and they therefore starve. Heaven is where each person uses a spoon to feed the person seated opposite.

How many people today even remember that a few years ago Chinese and Indian soldiers were battling on the border between China and India? How many people know that the "Kashmir dispute" is not only between India and Pakistan but also between India and China? Except that with China the border dispute includes another Indian state, Arunachal Pradesh, which together with Jammu and Kashmir (this is one state), "Beijing views as one of its main outstanding border disputes." But because of the growing economic links (Varshney's "associational" ties), Indian and Chinese diplomats have a powerful incentive they didn't have forty years ago to "hammer out a comprehensive agreement to resolve the conflicts involving their 2,200 mile border, and have assigned special envoys to work out a deal."[10]

It must have occurred to Prime Minister Vajpayee that his pointed statement about China applies very well to Pakistan. The hump India and Pakistan have to get over is how to convince both sides that the mutual benefits of their cooperation will vastly outweigh preoccupation with their differences.

If China and India succeed, we can reasonably pray that China may use its goodwill and regional influence with its historical ally Pakistan and broker a similar rapprochement between Pakistan and India. This would mean that the peace road from Delhi to Islamabad might go through Beijing. As has happened between the United States and China, growing bilateral trade has a way of dissolving disputes and making the disputes look like children's arguments over cheap toys. Trade in the India-Pakistan-China triangle would be an enormous boon to the region that includes Nepal, Tibet, Bhutan, and Bangladesh. If all parties take a time-out from hostilities and focus on economic development and increasing bilateral trade, within a decade or two solutions will be found to the sources of conflict. And Americans would be able to visit the Dalai Lama in Tibet.[11]

American bumper stickers during the 1960s read Make Love, Not War. We need bumper stickers that apply the more powerful lesson Create Jobs, Not War, for history has proven that a critical mass of good business relationships can put conflict into a whole different perspective. Growing bilateral trade is part of a vision that both parties should wish to achieve. Why have a beef over some cold Himalayan mountain land when peace can raise a mountain of real beef? Remember that the nature of wealth has evolved drastically over the past century. At one time land was the primary definition of wealth and power; until a little over a century ago one had to be a white male landowner to be able to vote in the United States. Today the wealthiest in the world, those on the lists in *Forbes* or *Fortune,* are not so because of land ownership but because of stock in companies or that peculiar thing we call money, which today consists of numbers held in accounts in banks located in crowded cities.

We don't hear much about applying this formula in ending conflict, terrorism, and extremism. Generally, people are willing to trade or sell one asset for another; this is the basis of any market. In addition, many are willing to trade away some of their own power in return for desired assets (usually money, which can be traded for other desirable assets). People will sometimes give another person a certain amount of power over themselves, as long as they are paid enough (in their own minds) for the control they are giving up. In personal and business relationships, this means that people's services, or their deferral to your preference, can be bought for the right sum of power assets or economic assets.

The limit to this formula is when the amount of money or power is enough to bend ethical boundaries, as when we sell our soul for the proverbial thirty pieces of silver. After two thousand years of inflation we might ask: What ethical violations would you consider for $30 million? Would you rat on Jesus in the Garden of Gethsemane for $300 million, for $30 billion? Or would you, like Jesus, refuse the offer to be president of the world (or the world's superpower) if it was purchased at the cost of your spiritual integrity? Perhaps you are impermeable to any price. But if we use this aspect of human nature (and we must be students of human psychology) for the good, we can provide carrots for people to promote peacemaking, friendship, and love. If we could find a way to pay Muslim preachers in the mosques and madrasas of Pakistan compensation packages rivaling those of midlevel generals in the Pakistani army to teach the Quranic principles of amity between Muslims and non-Muslims, and if we could bring them into dialogue with their Hindu counterparts in India, peace between India and Pakistan would be achieved for a much lower dollar cost than the expense of the nuclear warheads now facing each other across the India-Pakistan border.

Our insight into the role of power and economics in individual lives therefore has implications for our foreign policy. If, for example, we seek to help Iraq progress from the era of Saddam's regime to a more open society, providing security and improving its economy is even more urgent than giving people the right to vote. As we discussed earlier, having democracy when your home lacks security, electricity, running water, and food is not as desirable an option for most people as living well even if under a less democratic regime.

WHAT DIALOGUE AMONG CIVILIZATIONS CAN DO: WAGE THE WAR AGAINST TERRORISM

When Middle Eastern decision makers and intellectuals begin to consider how to democratize their countries, they face a bewildering variety of critical challenges and issues. They also may find few places to turn for advice that is free from bias and hidden agendas.

One fruitful approach for the Muslim world, especially in the Middle East, would be an ongoing program of thoughtful, roundtable dialogues and symposia aimed at bringing opinion leaders from individual Muslim countries together with scholars, heads of major institutions, and elected leaders from the United States and other Western countries. Functioning as an information exchange in nation building, these dialogues would focus on the challenge of adapting principles of democratic capitalism to Islamic cultures where such concepts are sometimes viewed as un-Islamic.

The world's track record of nation building is not as good as it should be. The know-how exists but rarely is the right peace team assembled to focus on the issues pertaining to the local context.

For example, if one were to ask the simple question of how to develop democratic governance in Iran, Iraq, and Saudi Arabia, the answer cannot be "one size fits all" but has to accommodate the on-the-ground reality in each country. In Iran, for example, there already is a nascent democracy movement. The need there is to encourage a separation and balance of powers and focus more on developing Islamic arguments for a healthy economic infrastructure to build a vibrant economy. In Iraq the focus should be on basic security, food, jobs, housing, and health services, on physical infrastructure such as roads, communications, and educational services, and on building a semblance of a functioning economy, so that creating a perfect democracy becomes a secondary priority. In Saudi Arabia the British model of a bicameral system of shared power between a House of Lords and a House of Commons might be an idea worth exploring with the ruling family. Here the analogy to the House of Lords would be the House of Saud, and the common folk would comprise the House of Commons.

These are just ideas to illustrate the point that the working out of the process cannot just be taking the American franchise and plunking it down elsewhere. Even McDonald's incorporates aspects of local mores and tastes in its hamburger outlets. For example, its Saudi outlets have separate spaces for families and single men.

The role of the United States becomes one of catalyst and supporter for stimulating and nurturing a constructive new wave of good governance discussions in the Muslim world. America can provide the Muslim world with safe, neutral, and unbiased venues in which to address such questions. A new forum—in which diverse, high-level secular and religious leaders might discuss these and related issues in a thoughtful atmosphere of constructive dialogue—could play an invaluable role in raising the level of dialogue about the challenge and promise of democracy in the Islamic world as well as about religion in the West.

A number of well-respected American institutions such as the Aspen Institute, the Chautauqua Institution, the Carnegie Endowment for Peace, and the United States Institute for Peace; major foundations such as Carnegie and Rockefeller; and a variety of universities and colleges could be invited to cohost a series of five-day, bilateral symposia, each convening a small group of twenty to thirty leaders to focus on the emerging issues in a particular Muslim nation. One such symposium might convene jurists and legal authorities to explore with Islamic scholars the idea of an independent judiciary and church-state issues within a specific country. In another case, an off-the-record meeting might be arranged between a group of American congressional representatives and emerging political leaders from a particular Islamic country.

One important focus of these bilateral nation-building dialogues would be institution building: the design of institutions of democratic capitalism that would be particularly suited to an Islamic culture. In America, because we take for granted the essential institutions on which our democratic system depends, we often overlook the reality that many such institutions don't even exist in developing nations. Some of these institutions are specific organizations while others are background social and civil systems that underlie and support the functioning of a free society.

A partial list of such democratic institutions would include a civilian police force, a fair (and functional) system of taxation, a free market economy with social safety nets, the rule of law and an independent judiciary, corporate and antitrust regulations to promote transparency and protect against monopolies, efficient capital markets, schools and education systems, free news media, and systems for environmental preservation and the protection of minorities. The West has tried to transplant such institutions into the developing world countless times in the past and has done so usually in a rather patronizing and naive manner that assumes the Western model will fit all cultures—which it

rarely does. The result has been a disappointing and often dismal failure rate in institution building as well as increased Muslim humiliation.

As an example of a culture-sensitive approach, the Quran offers
strong insights into the human proclivities that have led to the ecological
crisis faced by today's world. Environmentalism in the Muslim world
can be anchored in Islamic teachings as well as in modern science, but
such efforts have to accommodate the local need for economic well-
being. Likewise, Islamic teachings that advocate a just economic order
and the injunction not to pollute our environment or destroy our resources (including trees) could be marshaled to support such objectives.

Another variety of a "democracy dialogue" would be a country-to-
country citizen exchange, in which a larger group of leading citizens
from many walks of life—perhaps a hundred at a time—would be invited to visit the United States to meet with a comparable group of
Americans for discussions about culture, lifestyle, raising a family, making a living, and life generally in America and the Middle East. In a reciprocal gesture, American citizens would then travel to the visitors'
country to repeat the process. This citizen-to-citizen approach would
follow the highly successful model of the Chautauqua Institution's citizen exchanges with the Soviet Union in the 1980s. Sister Cities International might be invited to be an additional partner in such a venture.
These reciprocal community visits could be publicized and their "town
meetings" broadcast on Middle Eastern media, such as al-Jazeera, for
example, as a way of stimulating debate and fresh thinking.

American and foreign nongovernmental organizations are already
attempting some of the above, but the assistance of the United States
government as part of an enlightened, well-articulated, and concerted
U.S. foreign policy initiative would maximize the impact of these efforts, as would participation by American Muslim leaders.

WHAT AN AMERICAN IMAM IS DOING: THE CORDOBA INITIATIVE

Since the tragedy of September 11, I have dedicated myself to helping
heal the relationship between America and the Muslim world. This has
meant an overflowing schedule of church, synagogue, and mosque pre-
sentations; newspaper, radio, and television interviews; and journeys to

speak at interfaith gatherings and conferences of every sort on several continents. My commitment also led directly to the writing of this book.

Reflected in this book are the philosophy and goals of a nonprofit endeavor that I have cofounded: the Cordoba Initiative. It is named after the period between roughly 800 and 1200 CE, when the Cordoba Caliphate ruled much of today's Spain, and its name reminds us that Muslims created what was, in its era, the most enlightened, pluralistic, and tolerant society on earth.

Through partnering with Jewish, Christian, and Muslim organizations as well as secular institutions and foundations, the Cordoba Initiative is building a broad multifaith coalition to help repair the damage that has been done to Muslim-American relations over the last fifty years. The initiative invites American Muslims to play a leadership role in mediating between the Muslim world and America. It plans educational and cultural programs, off-the-record international dialogues between leaders, communications initiatives, and "difficult" interfaith conversations—all aimed at building understanding and peace, both at home and abroad. This book is an emanation of the "spirit of Cordoba."

WHAT INTERFAITH DIALOGUE CAN DO: HELP US SEE GOD'S IMAGE IN ONE ANOTHER

Religion is about connecting humanity with God and never about rousing the masses to violence and aggression. It is about peeling away those veils that prevent us from gaining knowledge of the sole true Reality. Our religious practice is measured by how well it achieves this goal, and it lacks value if it fails to call forth the love of God. When our voices are raised together to proclaim the unity of God and the unity of humankind, then our religiosity has attained its objective.

I mentioned earlier that God speaks in the Quran of the righteous and unrighteous of the People of the Book[12] as well as of the Prophet Muhammad's own followers. On Judgment Day, Muslims believe that humanity shall be divided into two groups: those who merit God's pleasure and those who merit God's displeasure. We therefore expect to find Christians, Jews, Muslims, and others on each side: in God's pleasure (heaven) and displeasure (hell).

Spirituality is about learning to see with God's eyes, and as we learn to do so, we find in this life Christians, Jews, Muslims, and others who emit the fragrance of Paradise, in whom God's pleasure is evident, as well as people across the religious spectrum in whom we detect the odor of God's displeasure, who make up the opposite group.[13]

This simple insight brings us to the conclusion that challenges many Muslims: that among those who confess to be of other faiths are those who in God's eyes share the same ultimate destiny.[14] Interfaith dialogue therefore engages us in each dimension of the two greatest commandments: the vertical, which is about fathoming the different ways people understand and worship God, and the horizontal, which involves developing coalitions of the righteous across the religious spectrum to work together toward the betterment of society. If we accept the principle that love of God requires love of our fellow humans, then dialogue between partisans having differing beliefs involves working with partners across the religious divides who see God's pleasure in each other, and it involves reminding ourselves of the theological and secular justifications for an authoritative and persuasive world vision of peace based on our traditions and sacred texts.

The ecumenical interfaith movement is utterly essential in this day and age. One of its most important objectives is to demonstrate to the public that religions, after all, are not the root causes of conflict. In *Interfaith Dialogue and Peacebuilding*, Rabbi Arthur Schneier, who convened four religious summits on peace and tolerance in the former Yugoslavia, insists that "in our era, religion is not the cause of conflict, although it is often used as the excuse; . . . religion, unfortunately, is often the most visible difference between contesting groups and, as a result, frequently is blamed for conflicts." It becomes paramount that "when conflicts arise strong voices be heard that characterize the conflict for what it is and distance religion from it, as well as promote compassionate understanding and tolerance." It is a travesty of religion, of God's directives to humanity, to be brutal, cruel, and inhumane in God's name. Schneier adds that a crime committed in the name of religion is the greatest crime against religion.[15] It is essential that the Cross, the Crescent, and the Star of David become symbols of peace, tolerance, and mutual respect.

Throughout history, dialogue and interaction have existed between people of differing faiths, even during the Crusades when Christians were warring against Muslims. At a time when many believe there is a "civilizational clash" between the West and the Muslim world, Muslims must challenge this wrong belief by committing themselves to a dialogue with all faiths, anchored on their conviction that God revealed His wisdom and His truths to every community throughout the world. Because Muslims accept as an article of faith that every society had its own messenger and prophet sent by the same God, and that the Prophet Muhammad himself dialogued with those who sought to destroy him and his message, it means that God wishes Muslims *to reach out to people of other faiths and "engage with them in the better way"* (Quran 16:125).

Historical experience has demonstrated the value and integrity of dialogue among faith-based partisans holding opposing beliefs on various matters of public importance. Theological and secular justifications exist for these conclusions, which experts from a range of faiths have authoritatively demonstrated from the teachings of our collective traditions and sacred texts. Working together to build a heightened human consciousness of God among humanity means that the work that lies ahead of us must be defined, both within our respective faith communities and in what we want from each other.

Initially, for the sake of our common shared goals, we must learn to view ourselves in relationship to others, whether religious or secular. Two major ground rules, simple and far-reaching, must be observed when we dialogue. First, compare equal to equal, and second, allow each party to define itself to the others.

Although obvious, the first rule is broken when apologists of our own faith are tempted to compare their tradition in its ideal form against the actual or bad forms of the other. For example, while many Christians correctly believe their faith to be the religion of love and peace, Jews and Muslims have seen the face of "Christian terrorism" over the centuries.

The second rule is to let others define who they are and what they feel to the others, and refrain from defining the other's religion in a manner that falsely enhances our own values and superiority. Thus, for example, Muslims ought not construe an Islamized, caricatured version of Hindu, Christian, or Jewish tradition and pay little attention to how the other faith sees and experiences itself. Nor should Muslims be insensitive to how other faith traditions see them. In particular, Muslims need to cogently explain why, if Islam is a religion of peace, acts of terrorism are committed in its name.

Muslims need to communicate the following:

1. Their special relationship to Christians and Jews and what this means for the followers of the Abrahamic tradition

2. That religious militancy is not found uniquely within the Muslim community and that such militancy would be attenuated if the political issues fueling it were addressed

Interfaith dialogue, sincerely conducted, has the power to reveal the fundamental truth that all human beings share a great deal in common at their deepest spiritual level. The same God created us all. And when, as human beings, we learn to recognize, identify with, and speak from the core human and spiritual values that we hold in common, we may transcend our superficial divisions and learn to embrace the cultural and theological diversity that only enriches the human family. Over time, interfaith dialogue can dissolve the concept of the Other, replacing it with a deeper realization that we are all—in fact—brothers and sisters.

Muslim skeptics abound who ask, Why spend time in dialogue? What does dialogue mean, and what does it accomplish? Having spent a few decades myself in interfaith dialogue, having been somewhat skeptical myself and realizing that it is hard work indeed, I therefore wish to conclude this chapter by offering the following suggestions as to how religions in dialogue can and do contribute to improving the human condition.[16]

Dialogue among people of faith, and across differences, opens our hearts to one another as human beings, reveals what is common among us, and deepens our quests for enduring truth. This is so because God can (and often does) speak to us through the "other"; we learn something about what is sacred from those different from ourselves and gain a deeper understanding of what our respective faiths require of us. In the process, we acknowledge that others may in fact also have a grasp of truth.[17]

Dialogue between the religions offers the opportunity for uncovering the common ground of shared values and goals that resonate in each of our faiths, even as we clarify real differences. Dialogue within a religion offers the opportunity for its adherents to be amazed at the authentic differences that arise from shared theology and ritual (orthodoxy and orthopraxy).[18] Dialogue forges personal bonds and relationships of trust, which carry the potential to strengthen the larger social fabric and make possible cooperative efforts where concerns and priorities overlap.

When religious spokespeople commit to speaking out in the public arena about peace, they contribute to an understanding and construction of a global notion of the common good. Our religions are unique sources of both public values—such as compassion and justice—and the moral energy and drive needed to practice these values in our daily lives. Speaking as people of faith in the public arena entails real challenges and sometimes dangers, yet with each challenge we overcome, we make a significant contribution. Among these challenges are:

- To make our religious language and images intelligible and meaningful outside our own religious context. Most religious spokespeople are not trained to speak to those outside their pale.

- To be careful in the way we employ our certitudes, knowing that ours are voices among many in the global arena. While we must not be shy to give public voice to the religious rationales underlying our statements and policy recommendations, in a pluralistic society public understanding and trust are increased by openness and clarity concerning the theology and sources of authority underlying our positions.

- To commit to a way of communicating and being together that affirms the humanity of all present. Interfaith dialogue is an intentional form of conversation, embodying our understandings of what our faith traditions expect of people in community, enhancing the potential for learning, discernment, and understanding. Dialogue requires that we come to this conversation with an honest intention of understanding and being understood and with a willingness to listen to different views without requiring others to convert to our point of view.

- To agree on how to disagree, and to identify the theological principles for disagreement while respecting the humanity of all participants. By validating forums of dialogue, we foster and encourage its fruits, which in the past have enriched our collective heritage as humans.

- To seek the common ground. Dialogue is not fundamentally a debate, nor is it a discussion necessarily aimed at resolving the core conflict. It involves seeking points of genuine overlap, and it requires listening fully to the other, suspending the need to defend or react, and listening for points of connection. Dialogue reveals that misunderstanding can be an opportunity for learning rather than an occasion for offense.

- To be respectful in speech and behavior, to pay attention to how the language we use affects and is understood by others, and to be honest about how others' language affects us. Dialogue requires virtues that must be enhanced in our current global social exchanges. It requires engaging with what people actually mean when they speak and not so much with what the listener thinks is meant or intended. It calls for bringing to the surface and acknowledging untested assumptions and preconceptions and being willing to ask and answer genuine questions.

By seeing beyond the narrow confines of cultural differences and historic enmities, spiritual leaders from the world's great religions are blessed with a unique opportunity to apply their combined wisdom and influence to meet the challenges of our day and to bequeath to future generations a globalized perspective that draws from the very best of our collective spiritual and religious heritage. I can think of no greater goal in the twenty-first century than ushering in the era predicted by the Old Testament prophet Isaiah: when nations "will beat their swords into plowshares and their spears into pruning hooks. Nation will not take up sword against nation, nor will they train for war anymore" (Isaiah 2:4 NIV).

On Pursuing Happiness

The world wants to like America. The guiding values that Thomas Jefferson articulated so eloquently—life, liberty, and the pursuit of happiness—resonate strongly around the world, transcending countless superficial and cultural differences, not because these are American values, but because they are universal values, embedded in the human heart. This is the reason that individual Americans are often treated with warmth and respect, even in countries whose governments are not considered friendly to the United States.

Nonetheless, in many regions of today's world, hostility toward the United States is the rule rather than the exception. In a world filled with threats—some real, some imaginary—the United States stands at a historic crossroads. One path leads in the direction of unyielding unilateralism. This path traverses the fields of fear—it elevates the war on terror above all other social, spiritual, and humanistic concerns. It leaves America standing alone, beleaguered, in a suspect, unfriendly world. Traveling this path, America endeavors to sleep at night by remaining heavily armed and constantly on guard.

The other path is quite different. It ascends the highlands of trust and faith, conveying us to a place where America acts as the Great Conciliator—instead of the Great Policeman—for the world's family of nations. This is the path of cooperation, of multilateralism, of dialogue, of building friendships. On this path, America sleeps well because it has many friends and few enemies. This is the path of hope.

Americans must outgrow the unbecoming arrogance that leads us to assert that America somehow owns a monopoly on goodness and truth—a belief that leads some to view the world as but a stage on which to play out the great historical drama: the United States of America versus the Powers of Evil.

The language of good versus evil is precisely the language of the fundamentalists whose worldview we oppose. Once we define as evil those who counter us, we lose the moral high ground and begin to descend an exceedingly slippery ethical slope. Sufis teach that we first must battle and destroy the evil within ourselves by shining upon it the good within, and then we learn to battle the evil in others by helping their higher selves gain control of their lower selves. To battle the evil of others by responding in kind and exhibiting equally violent aggressive behavior is to flout the very ethic of our religious traditions; it is also to violate Geneva conventions, international law, the United Nations, world opinion, and even our own Bill of Rights. *If we truly believe that God is on our side, rather than making sure that we are on God's side, we slip into the illusion that sees no measure as too extreme—a delusion that captivates every extremist heart.*

The United States has a greater destiny than to be perceived as the schoolyard bully of the twenty-first century. We have a higher spiritual calling than self-centered unilateralism. Throughout its history, America has been a beacon of hope for so many around the world. Its role as keeper and bringer of hope has left no doubt about what is right with America. This heritage is why the world wants to like us; and this is the true, good role to which we should always aspire, even when the path is steep and the misunderstanding that divides us from other cultures is profound.

We have two powerful tools with which to bridge the chasm separating the United States from the Muslim world: faith in the basic goodness of humanity and trust in the power of sincerity and dialogue to overcome differences with our fellow human beings. This faith and this trust are taught by all the Abrahamic traditions. They define the Abrahamic ethic, which lies at the core of our American Declaration of Independence, and America needs to rely more heavily on them, as do our fellow actors on the stage of history.

What's right with America and what's right with Islam have a lot in common. At their highest levels, both worldviews reflect an enlightened recognition that all of humankind shares a common Creator—that we are, indeed, brothers and sisters. In 1883, when Emma Lazarus wrote the words that celebrate the beautiful lady who stands so resolutely in New York's harbor, she was not imagining an isolationist empire-nation bent only on pursuing its own unilateral vision for the world. Rather, she had in mind a nation resting securely on its foundations of democracy, freedom, and human rights, of which Jefferson, Adams, Franklin, and the other great fathers and mothers of this nation dreamed. It is humanity's dream—rich with hope and idealism for a troubled world—that the great lady in the harbor symbolizes:

> *Not like the brazen giant of Greek fame,*
> *With conquering limbs astride from land to land:*
> *Here at our sea-washed, sunset gates shall stand*
> *A mighty woman with a torch, whose flame*
> *Is the imprisoned lightning, and her name*
> *Mother of Exiles. From her beacon-hand*
> *Glows world-wide welcome; her mild eyes command*
> *The air-bridged harbor that twin cities frame.*
> *"Keep, ancient lands, your storied pomp!" cries she*
> *With silent lips. "Give me your tired, your poor,*
> *Your huddled masses yearning to breathe free,*
> *The wretched refuse of your teeming shore.*
> *Send these, the homeless, tempest-tost to me.*
> *I lift my lamp beside the golden door!"*

To hold high the lamp of freedom, hope, and friendship is America's greatest gift to the world—and its sacred responsibility.

As I sailed into New York on the cold wintry morning of Wednesday, December 22, 1965, on the Italian SS *Michelangelo*, I beheld the Statue of Liberty and wondered what America had in store for me. Little did I realize then that I was to discover the riches of my faith tradition in this land. Like many immigrants from Muslim lands, I discovered my Islam in America.

I therefore entertain a wish, shared by my reading of my noble scripture, the Quran, regarding all religions, including Judaism and Christianity—the very same wish entertained by all who have taken part in interfaith dialogue across the ages. I wish for humankind to drink deeply from that rich, nourishing current of spiritual traditions— those immutable principles of divine origin that have been given form in so many ways in human societies. Religion must be more than mere custom or habit, more than the transient styles and cultural fashions of passing ages. Religion, which speaks to the eternal in us, must be the foundation of a robust, harmonious society and the animating principle of the whole life of a people.

A poem by Sheikh Muhyiddin Ibn al-'Arabi, regarded by some to have been the greatest Sufi master (ash-Shaykh al-Akbar), expresses the heart of this eternal quest. He describes the shift from a religion based on what is transient to one based on the eternal, and he inspires our hope that humanity itself may undergo such a transformation:

> There was a time when I took it amiss in my companion if his religion
>   was not near to mine;
> But now my heart takes on every form; it is a pasture for gazelles, a
>   monastery for monks,
> A temple for the tables of the Torah, a Ka'bah for pilgrims and the holy
>   book of the Quran.
> Love is my religion, and whichever way its riding beasts turn, that way
>   lies my religion and belief.

Acknowledgments

Most books we write. Others, like this one, write themselves through us—and we feel grateful for having been so honored. This genre of book has a mind of its own, deciding when it will make its appearance, who will be involved, when, how, and to what end. This book speaks its gratitude to all who assisted in its development.

First, thanks are due to the many who urged me to write this book. Not atypical was Jane Friedman, so utterly frustrated about the lack of progress toward peace in the Middle East that she offered to "resign my position if that could help make it happen." With the critical help of Claire Al-Kouatli, who worked tirelessly as my editorial assistant throughout the process, my literary agent, Joy Harris, helped me craft the proposal that allowed the book to present its case to the publisher, Steve Hanselman of Harper San Francisco, who saw it "fill a gap in our stable of books." Gratitude, gratitude, gratitude.

To Eric Brandt, Harper's very talented editor, who gently but very persuasively applied the alchemical process that transformed the book's graphite-like atoms into his sought-for "diamond-like" configuration, and to his gifted copyeditor, Priscilla Stuckey, who artfully set the diamond so that its light would reflect coherently in the eyes of its reader. To Roger Freet, whose suggestions flavored the book more than he could know. To Harper's Senior Managing Editor, Terri Leonard, for her grace in accommodating an author's agitations for the "perfect book" while keeping us all on schedule. This book speaks highly of their professionalism, and I cannot thank them enough.

To my congregation and students, thanks and appreciation for their patience with my absence, for their support and prayers, and especially to Behrooz Karjooravary, Naz Ahmed, and Faiz Khan for standing in for me. Special mention to Farzan Saleem for enhancing my laptop's performance—the modern author's pen and paper. To

Samira Husic for helping me painstakingly retrieve weeks' worth of work that my computer caused to vanish into the interstices of cyberspace.

To John Kiser, Reverend Joan Brown-Campbell, Edgar Bronfman, Rabbi Jack Bemporad, Professor Ali Asani, Dr. Faroque Khan, Omar Amanat, and Julia Jitkoff for invaluable suggestions and keen personal interest in this book's message.

To my wife, Daisy Khan, belongs those most special thanks for what only spouses know: "what a husband is like when he can't find his shoelaces." Throughout the process she saw to it that the book would extract only the very best of me and bore with the patience of Job the disappearance of our thirty-square-foot dining table and the rest of the dining room floor under a two-foot pile of books. To my mother, who made sure that the dining room's absence did not prevent me from being most lavishly sustained during the final stretch of finishing the book. But, most important, she has nourished me with her lifelong love, prayers, and blessings.

My deepest gratitude goes to John S. Bennett, cofounder of the Cordoba Initiative, which offers a blueprint for healing the relationship between the Muslim world and the West. Only God has treasures of sufficient depth and variety to thank him for his unflagging efforts in weaving the Initiative's ideas into the architecture of this book.

I am extremely grateful to all of the above, while exonerating them from responsibility for any of my errors or opinions. For God's acceptance and pleasure I plead on their and my behalf, and especially on behalf of my father and greatest teacher, Dr. Muhammad Abdul Rauf, and all the rest of my spiritual ancestors, teachers, and guides, notably Sheikh Muzaffer Ozak. It is through their collective teachings, example, spiritual guidance, spiritual upbringing, and blessings that I am who I am.

Fatwa Permitting U.S. Muslim Military Personnel to Participate in Afghanistan War Effort

In the Name of God,
the Compassionate,
the Merciful

LEGAL FATWA

This is the reply to the (religious) inquiry presented by Mr. Muhammad Abdur-Rashid, the most senior Muslim chaplain in the American armed forces. It concerns the permissibility of the Muslim military personnel within the U.S. armed forces to participate in the war operations and its related efforts in Afghanistan and elsewhere in other Muslim countries.

In his question he states that the goals of the (war) operations are:

1. Retaliation against those "who are thought to have participated" in planning and financing the suicide operations on September 11th, against civilian and military targets in New York and Washington (he then detailed the consequences of these operations.)

2. Eliminating the elements that use Afghanistan and elsewhere as safe haven, as well as deterring the governments which harbor them, sanction them, or allow them the opportunity for military training in order to achieve their goals around the world.

3. Restoring the veneration and respect to the U.S. as a sole superpower in the world.

Furthermore, he concludes his inquiry by mentioning that the number of the Muslim military personnel, in the three branches of the American armed forces, exceeds fifteen thousand soldiers. Hence, if they refuse to participate in fighting, they will have no choice but to resign, which might also entail other consequences. Finally, he asks if it is permissible, to those who can transfer, to serve in different capacities other than direct fighting.

The reply:

Praise be to God and peace and blessing be upon the messengers of God.

We say:

This question presents a very complicated issue and a highly sensitive situation for our Muslim brothers and sisters serving in the American army as well as other armies that face similar situations.

All Muslims ought to be united against all those who terrorize the innocents, and those who permit the killing of non-combatants without a justifiable reason. Islam has declared the spilling of blood and the destruction of property as absolute prohibitions until the Day of Judgment. God (glory be to He) said: "Because of that We ordained unto the Children of Israel that if anyone killed a human being—unless it be in punishment for murder or for spreading mischief on earth—it would be as though he killed all of humanity; whereas, if anyone saved a life, it would be as though he saved the life of all humanity. And indeed, there came to them Our messengers with clear signs (proofs and evidences), even then after that, many of them continued to commit mischief on earth." 5:32

Hence, whoever violates these pointed Islamic texts is an offender deserving of the appropriate punishment according to their offence and according to its consequences for destruction and mischief.

It's incumbent upon our military brothers in the American armed forces to make this stand and its religious reasoning well known to all their superiors, as well as to their peers, and to voice it and not to be silent. Conveying this is part of the true nature of the Islamic teachings that have often been distorted or smeared by the media.

If the terrorist acts that took place in the U.S. were considered by the Islamic Law (Shar'iah) or the rules of Islamic jurisprudence (Fiqh), the ruling for the crime of "Hirabah" (waging war against society) would be applied to their doers. God (Glory be to He) said: "The recompense of those who wage war against God and His Messenger and do mischief on earth is only that they shall be killed or crucified or their hands and their feet be cut off from opposite sides, or be exiled from the land. That is their disgrace in this world, and a great torment is theirs in the Hereafter. Except for those who (having fled away and then) came back with repentance before they fall into your power; (in that case) know that God is Oft-Forgiving, Most Merciful." 5:33–34

Therefore, we find it necessary to apprehend the true perpetrators of these crimes, as well as those who aid and abet them through incitement, financing or other support. They must be brought to justice in an impartial court of law and punish them appropriately, so that it could act as deterrent to them and to others like them who easily slay the lives of innocents, destroy properties and terrorize people. Hence, it's a duty on Muslims to participate in this effort with all possible means, in accordance with God's (Most High) saying: "And help one another in virtue and righteousness, but do not help one another in sin and transgression." 5:2.

On the other hand, the source of the uneasiness that American Muslim military men and women may have in fighting other Muslims, is because it's often difficult—if not impossible—to differentiate between the real perpetrators who are being pursued, and the innocents who have committed no crime at all. The authentic saying by the prophet states: "When two Muslims face each other in fighting and one kills the other, then both the killer and the killed are in the hell-fire. Someone said: we understand that the killer is in hell, why then the one who's being killed? The prophet said: because he wanted to kill the other person." (Narrated by Bukhari and Muslim.)

The noble Hadith mentioned above only refers to the situation where the Muslim is in charge of his affairs. He is capable of fighting as well as capable of not fighting. This Hadith does not address the situation where a Muslim is a citizen of a state and a member of a regular army. In this case, he has no choice but to follow orders, otherwise his allegiance and loyalty to his country could be in doubt. This would subject him to much harm since he would not enjoy the privileges of citizenship without performing its obligations.

The Muslim (soldier) must perform his duty in this fight despite the feeling of uneasiness of "fighting without discriminating." His intention (niyya) must be to fight for enjoining of the truth and defeating falsehood. It's to prevent aggression on the innocents, or to apprehend the perpetrators and bring them to justice. It's not his concern what other consequences of the fighting that might result in his personal discomfort, since he alone can neither control it nor prevent it. Furthermore, all deeds are accounted (by God) according to the intentions. God (the Most High) does not burden any soul except what it can bear. In addition, Muslim jurists have ruled that what a Muslim cannot control he cannot be held accountable for, as God (the Most High) says: "And keep your duty to God as much as you can." 64:16. The prophet (prayer and peace be upon him) said: "when I ask of you to do something, do it as much as you can." The Muslim here is a part of a whole, if he absconds, his departure will result in a greater harm, not only for him but also for the Muslim community in his country—and here there are many millions of them. Moreover, even if fighting causes him discomfort spiritually or psychologically, this personal hardship must be endured for the greater public good, as the jurisprudence (fiqhi) rule states.

Furthermore, the questioner inquires about the possibility of the Muslim military personnel in the American armed forces to serve in the back lines—such as in the relief services' sector and similar works. If such requests are granted by the authorities, without reservation or harm to the soldiers, or to the other American Muslim citizens, then they should request that. Otherwise, if such request raises doubts about their allegiance or loyalty, cast suspicions, present them with false accusations, harm their future careers, shed misgivings on their patriotism, or similar sentiments, then it's not permissible to ask for that.

To sum up, it's acceptable—God willing—for the Muslim American military personnel to partake in the fighting in the upcoming battles, against whomever, their country decides, has perpetrated terrorism against them. Keeping in mind to have the proper intention as explained earlier, so no doubts would be cast about their loyalty to their country, or to prevent harm to befall them as might be expected. This is in accordance with the Islamic jurisprudence rules which state that necessities dictate exceptions, as well as the rule that says one may endure a small harm to avoid a much greater harm.

And God the Most High is Most Knowledgeable and Most Wise.

Rajab 10, 1422 AH /
September 27, 2001

Signatories:

Sheikh Yusuf al-Qaradawi
[Grand Islamic Scholar and Chairman of the Sunna and Sira Council, Qatar]

Judge Tariq al-Bishri
[First Deputy President of the Council d'état, Ret., Egypt]

Dr. Muhammad S. al-Awa
[Professor of Comparative Law and Shari'a, Egypt]

Dr. Haytham al-Khayyat
[Islamic Scholar, Syria]

Mr. Fahmi Houaydi
[Islamic Author and Columnist, Egypt]

This English version was translated from the original Arabic, authorized and approved by authors of the statement.

Notes

FOREWORD

1. Wilfred Cantwell Smith, *Islam in Modern History* (Princeton: Princeton University Press, 1957), 305.

PREFACE

1. A popular saying goes as follows:
   He who knows, and knows that he knows, is a sage; follow him.
   He who knows, and knows not that he knows, is asleep; awaken him.
   He who knows not, and knows that he knows not, is ignorant; teach him.
   He who knows not, and knows not that he knows not, is dangerous; run away
      from him.

2. Charles Kimball, *When Religion Becomes Evil* (San Francisco: HarperSanFrancisco, 2002).

INTRODUCTION

1. To read the full report, log on to http://www.people-press.org (accessed January 23, 2004).

2. Some argue that this arose less as a reaction to religion per se and more in response to the dominant American Protestant (primarily Baptist and Methodist) views of religion, which often dominated other religions—particularly, at that time, Catholicism and Judaism. Some feared that the power possessed by this WASP establishment to promote its values in realms outside of religion, especially in science and education, was subtly curtailing freedom of thought. See Michael Ariens and Robert Destro, *Religious Liberty in a Pluralistic Society*, 2nd ed. (Durham, NC: Carolina Academic Press, 2002).

3. These ideals are all Islamic ones, but what the West achieved was *institutionalizing* these ideals through social safety nets such as Social Security, unemployment insurance, welfare benefits, and so forth.

CHAPTER ONE

1. Will Herberg, *Protestant, Catholic, Jew: An Essay in American Religious Sociology* (Chicago: Univ. of Chicago Press, 1960), 40.

2. This debate between human free will and predestination spilled over into a robust debate between the Prophet Muhammad and his skeptical contemporaries, who argued that God had determined them to be disbelievers, and they were therefore merely reflecting the divine will. See Feisal Abdul Rauf, *Islam, a Search for Meaning* (Costa Mesa, CA: Mazda Publishers, 1995), 53ff.

3. This in fact constitutes the core ideas of all divinely revealed religion, but we shall limit our focus in this book to the three known as the Abrahamic religions.

4. An important note to the non-Muslim reader: when a Muslim says, "The Quran states," it is taken to be equal to "God states" and therefore is part of a Muslim's belief.

5. The expression "the nature of God" (*fitrat allah*) holds two meanings: "God's nature" as well as "the nature that God made," upon which God created humanity (that is, God created humanity in the divine image). See Rauf, *Islam: A Search for Meaning*.

6. This idea is the basis of one of the great pieces of Islamic literature, the story of Hayy Ibn Yaqzan (literally, the Alive Son of the Aware), authored by Ibn Tufayl, who lived in Spain in the twelfth century. Hayy, raised by himself on a tropical island, comes to the realization of God on his own as the result of his own thinking process. In a sense his story recapitulates the Abrahamic search for God. See *Ibn Tufayl's Hayy Ibn Yaqzan: A Philosophical Tale,* trans. Lenn Evan Goodman (New York: Twayne Publishers, 1972).

7. The jinn (from which the English word *genie* comes) are beings created, according to the Quran, from smokeless fire, as humans are from clay and angels from light. They are capable of salvation or punishment like humans.

8. Quoted from Rabbi Jack Bemporad, "The Pontifical Biblical Document, The Jewish People and the Sacred Scriptures in the New Testament: A Jewish Perspective," *Bulletin Centro Pro Unione*, no. 63 (Spring 2003): 3–7.

9. "A woman got separated from her child and when she found it again, she pressed the child to her chest and breastfed it. The Prophet asked his companions, 'Could you imagine this woman throwing her child into the fire?' We said, 'No, by God! She could not bear to do such a thing!' The Prophet replied, 'Indeed, God is more merciful to his servants than this mother to her child'"; Muslim, *Sahih*, "Kitab al-Tawbah," chapter titled "The Extent of Allah's Mercy Is Wider Than His Wrath," hadith no. 4947.

10. This is the universal definition of the word *Islam*. Anyone who believes in the oneness of God and submits to a relationship to the one God as creature to Creator is thereby Muslim.

11. The story of Hargar's discovery of the well of Zanzam is mentioned in Genesis 21:19 of the Bible.

12. Bukhari, *Kitab al-Iman,* hadith no. 12.

13. The term used is *shara'a,* meaning "to ordain," thus implying that the fundamental religious laws established by the Prophet Muhammad are in keeping with the laws of Moses and Jesus, all of which flow out of the Abrahamic ethic.

CHAPTER TWO

1. One reason Muslims view themselves as having a special kinship with Jews and Christians is that they believe Muhammad is the Gentile (another interpretation of the word *unlettered*) Prophet, foretold in both the Old and New Testaments. John 1:19–21 speaks of Jews sending priests and Levites from Jerusalem to interrogate Jesus: "Who art thou?" (John 1:19) They kept probing: "Art thou Elias? . . . Art thou *that Prophet?*" (John 1:21, see also 1:25). Muslims believe the expression *that Prophet* is a New Testament reference to the Old Testament mention of the expected Prophet Muhammad. That Old Testament reference has Moses declaring, "The Lord thy God will raise up unto thee a Prophet from the midst of thee, of thy brethren, like unto me; unto him ye shall hearken. . . . I will raise them up a Prophet from among their brethren, like unto thee, and will put my words in his mouth; and he shall speak unto them all that I shall command him" (Deuteronomy

18:15, 18). Whereas Muslims regard Jesus as the Messiah, Muslims regard Muhammad as *that prophet* "like unto Moses," for Muhammad came with new legislation and did not teach except what he was taught by God.

2. As translated by the American master calligrapher Muhammad Zakariya. See http://www.zakariya.net (accessed February 5, 2004).

3. Muslim, *Sahih,* vol. 1, hadith no. 1.

4. Muslim, *Sahih,* "Kitab al-Iman," hadith no. 9.

5. In Judaism, the emphasis is on orthopraxy, and there is much greater flexibility in one's specific beliefs. A Jew may or may not believe, for instance, in a heaven or a hell, an afterlife, or a day of judgment, yet if he or she observes the Sabbath, the rules of circumcision, the Jewish holidays, and so forth, he or she is generally considered to be an observant Jew. In the Christian faith, the emphasis is on orthodoxy: as long as one believes that Jesus Christ is the savior, one is generally accepted as a Christian. Muslims are doubly bound, having both an orthodoxy, which must be believed in, and an orthopraxy, which must be practiced, if one is to be deemed an observant and practicing Muslim.

6. The story of Mary is beautifully told in the Quran 19:17ff., where God states that Jesus was conceived without a human father. Muslims therefore believe in the virgin birth of Jesus.

7. Quran 16:36 asserts, "And certainly We raised in every nation a messenger, saying: Serve God and shun the devil."

8. This verse differentiates between those who outwardly practice religion without any inner content of faith and belief, which defines one way the term *muslim* has been used, from the *mu'min,* believers whose inner spirituality is alive and whose ethics fulfill the Prophet's teaching that "no one is a believer (*mu'min*) until he loves for his brother what he loves for himself." What is noteworthy is that in addressing the Prophet's followers, the Quran always uses the phrasing *ya ayyuha-lladhina amanu* ("O you believers" or "O you who have believed"), never *ya ayyuha-lladhina aslamu* ("O you Muslims" or "O you who have submitted"). This almost suggests that the Quran is a book addressed more to believers (*mu'mins*) and less to those merely concerned with calling themselves by the label *muslim*—that is, to those concerned with the substance and reality of authentic faith rather than with the nomenclature and outer expressions of faith.

9. This is verse 2:255 of the Quran. It reads: "God! There is no god but He, the Live, the Self-Subsisting. Slumber and sleep do not touch Him. Who shall intercede with Him except by His Permission? Knowing what is before and behind them [that is, all of humanity], while they [humanity] do not embrace a jot of His knowledge except by His choice. His Throne [that is, power and dominion] extends [all through] the heavens and earth; and sustaining them tires Him not. And He is the Exalted, the Mighty." According to hadiths of the Prophet, reciting this verse protects the individual from evil.

10. The idea in Western universities of a "chair" of philosophy, for example, came from this image of the master seated on a chair, lecturing to his group of students.

11. For more on this, see Maurice Bucaille, *The Bible, the Qur'an, and Science* (Indianapolis: American Trust Publications, 1978).

12. Muslim, *Sahih,* hadith no. 6251.

13. In a hadith, the Prophet Muhammad indicated that (on Judgment Day), "You shall certainly see your Lord as you see this full moon, without any doubt"; Muslim, *Sahih,* "Kitab Mawaqit al-Salah," hadith no. 521.

14. Muslim 4937, also Tirmidhi 2376, Ibn Majah 4229, Ahmad Ibn Hanbal 16949.

15. Bukhari, *Sahih,* "Kitab al-Riquq," Bab al-Tawadu', hadith no. 6021.

16. *The Mathnawi of Jalaluddin Rumi,* trans. Reynold A. Nicholson (n.p.: Luzac, 1972), 5.

17. This hadith is not referenced in the standard Hadith sources.

18. Genesis 1:26–27. This is also in the Hadith: Bukhari 5759, Muslim 5075, Ibn Hanbal 7021.

19. *Mathnawi,* trans. Nicholson, bk. 2, p. 316, vv. 1852, 1853.

20. This is based on the Quranic verse 57:4: *wa huwa ma'akum ayna ma kuntum,* "He is with you wherever you are." This is in contrast to the philosophers who spent their time debating *"wujud* [reality of existence] versus *mahiyya* [quiddity]."

21. Shaikh Wali Raslan, *Risala fi't-Tawhid,* trans. Muhtar Holland as *Concerning the Affirmation of Divine Oneness* (Hollywood, FL: Al-Baz, 1997), 50ff.

22. John Kiser, *The Monks of Tibhirine: Faith, Love, and Terror in Algeria* (New York: St. Martin's Press, 2002), 9.

23. Quoted in *Ghazali: Deliverance from Error,* trans. R. J. McCarthy (Louisville, KY: Fons Vitae, 1999), 9, 12, originally published as *Freedom and Fulfillment* (Boston: Twayne, 1980).

24. Abd al-Ghafir al-Khatib, quoted in *Ghazali,* trans. McCarthy, 15–17, 75.

25. *Ghazali,* trans. McCarthy, 46.

26. Vincenzo M. Poggi, S.J., cited in *Ghazali,* trans. McCarthy, 332.

27. Margaret Smith, *Al-Ghazali the Mystic,* quoted in *Ghazali,* trans. McCarthy, 40.

28. *Ghazali,* trans. McCarthy, 38.

29. Poggi, quoted in McCarthy, 42.

30. *Ghazali,* trans. McCarthy, 43, 69.

31. The word *lahn* can also mean "barbarism."

32. *Ghazali,* trans. McCarthy, 78.

CHAPTER THREE

1. William Sloane Coffin, *A Passion for the Possible: A Message to U.S. Churches* (Louisville, KY: Westminster/John Knox Press, 1993), 3, 2.

2. Muhammad 'Abd al-Hadi Abu Ridah, quoted in Philip K. Hitti, *Makers of Arab History* (New York: St. Martin's Press, 1968), 191.

3. Muhammad Asad, *The Principles of State and Government in Islam* (Gibraltar: Dar al-Andalus, 1980), vi.

4. In discussing the Declaration of Independence and Constitution, I have drawn on Roger Pilon, preface to *The Declaration of Independence and the Constitution of the United States of America* (Washington, DC: Cato Institute, 1998).

5. Asad, *Principles of State,* 96.

6. "The Farmer Refuted" (1775), *American State Papers,* 123, quoted in F. Forrester Church, *The American Creed* (New York: St. Martin's Press, 2002), 32.

7. Thomas Jefferson, letter to John Hambden Pleassants, April 19, 1824, quoted in Church, *American Creed,* 33.

8. See Will Herberg, *Protestant, Catholic, Jew: An Essay in American Religious Sociology* (Chicago: Univ. of Chicago Press, 1960), 6–82.

9. Perry Miller, "The Location of American Religious Freedom," in *Religion and Freedom of Thought* (New York: Doubleday, 1954), 21.

10. Asad, *Principles of State*, 1.

11. Ibn al-Qayyim al-Jawziyyah, *I'lam al-Muwaqqi'in 'an Rabb al-'alamin* (Cairo, n.d.), 3:1.

12. This incident is referred to in the Quran, chap. 48.

13. "Obedience to God and to the Messenger" is a command that appears about a dozen times in the Quran and is commonly heard among Muslims. See, for instance, Quran 3:32, 3:132, 4:59, 5:92.

14. Quoted in Martin Lings, *Muhammad: His Life Based on the Earliest Sources* (New York: Inner Traditions International, 1983), 344.

15. Ibn al-Nadim, Fihrist, 280, and Ibn Qutaybah, Imamah, II, 156, quoted in Subhi Mahmassani, *Falsafat al-Tashri' fi al-Islam: The Philosophy of Jurisprudence in Islam*, trans. Farhat Ziadeh (Leiden: E. J. Brill, 1961), 25.

16. From Pilon, preface to *Declaration of Independence*.

17. See http://www.cdi.org/budget/2004/world-military-spending.cfm (accessed January 22, 2004).

18. An example of removal of separation of powers was what happened in 1997 when Pakistani prime minister Nawaz Sharif eliminated the independence of the judiciary.

19. *Microsoft Encyclopedia Encarta 98* (electronic resource) (Redmond, WA: Microsoft, 1997), s.v. "Federal Reserve System."

20. Although a number are state supported, such as PBS, C-Span, and Voice of America.

21. Fareed Zakaria, *The Future of Freedom: Illiberal Democracy at Home and Abroad* (New York: Norton, 2003), 17.

22. Church, *American Creed*.

23. For example, the disputes that occurred in the caliphate of al-Ma'mun as to whether the Quran was created or uncreated or whether performing the prayer with one's hands crossed on one's chest or hanging by one's sides was better—categories of issues on which Muslims may maintain diverging opinions.

24. For example, in the United States we often add a clause to an interstate contract that might say, "This contract shall be in accordance with New York State law." Two parties to a contract may agree to say, "This contract shall be governed by Hanafi law," even in a country like Saudi Arabia, where the law is Hanbali law.

25. Murray T. Titus, "Islam and the Kingdom of God," in *The MacDonald Presentation Volume* (1933; Freeport, NY: Books for Libraries Press, 1968), 395–96.

26. Antonin Scalia, "God's Justice and Ours," article adapted from remarks given at a conference sponsored by the Pew Forum on Religion and Public Life at the University of Chicago Divinity School, *First Things: Journal of Religion and Public Life* 123 (May 2002): 17–21, available at http://www.firstthings.com (accessed January 12, 2004).

27. Hadith in Ibn Majah, 3940.

28. Ahmad Ibn Hanbal, 21020.

29. Tirmidhi, 2092.

30. Asad, *Principles of State*, 39.

31. Church, *American Creed*, 139, italics mine.

32. Some add a fourth, namely, law of nations, dealing with what we would call international law. It was from this later development in Islamic law that the terminology of *dar al-Islam* ("house of Islam") and *dar al-harb* ("house of war") came about, and which some have misinterpreted to mean that Muslims are to be at war with those not

Muslims. Note also that the marriage contract falls under the law of transactions, since it is regarded as a contract between husband and wife.

CHAPTER FOUR

1. Wilfred Cantwell Smith, *The Meaning and End of Religion* (New York: Mentor Books, 1962).

2. Smith, *Meaning and End of Religion*, 103.

3. Smith, *Meaning and End of Religion*, 337.

4. Smith, *Meaning and End of Religion*, 103.

5. Smith, *Meaning and End of Religion*, 105.

6. Smith, *Meaning and End of Religion*, 12.

7. The Quran calls Jesus the Messiah, son of Mary; see Quran 3:45, 4:171–72, 5:17, 5:72–75. The Quran refers to Christians as "Nazarenes."

8. Wilfred Cantwell Smith, *Questions of Religious Truth* (New York: Scribner, 1967), 102–3.

9. Konrad Lorenz, *On Aggression* (New York: Bantam, 1971), x.

10. Mu'awiyah later established the Umayyad Dynasty, which lasted from 661 to 750 CE.

11. Richard Dawkins, *The Selfish Gene* (New York: Oxford Univ. Press, 1976), 3.

12. Dawkins, *The Selfish Gene*, 201, italics mine.

13. The real-life situation is more complex, and many other behavioral strategies exist that altogether work against each other, but the broad point remains valid, namely, that cooperation provides a greater payoff.

14. Ashutosh Varshney, *Ethnic Conflict and Civic Life: Hindus and Muslims in India* (New Haven, CT: Yale Univ. Press, 2002).

15. Varshney, *Ethnic Conflict*, 6.

16. 'Ayni, *'Umdat*, XXII, 83.

17. Bukhari, *Sahih*, hadith no. 1.

18. Mark Juergensmeyer, *Terror in the Mind of God* (Berkeley and Los Angeles: Univ. of California Press, 2000), 102, 104.

19. Juergensmeyer, *Terror*, 105–6, 112–16.

20. Quoted in Mariana Caplan, *Halfway Up the Mountain: The Error of Premature Claims to Enlightenment* (Prescott, AZ: Hohm Press, 1999), 401.

21. Juergensmeyer, *Terror*, 113.

22. Juergensmeyer, *Terror*, 114.

23. *The Mystical Teachings of al-Shadhili*, trans. from the Arabic of Ibn al-Sabbagh's *Durrat al-Asrar wa Tuhfat al-Abrar* by Elmer H. Douglas (New York: State Univ. of New York Press, 1993), 113–14.

24. See Robert Bellah et al., *The Good Society* (New York: Knopf, 1992).

25. Benjamin Barber, *Jihad vs. McWorld* (New York: Ballantine Books, 2001), xiv.

26. Barber, *Jihad vs. McWorld*, xiii.

27. Ahmad Ibn Hanbal, 18074; see also Ibn Majah, 4002, and Nasa'i, 4138.

28. See the appendix, Qaradawi's fatwa on the permissibility of U.S. Muslim military personnel to participate in the Afghan war.

29. *Sahih al-Bukhari*, 984.

30. *Sahih al-Bukhari*, 182.

31. Abu Daud, *Sunan*, vol. 2, p. 98.

32. *Al-Bukhari*, hadiths 2683 and 6012.

33. See Feisal Abdul Rauf, *Islam, a Sacred Law: What Every Muslim Should Know About the Shari'ah* (Battleboro, VT: Qiblah Books, 2000), 54.

34. This is analogous to variations in state laws within the United States.

35. Note the link to the values in the original phrasing of the Declaration of Independence: "life, liberty and property," later changed to "life, liberty, and the pursuit of happiness."

36. Emile Durkheim, *Suicide* (New York: Free Press, 1951).

37. Durkheim, *Suicide*, 16.

38. Durkheim, *Suicide*, 15.

39. Durkheim, *Suicide*, 14.

40. Durkheim, *Suicide*, 15–17.

41. Durkheim, *Suicide*, 298.

42. Durkheim, *Suicide*, 299–300.

43. Robert A. Pape, op-ed article, *New York Times*, September 22, 2003.

44. Note that the use of the term *Islam* here is not in the religious sense as a theology but as an identity tag of a society, a collective consciousness of a people who identify as such, the collective psychology that emanates from its history, and all that contributes to its sense of self.

45. Some of these principles are a two-state solution, withdrawal by Israel to pre-1967 borders, removal of illegal settlements, or a combination of return, resettlement, and compensation for Palestinian refugees.

46. Caryle Murphy, *Passion for Islam* (New York: Scribner, 2002), 75, 159.

47. Murphy, *Passion for Islam*, 310,

48. For more information on RAND Corporation reports, log on to http://www.rand.org.

49. Barber, *Jihad vs. McWorld*, xxv.

50. Pew Charitable Trust, "Views of a Changing World, 2003: War with Iraq Further Divides Global Publics," Pew Global Attitudes Project, available at http://people-press.org/reports/display.php3?ReportID=185 (accessed February 3, 2004).

51. Pew Charitable Trust, "Views of a Changing World, 2003."

52. Barber, *Jihad v. McWorld*, xvi–xvii, xv, xvii.

53. The *Lancet*, the journal of the British Medical Association, asserted on the basis of findings by a 1995 study team of the United Nations Food and Agriculture Organization that examined health and nutritional conditions in Iraq that since the end of the Gulf War, sanctions were responsible for the deaths of 567,000 Iraqi children; see Sarah Zaidi and Mary C. Smith-Fawzi, "Health of Baghdad's Children," *Lancet* 346, no. 8988 (December 2, 1995). A more recent and independent study by public health specialist Richard Garfield of Columbia University confirms that hundreds of thousands of children in Iraq have died prematurely and unnecessarily during this sanctions crisis. Garfield examined the studies that have been conducted on Iraq to date and found the numbers to be more like 106,000. For more information, see Richard Garfield, "Morbidity and Mortality Among Iraqi Children: Summary of General Findings," available as of January 15, 2004, at the Web site of the Fourth Freedom Forum: http://www.fourthfreedom.org.

54. Alan Cooperman, "Clergy Urge More Active White House Effort for Mideast Peace," *Washington Post*, December 2, 2003.

55. Edward Said, *Covering Islam* (New York: Vintage Books, 1997).

56. Said, *Covering Islam*, 172.

57. Said, *Covering Islam*, 173.

58. Edward Said, *The Edward Said Reader* (New York: Vintage Books, 2000), 174.

59. Economist friends advise me that Americans should be grateful to Muslim oil-producing countries for having continued to maintain the currency of oil in U.S. dollars. If they had decided to change it to the Euro or another currency, the impact on the U.S. dollar would have been disastrous.

60. Said, *Covering Islam*, 53.

61. An example of this in Africa was Nigeria, where more than two hundred different religious, tribal, and language groups were forced into a new nation-state identity called Nigeria. One by-product of this was the Nigerian-Biafran civil war (1967 to 1970).

CHAPTER FIVE

1. This is well documented in Stephen Kinzer's *All the Shah's Men: An American Coup and the Roots of Middle East Terror* (Hoboken, NJ: John Wiley & Sons, 2003).

2. Ibn Khaldun, *The Muqaddimah: An Introduction to History,* translated from the Arabic by Franz (Princeton: Princeton Univ. Press, 1967), 5.

3. Wilfred Cantwell Smith, *Islam in Modern History* (Princeton: Princeton Univ. Press, 1957), chap. 1.

4. Smith, *Islam in Modern History,* 21.

5. Smith, *Islam in Modern History,* 23.

6. The difference between the Islamic and Jewish conception of history is that in Islam, history ought to be subordinated to revelation, which is final. Classical Hebrew thought put what it learned from history into its scripture. For the Old Testament, revelation is itself a long-term process. Otherwise the Jewish and Muslim attitudes to the historical process are similar.

7. A saying of the Caliph Ali bin Abu Talib, cousin of the Prophet Muhammad.

8. Islamic history in the Quranic sense begins with Adam and God's creation of the universe.

9. Karen Armstrong, *Islam: A Short History* (New York: Modern Library, 2000), 27.

10. Armstrong, *Islam,* 29.

11. Such as the split of the *ummah* into Sunni and Shiah and the establishment of dynastic rule over rule by merit.

12. Armstrong, *Islam,* 46.

13. We have witnessed several twentieth-century attempts to establish an Islamic society: in Saudi Arabia, Pakistan, Iran, Sudan; and in Turkey, Algeria, and Egypt by segments of the population. Malaysia, meanwhile, has focused on the ingredients of an Islamic state and in my judgment has progressed the most in this regard.

14. *Encyclopedia of Islam* (CD-ROM, Leiden: Brill, 1999), s.v. "*bayt al-hikmah.*" See also s.v. "*dar al-hikmah*" and "*dar al-'ilm.*"

15. Philip K. Hitti, *Makers of Arab History* (New York: St. Martin's Press, 1968), 85, 92.

16. Hitti, *Makers of Arab History,* 93.

17. Armstrong, *Islam,* 61–62, 65.

18. We have mentioned above Imam Malik's fatwa that a pledge of allegiance (*bay'ah*) obtained under duress was not valid, which resulted in his being whipped (see above, chap. 3).

19. The development of Islamic law, the Shariah, was therefore a powerful way for the Muslims to develop a rational and historical basis to found the believer's sense of sacred transcendence in spite of and in the face of corrupt rulers. It was at this time that the pursuit of collecting hadiths to internalize the archetypal figure of the Prophet was catalyzed. The caliphs countered by circulating forged hadiths to bolster their position in power. That Malik Ibn Anas (d. 795) called his school *ahl al-hadith* ("people of hadith") probably had political overtones, suggesting that they were following to a greater degree the footsteps of the Prophet than the *ahl ar-ra'y* ("people of opinion"), a name given to the followers of Abu Hanifa's school in Kufa. This may have been a dig at Abu Hanifa's position in favor of the *murji'a* doctrine, that it was better not to get involved in the complex finger pointing about which caliph was better than the other or who had a better claim to be caliph. (The term *murji'a* was based on Quranic verse 9:106, which mentions some of the Prophet's companions who did not join the Prophet in an expedition and for whom judgment would be deferred [*arja'a*] and thereby left up to God to decide.) *Murji'a* doctrine suggested that we'd better leave that judgment to God. The majority of the community continued to sympathize with the family of the Prophet rather than with the Umayyad and Abbasid rulers, who suppressed and dishonored them.

20. The Iranians are predominantly Shiite.

21. The debates on compulsory public education in the United States were about the need to educate the future citizens of the republic. The current American concern about the madrasas in Pakistan and Saudi Arabia is that they are educating a generation of passionately anti-Western Muslims.

22. Ibn Khallikan, *Wafayat al-a'yan wa anba' abna' al-zaman* (Obituaries of the Famous, and News of the Sons of the Time) (New Delhi, 1996).

23. "We have revealed it [this Book] as an Arabic Quran, so that you might understand" (12:2); see also Quran 20:113 and 39:28, which say it was sent in Arabic, explaining God's promises, and "without crookedness" so that we might acquire piety.

24. Iranian activists could not go to Saudi Arabia because the Wahhabis were anti-Shiah. (Ayatollah Khomeini, for example, took refuge in Iraq and then in France before leading the Iranian revolution of 1979.) The Arab revolt against Ottoman rule in the early part of the twentieth century left a distaste in Turkey, which may have added to Kemal Atatürk's turn to a rapid Europeanization of Turkey.

25. *Encyclopedia of Islam*, s.v. "Indonesia."

26. Their efforts in trying to rid the Sudan of British rule is depicted in the film *Khartoum*, which starred Charlton Heston as Charles "Chinese" Gordon and the late Sir Laurence Olivier as the Mahdi.

27. Caryle Murphy, *Passion for Islam* (New York: Scribner, 2002), 44–49. For a deeper study of Muhammad 'Abduh, see Charles C. Adams, *Islam and Modernism in Egypt* (London: Oxford Univ. Press, 1933), and Yvonne Y. Haddad, "Muhammad Abduh: Pioneer of Islamic Reform," in *Pioneers of Islamic Revival*, ed. Ali Rahnema (London: Zed Books, 1994).

28. See Muhammad Iqbal, *The Reconstruction of Religious Thought in Islam* (1934; repr., Lahore, Pakistan: Kazi Publications, 1999).

29. *New York Times Magazine*, April 20, 2003. See also Paul Berman, *Terror and Liberalism* (New York: Norton, 2003).

30. "Whoever forges a way by which to seek knowledge, God will forge for him or her a way through that knowledge toward paradise. The angels unfold their wings with

pleasure upon the seeker of knowledge. All in the heavens and in the earth—even the fish in the ocean—pray for his or her forgiveness. The excellence of the seeker of knowledge over the mere worshiper is like the full moon over all the stars. Indeed, the people of knowledge are heirs of the prophets. The prophets bequeath neither *dinar* nor *dirham* [figuratively, neither dollar nor penny] but bequeath knowledge; so whoever takes of it has taken hold of an abundant fortune"; Abu Dawd, *Sunan*, "Kitab al-'Ilm," Bab al-Haththu 'ala Talib al-'Ilm, hadith no. 3157.

31. "The believer who has power is better and more beloved to God than the believer who is weak—and both are good"; Muslim, *Sahih*, "Kitab al-Qadr," hadith no. 4816.

32. Max Weber, *The Protestant Ethic and the Spirit of Capitalism* (1930; repr., New York: Routledge, 2001), xiii.

33. I owe many of the ideas in this section to the excellent book by John Micklethwait and Adrian Wooldridge, *The Company: A Short History of a Revolutionary Idea* (New York: Modern Library, 2003).

34. Micklethwait and Wooldridge, *Company*, xv.

35. Micklethwait and Wooldridge, *Company*, 43.

36. Quoted in Micklethwait and Wooldridge, *Company*, 54.

37. Quoted in Micklethwait and Wooldridge, *Company*, 18; see also Stephen Innes's comments on 201.

38. Thomas A. Tweed, "Islam in America: From African Slaves to Malcolm X, " National Humanities Center, Chapel Hill, NC, available at www.nhc.rtp.nc.us/tserve/twenty/tkeyinfo/islam.htm (accessed February 4, 2004).

39. Tweed, "Islam in America."

40. *Microsoft Encarta Encyclopedia 98* (electronic resource) (Redmond, WA: Microsoft, 1997), s.v. "Affirmative Action."

41. C. Eric Lincoln, *The Black Muslims in America* (Boston: Beacon Press, 1961), iii.

42. Lincoln, *Black Muslims*, iv.

43. Louis E. Lomax, *The Negro Revolt* (New York: Harper & Row, 1962), 184.

44. Lomax, *Negro Revolt*, 190.

45. Armstrong, *Islam*, 16.

46. Alim Islamic Software, *Al-Tirmidhi*, hadith no. 4939.

47. Armstrong, *Islam*, 16.

48. At one of the most important milestones in Islamic history, known as the Treaty of Hudaybiyah, the Prophet Muhammad took his wife Umm Salama's advice on what to do. The Prophet led his followers to perform the pilgrimage in Mecca for the first time since they had fled to Medina. They stopped at a place called Hudaybiyah, about twenty miles from Mecca. After intense negotiations, Muhammad agreed that the Muslims would wait another year before making the pilgrimage to Mecca. The pilgrims were disappointed, their expectations dashed. They stood in a group staring in shock at the Prophet and didn't make a move even when he commanded them to sacrifice their animals and cut their hair (rites traditionally done at the end of the pilgrimage, and only within the sacred precincts of Mecca). Concerned that he would lose their support, Muhammad retreated to his tent, where Umm Salama had been watching the events transpire. He asked her advice. "Go forth," she said, "and say no word to any man until you have performed your sacrifice" (see Martin Lings, *Muhammad* [New York: Inner Traditions, 1983], 254). Seeing the Prophet perform the ritual act, the Muslims immediately raced to perform their sacrifices, thereby releasing the tension that had built up. As

Karen Armstrong notes, Umm Salama had evaluated the situation exactly (see Armstrong, *Muhammad: A Biography of the Prophet* [New York: HarperCollins, 1992], 222). Umm Salama recognized that the Prophet's followers would emulate his actions even more readily than his verbal instructions. The Prophet Muhammad succeeded here based on her advice.

49. Alim, Prophet's Last Sermon.

50. *Encyclopedia of Islam,* s.v. "Khadidja."

51. *Encyclopedia of Islam,* s.v. " 'A'isha Bint Abi Bakr."

52. American Muslims generally believe, rightly or wrongly, that the Patriot Act is primarily targeted against them.

53. Herberg, *Protestant, Catholic, Jew,* 142.

54. Herberg, *Protestant, Catholic, Jew,* 143.

55. Theodore Maynard, *The Story of American Catholicism* (New York: Macmillan, 1941), 285.

56. Thomas Sugrue, as expressed in Herberg, *Protestant, Catholic, Jew.*

57. In addition to educational institutions, there were Catholic hospitals, homes, and orphanages; Catholic charities and welfare agencies; Catholic Boy Scouts and War Veterans, Catholic associations of doctors, lawyers, teachers, students, and philosophers; Catholic leagues of policemen, firemen, and sanitary workers; and a Catholic Youth Organization. The immense system constitutes a self-contained Catholic world with its own complex interior economy and American Catholicism's resources of participation in the larger American economy; see Herberg, *Protestant, Catholic, Jew,* 154.

58. Herberg, *Protestant, Catholic, Jew,* 149.

59. James Cardinal Gibbons, "The Church and the Republic," quoted in Herberg, *Protestant, Catholic, Jew,* 150.

60. "The Catholic Church in American Democracy," press release of the National Catholic Welfare Conference, January 26, 1948.

61. Herberg, *Protestant, Catholic, Jew,* 152.

62. Herberg, *Protestant, Catholic, Jew,* 161.

63. The Jewish Reform movement was set in motion in America by Isaac Mayer Wise, who among his accomplishments compiled a new prayer book and order of service according to the American Custom (*Minhag America*). In 1873 he formed the Union of American Hebrew Congregations and in 1875 established a theological seminary, the Hebrew Union College in Cincinnati. In 1889 he launched a rabbinical association under the name of the Central Conference of American Rabbis.

64. Herberg, *Protestant, Catholic, Jew,* 177.

65. See Norman Bentwich, quoted in Herberg, *Protestant, Catholic, Jew,* 202.

66. Oscar Handlin, quoted in Herberg, *Protestant, Catholic, Jew,* 288.

67. Herberg, *Protestant, Catholic, Jew,* 191.

68. Herberg, *Protestant, Catholic, Jew,* 222.

69. Herberg, *Protestant, Catholic, Jew,* 198.

70. Herberg, *Protestant, Catholic, Jew,* 236.

71. Quoting the Beth Din Web site, http://www.bethdin.org/services.htm (accessed January 20, 2004).

72. Quoted in David Fromkin, *A Peace to End All Peace* (New York: Henry Holt, 1989), 257.

73. Fromkin, *Peace to End All Peace,* 258.

74. Fromkin, *Peace to End All Peace,* 259.

75. Quoted in Fromkin, *Peace to End All Peace,* 262.

76. Quoted in F. Forrester Church, *The American Creed* (New York: St. Martin's Press, 2002), 90.

77. Quoted in Church, *American Creed,* 92.

78. Church, *American Creed,* 91.

79. See Kinzer, *All the Shah's Men.*

80. *Microsoft Encarta Encyclopedia 98,* s.v. "Afghanistan."

81. John Micklethwait and Adrian Wooldridge, *A Future Perfect: The Essentials of Globalization* (New York: Crown Business, 2000), xix.

82. Francis Fukuyama, *The End of History and the Last Man* (New York: Perennial Reprint, 2002), xii.

83. Michael Novak, "The Most Religious Century," op-ed piece, *New York Times,* May 24, 1998.

84. Novak, "Most Religious Century."

CHAPTER SIX

1. In it he said,

It should be clear to all that Islam, the faith of one-fifth of humanity, is consistent with democratic rule. Democratic progress is found in many predominantly Muslim countries: in Turkey, Indonesia and Senegal and Albania and Niger and Sierra Leone. Muslim men and women are good citizens of India and South Africa, the nations of Western Europe and of the United States of America. More than half of all Muslims live in freedom under democratically constituted governments. They succeed in democratic societies, not in spite of their faith, but because of it. A religion that demands individual moral accountability and encourages the encounter of the individual with God is fully compatible with the rights and responsibilities of self-government.

The text of Bush's speech is available at http://www.nytimes.com/2003/11/06/politics/06TEXT.BUSH.html.

2. Unlike in the United States, in many Muslim countries the government owns certain industries, like the oil, transportation, and communication industries. These industries need to be privatized and broken up, as has happened in America.

3. Anwar Sadat of Egypt, for example, was assassinated within a year of having himself proclaimed president for life.

4. "Mixing Growth with Islam," *Wall Street Journal,* November 7, 2003.

5. This problem is now being played out in France with the scuffle about headscarves in French schools. The best way to solve this is to create a win-win situation. My wife suggests, Why can't the French authorities ask their top designers, such as Cacherel, Hermes, Yves St. Laurent, and others, to design a headscarf for Muslim schoolgirls that addresses Islamic concerns and is in keeping with French aesthetics of haute couture? Headgear has always been a fashion item throughout human history; this can grow into a billion-dollar business, meaningfully contribute to a culturally French Islam, and be an economic boon.

6. Marc Gopin, *Holy War, Holy Peace* (New York: Oxford Univ. Press, 2002), 181–82.

7. One example of such a workable framework that might be implemented was provided by the Geneva Accord, negotiated between Yossi Beilin and Yasser Abed Rabbo, who were parties to previous negotiations between Israel and Palestine.

8. *New York Times,* "Top Evangelicals Critical of Colleagues Over Islam," Laurie Goodstein, May 8, 2003.

9. "China and India Move Closer, Seeing Trade Gains," *Wall Street Journal,* November 11, 2003.

10. "China and India."

11. Barely four weeks after I wrote this passage, the *Wall Street Journal* published an article under the headline "China Steps Up Diplomatic Role," by Jay Solomon, Charles Hutzler, and Zahid Hussein, with subtitles "Beijing Takes the Initiative with India and Pakistan" in pushing for a peace pact and "From Guns to Butter, Better China-India Ties . . . Could speed détente between South Asian rivals." The article is full of ideas that demonstrate, in effect, how to apply Varshney's insights on associational ties and Dawkins's insights on increasing the payoffs to avoiding violence that I have tried to highlight in building peace.

12. Quran 3:112–16. This teaching is similar to Jesus's parable of the weeds mentioned in Matthew 13:24–30.

13. The Quran points out, for example, that even "among your spouses and your children there are enemies to you" (Quran 64:14).

14. These points apply as well to adherents of other faiths.

15. Arthur Schneier, "Religion and Interfaith Conflict," chapter 7 of *Interfaith Dialogue and Peacebuilding,* ed. David Smock (Washington, DC: U.S. Institute of Peace Press, 2002), 112.

16. I am indebted to the following: Daniel Yankelovich, *The Magic of Dialogue* (New York: Simon & Schuster, 1999); Mary Jacksteit and Adrienne Kaufmann, *Finding Common Ground in the Abortion Conflict: A Reference Manual,* available from Search for Common Ground, http://www.sfcg.org, or the National Association for Community Mediation, http://www.nafcm.org.

17. I noted earlier that early Muslim history is replete with learning gained from the non-Arab communities among whom Muslims lived and that later Jewish scholars such as Maimonides and Ibn Paqoda applied principles learned from their Sufi Muslim contemporaries such as al-Ghazali.

18. For example, when I studied the field of Islamic law that categorizes the differing laws in the Islamic schools of jurisprudence and the reasoning that led each jurist to his opinion, classically called *'ilm al-khilaf* (literally, "knowledge of differences"), it gave me a deeper appreciation of the compelling reasons of each school, resulting in my being more tolerant and accepting of differing views within Islam.

Index

314   *Index*

terrorism *(continued)*
    155; Palestinian-Israeli conflict and,
    154–55, 160–61; September 11, 2001, xix,
    xx–xxi, xxii, 134, 138, 145, 146, 189, 243,
    243; social conditions and, 151–52; solution
    to, 155; suicide bombers, xix, xx, xxi, 126,
    139, 143–48; United States as target of, 152;
    war on, as new Cold War, 152–55. *See also*
    conflict
Throne verse *(ayat al-kursi)*, 60
Titus, Murray, 105
tolerance, 2, 14, 33–40
Turkey: admission to EU denied, perception
    of reason, 8; alliance with West, 239; divi-
    sion of, post–World War I, 234; Istanbul,
    190, 191; Kemal Atatürk and Europeaniza-
    tion, 4–5, 170–71, 193, 204, 234; Kurds in, 5,
    193; Mamluks, 189; Seljuks, 190, 192, 193;
    woman head of state, 217; women in, 220.
    See also Ottoman Empire

Umar, Caliph, 142, 149, 168, 181
'Umar bin al-Khattab, 89
United Nations, 236; Universal Declaration of
    Human Rights (ECOSOC), 238–39, 243
United States: Abrahamic ethic in, 80, 82, 83,
    85, 97, 105, 207, 215, 231, 238; affirmative
    action policies, 213; Afghanistan invasion
    and development, 149, 162, 244; American
    (as term), 115–16; American Christians and
    Jews, 8–9, 85, 169, 220–30, 261–66; Ameri-
    can Muslims, xix, 9, 27, 79, 221, 222–23, 225,
    227, 228, 230, 257–60, 261; anti-Americanism
    by Muslims, xvii, 1, 7–8, 40, 166, 251; antire-
    ligious secularism in, 6; arrogance of, per-
    ceived, 281–82; bias against Muslims in,
    165–66, 265–66; civil rights and Black Mus-
    lims, 211–16; Cold War with Soviet Union
    and foreign policy, 204–5; congruence with
    Islamic values (what's right with America,
    79–111; Constitution, 81–82, 85, 91, 105,
    106–7, 107, 178, 248; Constitutional Amend-
    ments, 92, 97–100, 206, 212, 216–17; Decla-
    ration of Independence, globalization of,
    234–39, 281; Declaration of Independence,
    inalienable rights (as consistent with
    Islamic law), 17, 40, 81–83, 85, 86, 87, 105,
    107, 178, 206, 243; democracy in, 80, 246;
    democratic capitalism and, 6, 8, 208–11,
    232–33; economic aid to Muslim world,
    237, 253; European idea of supremacy in, 5;
    Federal Reserve Bank, 93, 96–97; foreign
    policy and the Muslim world, 157–61, 163,
    239–43, 252–57; freedom of speech, the
    press, and religion ("establishment
    clause"), 97–100; global religion, impact on,
    8–9; global village and, 243–49; as Great

Policeman, 281; as Great Satan, xvii, 266;
    history, 206–30; injustice and unconstitu-
    tionality, 149–50, 152; Iraq War, xviii, 136,
    161, 243; isolationism in, 164; Israeli-
    Palestinian conflict and, 160–61; Judeo-
    Christian ethic, 207, 217, 220–30; law in, as
    Shariah-compliant, 86–88, 104, 107; law in,
    proposed Islamic changes for, 86, 109–11;
    liberty, ideal of, 5; military, 93–96; Muslim
    world and, healing the relationship,
    251–80; political right, shift to, xxi, 189;
    Protestant ethic and Puritanism, 207–8, 225;
    Protestantism, evangelical, 207; religious
    foundations of, 104–8, 206, 249; religious
    pluralism in, 5, 33, 85–86, 104, 108, 170, 189;
    Roosevelt and the Four Freedoms, 237–38,
    253, 254; Roosevelt and the New Deal,
    232–33; separation of church and state, 6, 7,
    102–4, 104–11; separation of powers (sys-
    tem of checks and balances), 90–97,
    100–101; slavery in, 211–12; Social Security
    Act, 233; terrorism used against, xix,
    xx–xxi, xxii, 134, 138, 145, 146, 152, 189;
    way of life as American religion (to Mus-
    lims), 84–86, 103, 178; Wilson administra-
    tion, New Freedom and, 230–32, 254; Wilson
    administration, World War I and peace pro-
    posals, 234–36; women's suffrage in, 216–17,
    232; World War II and, 236–39
Uthman, Caliph, 182
Uzbekistan, 5, 167
Uzbeks, 5, 167

Vajpayee, Atal Bihari, 269
Varshney, Ashutosh, 127, 268
"Views of a Changing World 2003" (Pew
    Global Attitudes Project), 1
Vines, Rev. Jerry, 265–66

Wahhabis, 193, 194–98, 200, 204, 240–42
Waliyullah, Shah, 193
Walters, Barbara, xviii
Washington, George, 108
Weber, Max, 208
When Religion Becomes Evil (Kimball), xx
Wilson, Woodrow: Fourteen Points, 235; New
    Freedom, 230–32; peace settlement, World
    War I, 235–36
women: American, suffrage movement,
    216–17, 232; Islam and, xviii, 216–20; piety
    of man judged by treatment of, 44; sup-
    pression of, xix, 31; veils *(chadors)*, 171

zakah. See charity
Zakaria, Fareed, 100
Zawahiri, Ayman, 151